PRIVATE
PRISONS

CONS AND PROS

CHARLES H. LOGAN

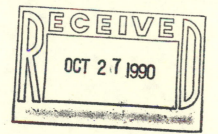

New York   Oxford
OXFORD UNIVERSITY PRESS
1990

Oxford University Press

Oxford   New York   Toronto
Delhi   Bombay   Calcutta   Madras   Karachi
Petaling Jaya   Singapore   Hong Kong   Tokyo
Nairobi   Dar es Salaam   Cape Town
Melbourne   Auckland

and associated companies in
Berlin   Ibadan

Copyright © 1990 by Oxford University Press, Inc.

Published by Oxford University Press, Inc.,
200 Madison Avenue, New York, New York 10016

Oxford is a registered trademark of Oxford University Press

Library of Congress Cataloging-in-Publication Data
Logan, Charles H.
   Private prisons: cons and pros/ Charles H. Logan.
      p. cm.   Includes bibliographical references.
   ISBN 0-19-506353-8
      1. Prisons—United States. 2. Privatization—United States.
3. Corrections—United States—Contracting out.   I. Title.
HV9469.L64   1990
365'.973—dc20   89-49028

9 8 7 6 5 4 3 2 1

Printed in the United States of America
on acid-free paper

For Sharla, Daniel, and Christopher

Acknowledgments

I am grateful to the National Institute of Justice for the Visiting Fellowship (86-IJ-CX-0062) that made possible all the research for this book. The views expressed here are my own and do not necessarily reflect Department of Justice policy. I am especially indebted to James K. Stewart, Director of the Institute, for his enthusiasm, his intellectual support, and his friendship. No other person has done as much as he to promote nationwide research, discussion, and action on private-sector involvement in corrections.

Others at the Institute were also helpful in many ways, especially Joel Garner, Bonnie Gowdy, Dick Linster, Marty Lively, Renee Trent, Neille Russell, and Ed Zedlewski. Barry Ruback, as a fellow Visiting Fellow, offered much social support and editorial help during the early stages of my work. George Cole, also a Visiting Fellow, was there for me at a later point.

Many government officials involved in prison or jail contracting were generous with time and information. Officials in Bay County, Florida, were very helpful, particularly John Hutt and Larry Davis. In Hamilton County, Tennessee, special thanks go to Floyd (Flop) Fuller, Superintendent of Corrections, and Bill McGriff, County Auditor. Bill contributed so much to my chapter on costs that he is co-author of a separate report derived from it. Bob Schmidt, now retired from the Immigration and Naturalization Service, provided a flood of information.

In general, I found that private corrections companies are at least as open to investigation and research as are public agencies, and sometimes more so. While I have talked with people at many companies, including Corrections Corporation of America (CCA), Buckingham Security Limited, Wackenhut, Behavioral Systems Southwest, U.S. Corrections Corp., and Pricor, my closest contacts have been at CCA and Buckingham. Charles and Joseph Fenton, the founders of Buckingham Security, were open and candid in all conversations.

No study of private corrections today can go very far without access to information on CCA, the industry leader. Fortunately, I don't see how any company or government agency could be more generous with its time and information than CCA, or more open to scrutiny by outsiders, including researchers, journalists, and even critics and opponents of the industry. So many people at CCA were helpful to me in supplying materials and providing access to facilities that I have to apologize to those whose names I omit. At one time or another, I had special help from Tom Beasley, Linda Cooper, Richard Crane, Doctor Crants, Don Hutto, Greg McCullough, and Peggy Wilson. David Myers, Vice President for Facilities Management, was a crucial link for me in getting information about, and access to, CCA's facilities.

Other researchers in this area have been helpful in sharing information and perspectives, including Diane Bast, Bruce Benson, Jan Brakel, Douglas McDonald, Joan Mullen, Charles Ring, and Ira Robbins.

Finally, I have saved special thanks for two people most important to this project and to me. Charles Thomas, Professor of Criminology and Associate Dean at the University of Florida, is a leading academic authority on private prisons. He knows more about this field than anyone else outside the industry, and he was most generous in sharing his information, materials, and contacts with me. Last on my list, but first in my life, is Sharla P. Rausch, my wife and frequent co-author, whose encouragement, assistance, advice, and support are always deeply appreciated.

Contents

PRIVATE PRISONS

Introduction

Americans both love and hate their government; trust and fear it. Traditionally, their political philosophy has been basically libertarian, though not consistently so. They believe in limiting the power of government in many ways, yet they also want to use government to pursue various special goals or interests. This ambivalence toward government is particularly evident in the area of criminal justice.

Those earliest of American reformers, the founders, established a Constitution premised on a lack of faith in the benevolence and wisdom of governors. Shortly thereafter, another group of American reformers established a penitentiary system premised on faith in the redemption of sinners and in the benevolence and wisdom of at least some authorities whose job it would be to coercively save those sinners.

This faith in the good intentions of penal authorities and in their competence to rehabilitate lawbreakers has been strongly challenged in the past two decades, for a variety of reasons. The reason most relevant here is a growing disenchantment with government generally. From the late 1950s to the mid-1970s, self-reported trust in government declined from almost 80 percent to about 33 percent.[1] This was part of a general lowering of public confidence in American institutions and leadership.[2] By the 1980s, taxpayers had begun to revolt and a presidential candidate with a platform of "getting the government off our backs" was elected with great popular support. This was also a time of growing interest in "pri-

3

vatization": the transfer of assets, and of the production of public goods and services, from government to the private sector.

The privatization of corrections, or punishment, is an especially significant part of the broader privatization movement. By challenging the government's monopoly over one of its ostensibly "core" functions, this idea directly threatens the assumption that certain activities are essentially and necessarily governmental.

How does one determine what government functions are necessary or essential? Historical tests are unavailing. No role has always been the exclusive province of the government. Nor can current practice be taken as definitive. Ronald Cass, Commissioner of the U.S. International Trade Commission and Professor of Law at Boston University, has pointed out the fallacy in using historical tests to define essential government functions: they produce a "one-way ratchet" for government expansion. Whatever the government does or has done becomes an essential government function, and contraction of the scope of government becomes impossible.[3]

Thus, privatization in the area of criminal justice generally, and of imprisonment particularly, plays an important part in a broad, ideological debate over the proper scope and size of government. This book contributes to that broader debate, even though its topical focus is rather narrow.

Proposals for the privatization of functions such as garbage collection or mail delivery have urged the government to divest itself partially or even entirely of specific responsibilities. In contrast, recent proposals for private prisons and jails have suggested only that it might be more efficient for government to lease these facilities or to contract for their operation and management by private companies. A completely private criminal justice system—or, indeed, the total dismantlement of the state—may be interesting to discuss at a theoretical level, but there are no viable policy proposals along those lines today.

Current proposals for private prisons refer only to private contracting, not to complete privatization in the sense of divestiture. Nonetheless, penal justice, even in the form of contracting, represents an extreme test of the limits of privatization. As a result, all of the arguments against contracting of other public services have been directed with great intensity against prison and jail contracts. If those objections can be answered in this context, it is doubtful that they could have greater power or validity in other areas of government activity. So the ideological stakes in the debate over correctional contracting are high.

My goal in this book is to examine critically all of the objections to private prisons that have been or could be raised, and to assess both their validity and their weight. Ten sets of issues will be explored in separate chapters, covering problems of propriety, cost, quality, quantity, flexibility, security, liability, accountability, corruption, and dependence.

In evaluating private prisons on these dimensions, there must be no double standard between private and public prisons. In particular, private prisons should not be judged against absolute or ideal standards without reference to the performance of government-run prisons. It is too easy to find problems, or to anticipate potential problems, in either type of prison if we fail to make relevant comparisons.

Arguments against private prisons vary in soundness and plausibility, but in no area have I found any potential problem with private prisons that is not at least matched by an identical or a closely corresponding problem among prisons that are run by the government. It is primarily because they are prisons, not because they are contractual, that private operations face challenges of authority, legitimacy, procedural justice, accountability, liability, cost, security, safety, corruptibility, and so on. Because they raise no problems that are both unique and insurmountable, private prisons should be allowed to compete (and cooperate) with government agencies so that we can discover how best to run prisons that are safe, secure, humane, efficient, and just.

1

The Iron Fist Meets
the Invisible Hand

Government production of goods and services is often defended as being a necessary response to market failure. Where the "invisible hand" of the market fails to produce goods and services of adequate quality, or in sufficient quantity, or at an appropriate price, or to distribute them properly, the "iron fist" of the state must take action. Conversely, privatization is often seen as a remedy for government failure in these matters. Does imprisonment represent an area of "government failure" today?

Imprisonment: Demand and Supply[1]

Imprisonment, since it serves the public as a whole rather than individual consumers, can be characterized as a public good. Public goods are generally financed and arranged for (but not necessarily produced) by government. Like other goods, they can be analyzed in terms of supply, demand, quality, and price. In the case of imprisonment, a clear pattern has emerged, one that is characteristic of goods or services produced under monopoly conditions. Quality is low, prices are high, and the supply has not kept up with demand.

The number of state and federal prisoners totaled 581,609 by the end of 1987, up 76 percent from 1980. Prison capacity, however, has not kept up with the increasing population. Overall, state prisons in 1987 were filled to somewhere between 105 percent and 120 percent of capacity, depending on how capacity is measured, while federal prisons held between 37 percent to 73 percent more than the maximum number of prisoners that they were meant to house. Over 12,000 state prisoners had to be held in local jails because other facilities were overflowing.[2] Due to a virtual moratorium on new construction during the 1970s, these overcrowded prisons are also deteriorating with age. The average inmate sleeps in a cell that is nearly 40 years old, and 10 percent are locked in prisons built before 1875.[3] Consequently, in 1987 prisons in 42 states and the District of Columbia were under court orders because of crowding and other conditions ruled unconstitutional.[4]

The Cost of Imprisonment

The cost of constructing and operating prisons is enormous, and usually it is underestimated. Cost estimates for construction vary according to region, type of prison, program needs, use of prison labor, recency of data and techniques of adjusting for inflation, reference to past or planned construction, and definition of what is included in "cost." The U.S. Department of Justice, using 1982 dollars, cites average construction costs per bed of $26,000, $46,000, and $58,000, for minimum, medium, and maximum security prisons, respectively. Because they are based on a systematic survey of all states and are specified by prison type, these figures probably come closest to reflecting average costs nationally.

Most estimates of construction cost, however, are probably too low, because they ignore such considerations as land purchase, site preparation, financing cost, overruns, and hidden cost.[5] Taking all of these factors into account, plus a conservative estimate of $14,000 per inmate in annual operating cost, one economist has estimated that a 500-bed prison ostensibly costing $30 million to build today could end up costing $350 million altogether over a 30-year period.[6]

As with construction, figures on operating costs vary widely. The most common estimates are in the mid-teen thousands, reflected by the American Correctional Association's figure of $15,000,[7] and the federal prison system's figure of $13,000.[8] Most estimates of operating costs are too low because they do not take into account fringe benefits, interagency services, federal grants, and other off-budget items. Studies of state corrections budgets have shown actual expenditures to be about one-third (Indiana) or 30 percent (New York) higher than the official budgets reported.[9]

In short, the current costs of constructing and operating prisons, while difficult to calculate precisely, are obviously quite high and are probably much higher than most people, even knowledgeable ones, assume. Moreover, these costs continue to grow rapidly. Over the last six years, the budget for care of juveniles in the custody of the Colorado Division of Youth Services has grown by 76.5 percent, which is over four times as fast as the general rate of inflation, as measured by an increase of 17.9 percent in the Consumer Price Index over the same period.[10] Nationwide, per capita spending on corrections at the state and local level has grown faster in the last 25 years than government spending in most other categories. From 1960 to 1985, per capita spending in constant dollars increased by 218 percent for corrections. Spending in other categories increased less: public welfare, 216 percent; hospitals and health care, 119 percent; police, 73 percent; education, 56 percent. Spending on highways declined by 21 percent.[11] In Tennessee, the corrections budget has increased 1,790 percent over the last 20 years, compared to an increase of 648 percent in the total General Fund and an increase of 810 percent in higher education (the single program with the next largest growth).[12]

The Privatization Option

Faced with overflowing and aging facilities, with court orders demanding immediate reforms, with already straining budgets and voter rejections of prison construction bond issues, and with mandatory sentence laws, toughening public attitudes, and "wars on drugs" that promise even larger prison populations, government authorities are ready to consider many different options to help relieve the strain. Some of these options include: emergency early release provisions; policies of selective incarceration and release; community corrections; home confinement with electronic monitoring; intensive supervision probation; increased use of fines; and contracting with other jurisdictions for jail and prison space. All of these options are aimed at either decreasing the prison population or using existing prison capacity more efficiently.

Another option is to contract with the private sector to finance, construct, own, and operate prisons and jails. This option does not conflict with any of the above options; rather, it supplements them. Its greatest potential is that of flexibility. It has the capability to do for corrections what entrepreneurial activity is supposed to do best: anticipate needs and meet them. In response to the space crunch in today's prisons, commercial confinement companies offer an immediate prospect of relatively rapid and efficient increases in overall confinement capacity. However, contracting need not always be aimed at increasing the number of available prison cells. If the need for secure confinement should decline, or if a viable alternative is developed, it should be easier to alter contracts or change contractors than to restructure entrenched public bureaucracies.

Private prisons and jails are not meant to be used in lieu of existing facilities, but to widen and diversify the prison system. One purpose of competition, in addition to cost containment, is to maximize choice. The prison crisis described above has caused government managers to see the urgent need for alternatives. In the early 1980s, the private sector responded to this need in the form of proprietary (i.e., privately owned) companies specializing in the management of correctional and confinement facilities. These companies, and the facilities they have been running, will be described in the next chapter.

Sources of Opposition

Opposition to contracted prisons comes from several sources. Organizations that have either opposed or called for a moratorium on private prisons include the American Federation of State, County, and Municipal Employees (AFSCME), the National Sheriffs' Association, the American Civil Liberties Union (ACLU), and the American Bar Association (ABA).

It is interesting to note that contracting provoked relatively little controversy during the many years when the only people being held against their will in private facilities were mental patients and juveniles. It may also be significant that most of the adult confinement facilities under private contract in the early 1980s were for the detention of illegal aliens. Finally, in this vein, the first privately contracted state prison holding adults at all levels of security is a facility for females.

It would be a mistake, however, to infer from this pattern that those who object to private prisons care less about the rights and welfare of mental patients, juveniles, aliens, or women than they do about those of healthy adult male citizens. Rather, the issues loom larger now because greater numbers of people, and therefore greater interests, are at stake. Neither governmental monopoly over the confinement function nor government employee monopoly over the relevant jobs was seriously threatened until privatization began to encroach on the vast heartland of corrections. That's when the real turf battles began and opposition was organized by the AFSCME, the National Sheriffs' Association, and other groups.

Employee unions and sheriffs' associations are opposed to private prisons largely for personal reasons: contracting threatens their jobs and, more significantly, their power.[13] Some correctional officials, too, view contracting as a challenge to their professional status and as a means of lessening their control. Others, however, believe that contracting will extend their capabilities as managers of contracts.

Probably the most powerful opponent to private prisons is the AFSCME, which is the sixth largest of all the AFL-CIO international unions.[14] It represents over 50,000 corrections workers nationally.[15] As of 1981, correctional employees were unionized in 29 of 52 jurisdictions (state, federal, and District of Columbia).[16] Union strength is weakest in the southern tier of the United States, which is where the private prison industry has concentrated most of its efforts. The AFSCME and other public employee unions are opposed to contracting out virtually all public services, but their opposition to prison privatization seems especially vehement.

Unions were the major force behind legislation in Pennsylvania imposing a one-year moratorium on new privatization of prisons or jails. They also forced the nonrenewal of a jail management contract in that state when the AFSCME threw its support behind two candidates for county commission running on a "take back the jail" platform. In San Diego County, California, the probation and correctional officers union in 1982 prevented Radio Corporation of America (RCA) from receiving a contract to run a 100-bed juvenile detention facility, by invoking an old county bylaw that prohibits contractors from running public facilities.[17]

The ACLU, a longtime champion of the rights of individuals against encroachment by the state, apparently fears private enterprise even more than government. ACLU officials are concerned that prisoners' due process rights are more likely to be jeopardized in private than in government-run prisons. Indeed, they believe that private prisons are intrinsically threatening to civil liberties.[18] A substantial part of the ACLU's opposition to private prisons, however, stems from its belief that there is already too much incarceration and privatization would only lead to more.

In February 1986, the House of Delegates of the American Bar Association passed a resolution recommending that "jurisdictions that are considering the privatization of prisons and jails not proceed . . . until the complex constitutional, statutory, and contractual issues are satisfactorily developed and resolved."[19] The president-elect of the ABA was quoted at that time as declaring: "I am personally hostile to the notion [of private prisons]."[20] According to Thomas Beasley, Chairman of Corrections Corporation of America and a member of the ABA, the resolution was brought forward with three speakers in favor but without any opportunity for opposing debate.[21] The report that accompanied the ABA resolution was written by a vigorous opponent of private prisons.

In later chapters, I will examine in detail the issues raised by these and other critics of privatization. First, however, the following chapter gives a descriptive overview of current or recent contracts for the private operation of secure confinement facilities—private prisons and jails.

2

Private Prisons Today:
A Descriptive Overview

"Private prison" is not a very precise term, though its general meaning is fairly clear. It refers to a place of confinement that is managed by a private company. "Prison" will be used broadly in this book to include any place of involuntary confinement within the justice system. This would include facilities of the Immigration and Naturalization Service (which is part of the Department of Justice) and juvenile justice facilities, but not places for involuntary civil confinement of the mentally ill. Within the current context, "prison" will be more or less synonymous with a "detention," "confinement," "correctional," or "penal" facility.[1] These are not primarily residential facilities, like foster homes, group homes, halfway houses, or community treatment centers. Prisons, detention centers, jails, reformatories, and similar institutions are places of incarceration.

The term "private" (or, sometimes, "proprietary") prison implies private ownership, at least of the management company, and sometimes of the facility's buildings and grounds. Private prisons are those that are privately owned, operated, or managed,[2] under contract to government. No prison today is completely private, in the sense of being independent of government authority, control, and revenue. Private prisons now operate only under contract to government. Hence, they may often be referred to simply as "contractors," "vendors," or "service providers."

Reference to "proprietary" or "commercial" prisons will reflect the fact that these are businesses. However, they may be organized on either a for-profit or a not-for-profit basis. They may be closely held, publicly traded, or employee owned (profit sharing). What they all have in common is that they are private entities operating under contract to government. They perform government functions and may be regarded for some purposes as "quasi-governmental," but they are not governmental in organizational form.

Correctional facilities can be divided into four general types: (1) juvenile open facilities; (2) juvenile institutional facilities; (3) adult community facilities; and (4) adult confinement facilities. The Bureau of Justice Statistics (BJS) classifies juvenile facilities as "open" or "institutional" based on degree of access to community resources and on the degree of security provided by the personnel and the physical plant.[3] Most open facilities are shelters, halfway houses or group homes, a few are set up as ranches. Institutional facilities include detention or diagnostic centers, training schools, and ranches. Adult facilities are classified by BJS as either "community" or "confinement," depending on whether the proportion of residents who are regularly allowed to depart unaccompanied (e.g., for work or study) is greater than half (community) or less than half (confinement).

Proprietary facilities are found among all four correctional situations. Since they are part of the criminal and juvenile justice systems, they all involve the exercise of state authority and at least some deprivation of liberty. Thus, although the concept of "proprietary prisons" is mainly associated with confinement or institutionalization, it could be taken to include open environment and community facilities as well. However, the private community-based and open facilities are so numerous, so widespread, and so broadly accepted that they will be described here only briefly, in statistical outline. The more recent, unfamiliar, and controversial examples of institutional and confinement facilities will be described in greater detail, including case histories.

Juvenile Open Facilities

Private, low-security juvenile facilities have been part of the corrections system in America since the nineteenth century. There has been relatively little controversy about these facilities, whether run by nonprofit or for-profit organizations. Indeed, there has been much praise, even from individuals and organizations opposed to private prisons, for the substitution of private community-based programs in place of state institutions of juvenile justice. For example, Jerome Miller has been widely applauded for changing the juvenile justice system of Massachusetts from a network of state institutions in 1969 to mostly community-based programs by 1974.[4] The Massachusetts Division of Youth Services now operates all of its community-based facilities (and half of its secure programs) through private contractors.[5]

The Bureau of Justice Statistics counted 82,272 persons held in 2,900 juvenile detention and correctional facilities on February 1, 1983.[6] The 1,877 private facilities, found in every state but Delaware, outnumbered the 1,023 public facilities by a large margin. While the privates comprised 65 percent of all facilities, they held just 38 percent of the juveniles in custody, since they were generally smaller units and provided more long-term care.[7]

In juvenile facilities with open environments, private contracting is now standard practice. Eighty-one percent of such facilities were privately operated as of 1983 and they housed about three-quarters (72 percent) of the juveniles held in that type of custody.[8]

One reason for the wide acceptance of private facilities with open, or noninstitutional, environments may be that they are not perceived as examples of the private exercise of state power. However, even open facilities are basically coercive in nature when they are used by the juvenile justice system. That is, they exercise authority backed up by actual or potential use of state force. Any court placement, even in the most open environment (like a group home), carries with it the possibility of subsequent judicial or other official intervention. Only 18 percent of the 25,855 admissions to private open facilities during 1982 were voluntary without adjudication.[9] Because the vast majority of residents in facilities with "open" environments were placed there involuntarily, the phrase "open facility" does not imply complete freedom to come and go. Unpublished data from the 1982–83 *Children in Custody* census show that 97 percent of the private open facilities were nonsecure in terms of hardware or guarded exits. In terms of custody, however, about 18 percent of the private, open facilities were classified as medium or strict.[10]

Adult Community Facilities

As of June 30, 1986, according to the *Directory of Juvenile and Adult Correctional Departments, Institutions, Agencies and Paroling Authorities*, published by the American Correctional Association (ACA), there were 4,758 adult state correctional inmates in community homes, of whom 61 percent were in contracted facilities. One survey found adult community-based facilities under contract in 32 states.[11] The International Halfway House Association estimates that about 1,000 of its members are private vendors providing community programs for correctional agencies.[12] At the federal level, the Bureau of Prisons relies exclusively on contracts to place offenders in community treatment centers. Of 310 separate contracts, 218 (or 70 percent) are with private providers; the rest are with local public agencies. However, many of the public contracts are low volume, so that nearly all of the actual placements are in privately operated centers. Thus, in June of 1989, 94 percent of the 3,287 federal offenders placed in community treatment were placed in private facilities.[13]

I will have little more to say in this book about correctional facilities that are community-based and residential. For nonsecure facilities, both juvenile and adult, the practice by government of contracting with private parties for operation and management is widely accepted. That level of acceptance is significant, because even nonsecure facilities involve the exercise of authority by the criminal justice system, albeit at an ostensibly low level of coercion. This suggests that the private exercise of authority usually reserved for the government is not categorically objectionable; rather, it is controversial primarily in proportion to how overtly coercive it appears. Thus, to set the stage for the debate over "private prisons," I will give more detailed descriptions here only of juvenile and adult facilities designed for relatively secure confinement.

Juvenile Institutional Facilities

Juvenile correctional facilities having an institutional environment are most often run by government employees. Still, there are many that operate under private contracts. In the 1982–83 census, there were 808 institutional facilities nationwide, of which 187 (23 percent) were private.[14] While almost all (91 percent) of the public institutional facilities were secure in terms of hardware or guarded exits, only 39 percent (73) of the private institutional facilities had that sort of security. What made these facilities "institutional" in BJS terminology was primarily their self-description as having a strict or medium level of custody (true of 92 percent of this group).[15]

This category—private juvenile detention and correctional facilities identified by BJS as having an institutional environment—may contain several examples of what I am calling "proprietary prisons." Unfortunately, it is impossible to trace the identities of those facilities directly, because of confidentiality guarantees provided by the Bureau of the Census, which gathers these data, and by the Bureau of Justice Statistics, which analyzes them. However, several such facilities have been identified by journalists and researchers in recent years.

Weaversville Intensive Treatment Unit

Of the currently operating institutions for secure confinement of juveniles, perhaps the longest-running for-profit enterprise is the Weaversville Intensive Treatment Unit, which opened in North Hampton, Pennsylvania, in 1975. When the Attorney General of Pennsylvania ruled that even hard-core delinquents could not be confined with adult offenders, officials turned for help to RCA Services, a division of the Radio Corporation of America that had previously run treatment programs for the state. In ten days, RCA renovated a state-owned building to establish Weaversville and was given a contract to run it.[16]

High security and control are maintained at Weaversville by a fence, locked internal and external doors, intensive supervision (35 staff members for 22 youths), and room restriction when necessary.[17] The security is necessitated by the nature of the population: boys aged 15–18 who have failed in or run from other programs and who have committed violent or otherwise serious crimes, such as burglary, robbery, assault, sex offenses, weapons offenses, arson, vandalism, and theft.[18] In spite of the far-reaching security, however, the atmosphere is relaxed. Each resident has his own carpeted room, with his own key.[19] Length of stay averages six months. The program emphasizes behavior modification, education, and vocational training. Contract renewal has been competitive, originally on a yearly basis, later changed to every three years.[20]

Eckerd Youth Development Center

While Weaversville was a first for the private sector in terms of its high-security custody for chronic and serious offenders, it remained in the tradition, for private facilities, of very small size. By the end of the 1970s, the private sector had not yet been entrusted with a large and secure correctional institution.

That threshold was crossed in the summer and fall of 1982, when the Florida School for Boys at Okeechobee, one of Florida's three large juvenile institutions (with 400 to 450 inmates), became the Jack and Ruth Eckerd Youth Development Center. The state retained ownership, but issued separate contracts for operating the program and for managing the facility. Both contracts were awarded (through open competition, but with only one responding bidder) to the Eckerd Foundation, a nonprofit arm of the Eckerd Corporation, a major drug manufacturer and drugstore chain.[21] Prior to 1982, the Eckerd Foundation had for many years run programs in Florida for emotionally disturbed and delinquent youths.

The state had planned to close the Okeechobee school but found that it could not afford to do so. For years it allowed the facility to deteriorate, with no money budgeted for physical improvements. Conditions were bad, and led to a lawsuit filed by the ACLU and other groups, charging "cruel and abusive conditions of confinement." The suit named Okeechobee and two other state-run institutions, but not the Eckerd Foundation, which the critics agree simply inherited the conditions. The Foundation donated $280,000 of its own money to upgrade the staff and worked to improve the physical plant and equipment.[22]

The population, aged 14 to 18, is predominantly hard-core, serious felony delinquents, with a complicating mix of severely disturbed and first-time offenders. High security is provided by close supervision, a fence with electronic sensors, and the isolated location of the training school. The average stay is about six months.

Florida Environmental Institute

The Florida Environmental Institute, a program of the nonprofit Associated Marine Institutes, is at least partially institutional and secure. Run since 1983 under contract to the Florida Department of Health and Rehabilitative Services, this is a three-phase program for Dade and Broward counties. The third phase is an open, non-residential program of participation in one of the marine biology programs operated by the Associated Marine Institutes. However, phases one and two, which consist of work, vocational, educational, and values training, occur in tents and trailers in an isolated swamp.[23] These phases are institutional in the sense of having no interface with an outside community, and they have at least a minimal level of security in the form of isolation. The program handles serious juvenile offenders.

Shelby Training Center

Another institutional juvenile facility is managed by Corrections Corporation of America, the leading proprietary prison company in the country (CCA will be described in more detail in the next section). Opened in May 1986, the Shelby Training Center in Memphis, Tennessee, was built for Shelby County by CCA—in ten months with an investment of $6.5 million of company funds—to hold male delinquents, primarily property offenders. The Training Center is a secure lockup, with close supervision, locked windows and doors, and a fence, though it looks like a college campus from the street. The complex consists of six housing units with 150 single rooms; six classrooms; library; music and art room; mechanical, woodworking, and electrical shop; dining area; and kitchen. It has 84 employees. The facility is accredited as being in accordance with American Correctional Association standards, as is its sister facility, Tall Trees, a 50-bed, nonsecure, community-based juvenile facility.

Under a state law effective in 1982, the state pays the county a per diem fee to hold locally those offenders who would otherwise be placed in state institutions. The county passes this per diem on to CCA, minus 2 percent for administration costs. While the facility has a capacity of 150, the population has been held to 110, which has been the limit that the state will reimburse, though that may change.[24]

Artesian Oaks

Artesian Oaks, in Saugus, California, is a fenced-in campus for juvenile parole violators. This 100-bed facility is operated by Management and Training Corporation of Ogden, Utah, a company that manages federal Job Corps training centers.[25]

Adult Confinement Facilities

The most recent and most controversial form of proprietary prison is the adult confinement facility, in which unchaperoned access to the community is not permitted for most of the population. Private versions of these facilities began to appear with increasing frequency during the 1980s.

By mid-1989, about a dozen private companies were running about two dozen adult confinement institutions totaling some 7,000 beds in about a dozen states. If that last sentence seems obsessed with qualifiers, it is because it is not always clear whether to classify a particular institution as a "confinement facility" or as a "residential program," and because contractual prisons and jails can spring so rapidly into or out of existence (as this book goes to press in late 1989, there are now about 9,000 of these beds). Thus no definitive census of these facilities exists.

The types of adult confinement facilities currently under contract include: jails; regular state and county prisons; facilities for offenders nearing release to parole; lockups for return-to-custody parole violators; and detention centers for the Immigration and Naturalization Service. They can be divided into three groups: federally contracted, state-contracted, and locally contracted.

Federal Contracts

Hidden Valley Ranch

In 1984, the federal Youth Corrections Act expired, leaving the federal Bureau of Prisons with a number of young adult offenders, aged 18–26, with remaining sentences to serve for such acts as bank robbery and mail fraud. The BOP signed a three-year contract with Eclectic Communications, Inc., a for-profit company, to house about 60 of these offenders at Hidden Valley Ranch in La Honda, California. The ranch, located in the mountains on 3.5 acres leased from San Francisco County, has the air of a suburban school, but is surrounded by a 12-foot chain link and razor-wire fence.[26] The staff of 30 is headed by Tom Keohane, a 27-year veteran of the Bureau of Prisons.[27]

The Bureau of Prisons was not the first federal agency to contract for confinement, nor the one to make the most use of that arrangement. That distinction belongs to the U.S. Immigration and Naturalization Service. The INS has contracted at least half a dozen facilities for the detention of illegal aliens awaiting deportation. These facilities are generally minimum to medium security and often include arrangements for families. Contracting provided the INS with a rapid, flexible, and cost-effective response to dramatic increases in illegal immigration, particularly in the Southwest. Jails and other facilities operated by local governments could no longer handle the overflow. Even if overcrowding was not a problem, existing facilities were unable to accommodate families, and they were expensive to operate, having been built for a higher level of security than the INS needed.

Behavioral Systems Southwest, INS Contracts

In 1980, the INS awarded its first facility management contract via competitive bidding to a for-profit company, Behavioral Systems

Southwest. BSS was founded as an offshoot of a behavioral modification training program by its current President, Theodore R.
Nissen, and Vice President, Tamara S. Lindholm. Both Nissen and
Lindholm had long careers in the California Department of Corrections. BSS now manages several holding facilities for the INS,
community treatment centers for the federal Bureau of Prisons,
and re-entry programs for the corrections departments of Arizona
and California.[28] With 130 employees, many of them ex-convicts,
BSS in 1986 supervised 465 inmates.[29]

For its first facility—the Pasadena Immigration Holding Facility—BSS converted a former convalescent home to house 125 men,
women, and children.[30] Over 3,000 aliens a year are processed by
the Pasadena facility.[31] BSS later won contracts for other INS
holding facilities in San Diego and Aurora, Colorado, near Den-
ver. The buildings have locked doors and razor wire on the roof;
the staff is not armed.[32] BSS leases its buildings for ten years on
the private market and operates them for the INS on annual contracts, thus exposing itself to some risk if a contract is not renewed.[33] The company did, in fact, give up its contract to run the
Aurora facility in 1987, when the INS contracted with the Wackenhut Corporation to build a new facility there. However, they
were able to convert the facility to another use for the remaining
two years of their lease. They had originally converted a warehouse
into the 85-bed facility at a cost of $150,000.[34]

BSS has been reported to carry insurance of $5 million and
its profits have been variously reported as 8 percent on a gross
of $6 million annually,[35] or 3.5 percent on revenues of $4.5
million.[36]

Corrections Corporation of America, INS Contracts

Another INS contractor is Corrections Corporation of America (CCA), which is now the leading proprietary manager of
correctional facilities. As of summer 1989, CCA operated 16 correctional facilities in 5 states with 4,238 beds.[37] Originally financed with $10 million in venture capital from the Massey
Burch Investment Group, the same firm that started Hospital
Corporation of America,[38] CCA is now a publicly traded corporation with assets of over $60 million in 1989.[39] CCA is self-

insured for $5 million in general liability coverage, which includes personal coverage of company officers while acting in their official capacities.[40]

The company, headquartered in Nashville, was founded in 1983 by Thomas Beasley, a Tennessee businessman, attorney, and former Tennessee Republican Party chairman,[41] and by T. Don Hutto, a former commissioner of corrections in Arkansas and Virginia and President of the American Correctional Association from 1984 to 1986.

In April 1984, CCA opened the Houston Processing Center, a 350-bed dual-purpose facility holding adult illegal aliens awaiting deportation by the INS and convicted alien offenders in the custody of the Bureau of Prisons. The company owns the facility, and operates it under annual contracts with the INS and the BOP. CCA took just seven months to locate a site and finance, design, and construct the $5 million facility.[42] During part of the construction period, CCA leased a former motel to house 140 aliens temporarily.[43]

On the outside, the Houston facility resembles an office building, including landscaping, while inside it is like a dormitory. Locked doors provide perimeter security and no weapons are carried inside.[44] CCA maintains a staff of 55 full-time employees[45] and provides space for several INS officials, whose duties include on-site monitoring of the CCA contract.[46] The Houston Processing Center is fully accredited by the Commission on Accreditation for Corrections,[47] and operates under the regulations and standards of the INS.[48]

In a second contract that began in March 1985, CCA operates the Laredo Processing Center for the INS in Laredo, Texas. CCA constructed this 200-bed facility, at a cost of $3 million, in just 145 days.[49] Unlike the Houston facility, which is restricted to adults, the Laredo facility is designed for men, women, and children.

Wackenhut Corrections Corporation, INS Contract

The Wackenhut Corrections Corporation (WCC) is a subsidiary of the $300-million Wackenhut Corporation of Coral Gables, Florida, one of the world's largest providers of security and related services. Wackenhut, which operates in 40 different countries on 6 continents, has offices in over 100 U.S. cities and 35,000 employees worldwide.[50] On May 4, 1987, just five months after signing a contract with the INS, Wackenhut opened a new 150-bed facility in Aurora, Colorado, near Denver, to hold illegal entrants and immigration offenders who have finished serving sentences in BOP prisons and are awaiting deportation.[51] Actual construction time was just three months.[52] The facility is owned outright by Wackenhut; it was not financed through third parties. The facility administrator is Craig Dobson, a 20-year veteran of the Bureau of Prisons and the founder and first director of the National Institute of Corrections Jail Center in Denver. In August 1989, the facility was accredited as meeting the standards of the American Correctional Association.

State Contracts

Marion Adjustment Center

The first facility to have the full combination of private ownership, private operation and management, incarceration of adult felons sentenced by a state, and a classification level (on paper) of at least "minimum security,"[53] was the United States Corrections Corporation's Marion Adjustment Center in St. Mary's, Kentucky, which began receiving inmates on January 6, 1986.

Without detracting from this distinction, it should in fairness to history be noted that other vendors had previously achieved all of these elements and more, though not in full combination at one facility. Most notably, on October 1, 1985, Corrections Corporation of America assumed exclusive possession (but not title) and full operation of the Bay County (Florida) Jail. With a level VI (highest) security wing holding serious offenders such as capital murderers and rapists, with postconviction as well as pretrial inmates, with federal and state in addition to county commitments, and with cells for men, women, and juveniles, this facility had it all . . . except for private ownership simultaneous with operation. That element was added later with CCA's construction and ownership of the Jail Annex, which opened on April 30, 1986.[54]

Still, the opening of Marion Adjustment Center was a milestone in the history of proprietary prisons. Whether the label of "prison" is accurate or not, the mere fact that it is widely referred to as the first contracted state prison in modern times makes Marion a political test of public perceptions of private prisons.

On legal, as opposed to political grounds, however, perhaps the U.S. Corrections Corporation (USCC) should not be too eager to identify itself as the first overseer of a privately owned and operated state "prison." Under a 1972 statute, the Kentucky Corrections Cabinet is authorized to establish "community residential centers" to hold convicted felons. The state attorney general, however, defines the Marion Adjustment Center as a minimum security prison, for which no specific contract-authorizing legislation exists. A citizens' group has brought a lawsuit against the state based on that opinion.[55]

USCC was incorporated in January 1983 by co-owners Milton Thompson, an architect, and J. Clifford Todd, a builder and developer, with an initial investment of $1.9 million.[56] To support their bid for the two-year contract, they purchased an old seminary, St. Mary's College in St. Mary, Kentucky, for $695,000. They were able to open the facility without any remodeling at first; residents were employed at that task later.[57]

The population at Marion is drawn from state prisoners nearing their parole eligibility dates.[58] The state selects cases for Marion on the basis of low risk, and USCC can reject any they regard as unsuitable. This selection process may help explain why 63 percent of Marion residents are in educational programs, compared to 20 percent of the inmates in other state institutions.[59] During the first 7 months of operation, there were 4 walk-aways, 3 of whom were recaptured within 24 hours. In a comparison state facility, walk-aways averaged 1.5 per week.[60] The staff in 1986 numbered 46, with 33 of them in security. An on-site state employee monitors the contract.

The facility initially had a physical capacity of 400 and an authorized capacity of 200.[61] Kentucky guaranteed USCC a minimum daily population of 175. Such an arrangement has the advantage, over a minimum payment clause, of ensuring that the state gets what it pays for, while protecting the contractor.[62] In late 1988, under a second contract from the Kentucky Corrections Cabinet, a new unit was opened with 250 beds, bringing the authorized capacity to 450.

USCC carries insurance that will cover up to $1.5 million per incident.[63]

New Mexico Women's Correctional Facility

On July 1, 1988, the state of New Mexico signed a contract with Corrections Corporation of America calling for a new 200-bed prison to be designed, financed, constructed, and then operated by CCA commencing April 1, 1989. Because the state was tardy in appropriating funds, the facility did not actually open until June 1, 1989. Its purpose is to hold all of the state's female felons, anticipated to number about 160 (any excess beds, up to the capacity of 200, may be filled by CCA with inmates from federal or other state jurisdictions). Located on 40 acres in Grants, New Mexico, this prison has high external security and internal security at all levels of custody. This makes it the first minimum through maximum security contemporary state prison to be run by a private contractor.

Prior to mid-1989, New Mexico held its female prisoners in another penitentiary in Grants that doubled as a reception and diagnostic center. When the CCA facility opened, all current employees had the option of either becoming part of CCA's staff of 85 full-time employees, or remaining with the state. The state is responsible for preservice training of all new CCA employees.

The contract has a 4-year initial term, with an option for successive 2-year extensions, up to 20 years. The extension option must be exercised after the first 2 years and every 2 years thereafter, thus occurring always in the middle of 4-year terms. If the contract is terminated, the state will buy the facility and all associated property from CCA, or it may, at its option, make this purchase anytime during the contract, at a decreasing percentage of the property's initially appraised value. If the contract runs the full 20 years, the state may buy the property for one dollar.

CCA, which is just beginning its operation at Grants as this is being written, will offer a program of services to include education, recreation, counseling, and medical and dental care. The contractor will run an inmate work program, a work- and school-release program, and a furlough program. In addition, space will be provided for an industry program to be run by the state.

CCA will classify inmates, using the state's classification manual, and will impose discipline, with grievance procedures, in accordance with New Mexico Corrections Department (NMCD) policy and procedures and state law. However, the NMCD retains final review and authority over all major decisions affecting inmates: classification as it affects custody level; discipline; grievances; allocation or revocation of good time; computation of parole eligibility or discharge dates; and approval of work, medical, or temporary furloughs. CCA may take no action on these without a prior written decision by NMCD. The NMCD will provide a contract monitor, who will have office space in and full access to the CCA facility.

CCA must maintain property, general liability, and civil rights liability insurance, naming the state as an additional insured, and it has pledged to defend the state in any lawsuit. In addition, CCA has indemnified the state against any claims, and all costs of defending against claims, arising out of the operation of the prison.

The contract obliges CCA to seek and obtain ACA accreditation within 24 months of operation.

Texas Preparole Facilities

As of this writing (summer 1989), the Texas Department of Corrections is in the process of bringing on line four major contracts to add 2,000 beds to their system. Wackenhut and CCA are each building, and will operate, two 500-bed minimum security prisons to hold state felons who are within two years of their release dates. The first of these facilities was opened by Wackenhut in Kyle, Texas, on June 28, 1989. Scheduled to open later in the summer are the second Wackenhut facility, at Bridgeport, Texas, and the two CCA facilities, at Cleveland, Texas, and Venus, Texas.

The Texas Board of Pardons and Paroles also has three other

prerelease facilities under private contract: Pricor Incorporated (described later, under local jail contracts) is providing 210 beds at the Sweetwater Reintegration Center and 223 beds at the Houston Reintegration Center; and CCA provides beds for 200 pre-parole cases at its Houston Processing Center (where it also holds INS detainees).

On the other side of the parole process, Wackenhut Corrections Corporation operates the 619-bed Central Texas Parole Violator Facility for offenders from all over the state who have violated their paroles.[64] This kind of lockup is often referred to as a Return-to-Custody (RTC) facility and the State of Texas is loooking to contract for several more. At least one other state, California, also views the RTC as a prime candidate for privatization.

California Return-to-Custody Facilities

As of the summer of 1989, the California Department of Corrections had six RTC facilities under contract, with plans to add more later. Although minimum security, these are real prisons, with razor wire and other security measures. Without going into individual details, the six prisons and their contractors are: (1) a 200-bed RTC at McFarland contracted to Wackenhut; (2) a 200-bed RTC at Mesa Verde (Bakersfield) contracted to Gary White and Associates; (3) the 200-bed Eagle Mountain RTC contracted to Management and Training Corp.; (4) a 200-bed RTC at Baker contracted to Eclectic Communications Inc. (ECI); (5) Hidden Valley Ranch, an 88-bed RTC at La Honda contracted to ECI[65]; and the Leo Chessley Center at Live Oak, a 100-bed RTC for females, also contracted to ECI.

In addition to the contractors' own staff at these RTCs, the state provides California corrections officers to supervise security. Despite reservations about privatization in the Department of Corrections, and opposition from correctional employees' unions in the legislature, the department plans to contract more facilities like these.[66] Such contracts allow the state to respond quickly to rapid increases in cases, without the long-term commitment entailed in construction and civil service employment.

Local Contracts

While no state has yet contracted for the operation of a medium or maximum security prison for males, something like that has already occurred on a small scale at the local level, in contracts for the management of jails. By their nature, jails must be equipped to hold and process all types of offenders as they enter the criminal justice system. In addition, jails often serve as temporary catch-basins for the runoff and spillover from all sorts of other institutions. Thus, overcrowding anywhere aggravates the already serious overcrowding in local lockups. Traditionally the poorest level of government, counties have been under the greatest pressure to find alternative solutions to crises in the demand for and supply of prisons. Despite organized opposition from the National Sheriffs' Association, one solution being explored by counties is private contracting.

Bay County Jail and Annex

A few years ago, Bay County, Florida, was devoting 65 percent of its budget to its jail, yet it faced overcrowding, medical problems, violations of state regulations, and lawsuits, including one inmate rape case in which corrections officers testified that they had not been on the floor for over two hours.[67] At the suggestion of a local newsman, the county commission considered the option of privatization. After an open and competitive process of Requests for Qualifications and subsequent bids, the county awarded a contract to Corrections Corporation of America.

Under the contract, CCA assumed full management of the Bay County Jail starting October 1, 1985, and agreed to build (and own) a new jail annex in addition to renovating the jail. The annex opened on April 30, 1986. Its facilities for 200 men, women, and (separately housed) juveniles supplemented the 204 beds for adult men at the main jail. The Bay County/CCA facilities hold every type of offender, from misdemeanants to capital murderers. Pretrial detention cases and convicted offenders awaiting transfer or serving sentences of one year or less are also placed here. Most are county inmates, but some are state or federal prisoners.

The Bay County Jail is secured by means of locked exits, locked internal gates, and locked cells. The annex has a chain-link and razor wire fence, internal gates, and some locked cells in addition to the more open, dormitory-style housing areas. Both facilities have remote monitors and lock-control stations. Consistent with Florida policy followed in all county jails, no arms are carried inside either facility, but some CCA security guards are certified to carry arms outside.

A county employee monitors the contract and has final authority over all recommendations regarding "gain time" made by CCA personnel in disciplinary actions. Rules for inmates and procedures for discipline and allocation of gain time were established in conformity to Florida statutes and Department of Corrections policies. Where not in conflict with Florida law or policy, CCA abides by the often more exacting standards of the American Correctional Association. Under contract, CCA is required to provide insurance and to indemnify the county against all legal damages resulting from the operation of the jail. At first, CCA carried a purchased policy; later they instituted a self-insurance plan.

Bay County Sheriff Lavelle Pitts was strongly opposed to the contract. He retained all of his salary and duties as sheriff except for administration of the jail, but 70 of the 75 deputies who previously worked in his jail became CCA employees on completing 40 hours of training by CCA.[68] CCA paid them for accrued vacation time and gave them raises ranging from 10 percent to 20 percent. After one year with the company, employees are eligible to participate in an employee stock ownership program.[69]

The 20-year contract with CCA specifies conditions for termination by either party. The fee charged by CCA may increase with inflation, but by no more than 5 percent a year. There is a provision, however, for negotiating adjustments every three years in the event of unforseen circumstances. A budget limit is set each year based on projected population size and projected inflation. The fee varies by population level, with lower per diem charges above specified population breakpoints. The contract specifies a minimum payment by the county of an amount equal to the charge for 285 prisoners per month. CCA may rent unused space to other jurisdictions, at a price at least equal to that charged to Bay County. Any excess is shared equally by the county and CCA.

Silverdale Detention Center

On October 15, 1984—one year before it took over the Bay County Jail—CCA assumed management of the Silverdale Detention Center, a minimum to medium security work farm for adults under the jurisdiction of Hamilton County, Tennessee, at Chattanooga. Silverdale has a capacity of 400, including 100 beds for females. Since the Hamilton County jail has no arrangements for females, some of the women at Silverdale are pretrial detainees; the rest of the prisoners are convicted offenders. As reported in the *New York Times*, Silverdale "houses state prisoners serving long terms for felonies, including murder, county prisoners serving less than a year for misdemeanors, and a growing number of prisoners serving mandatory 48-hour sentences for driving while intoxicated. Also growing in number are second offenders serving a minimum of 45 days and third offenders serving a minimum of 120 days under Tennessee's tough laws on driving while drunk."[70] The maximum sentence is 6 years, and about one-third serve more than one year, but the average stay is short, about 45 days.[71]

As part of the contract, Hamilton County leases the Silverdale facility to CCA. All buildings and grounds remain the property of the county, including the $1.6 million in renovations and additions invested by CCA during its first year of operation. If the county terminates the contract, however, it must reimburse CCA for any remaining unamortized portion of this investment. The contract runs for 32 years and is automatically renewable at 4-year intervals, though conditions for termination are included. Payment rates, however, are renegotiated every year.

All county employees at Silverdale were retained by CCA, but there was 50 percent turnover within two years.[72] The warden of Silverdale under its operation by the county is now the Hamilton County Director of Corrections and the monitor for the CCA contract. Unlike Sheriff Pitts, the displaced warden in Bay County, the Hamilton County corrections director is favorably impressed with the new management of his old facility, in spite of his initial skepticism toward the idea of a proprietary operation.[73]

CCA expanded bed space and introduced many changes at Silverdale. A list prepared by the warden identifies 74 innovations effected by CCA during its first year.[74] Public officials doubt that the county could have afforded to make these improvements on its own.[75]

In contractually mandated pursuit of accreditation, corrections officers receive more training than was previously provided by the county, and many operating procedures are tighter than before.[76] As in all CCA facilities, the officers inside are unarmed; after experiencing a minor disturbance, Silverdale obtained riot equipment, including mace, shields, and riot guns, to be issued if needed.[77] Procedures for the discipline of inmates and the allocation of gain time are specified in CCA's contract and are similar to those for the Bay County Jail.[78]

Santa Fe County Jail

Santa Fe County, New Mexico, is the site of a third CCA contract at the local level of government. After running its new jail for a year, the county decided to consider the private alternative. As a result of competitive bidding among five contenders, the county awarded a three-year contract to CCA, commencing August 1, 1986.[79] The jail—the Santa Fe County Detention Facility—has 147 beds, plus a section for juveniles with 20 housing cells and 4 booking cells.[80]

Through supplemental contracts, CCA also rents some of its beds at the Santa Fe County Detention Facility to other jurisdictions, including the city of Santa Fe, the Federal Bureau of Prisons, the U.S. Marshall's Service, San Miguel County, and Pecos and Rio Arriba, New Mexico.[81] CCA has posted a $325,000 certificate of deposit as collateral on a performance bond for this contract.[82]

CCA assured the staff of 58 that they would retain their jobs and salaries but that there would be retraining and reorganization required. The company "also promised to assume employees' accrued vacation; [to] offer 10 paid holidays [plus optional unpaid holidays], 12 days of annual leave and 12 sick days; [and to] provide comprehensive medical and life insurance and a stock ownership plan." [83]

A 1984 New Mexico statute authorizes contracting for two county jails as pilot projects.[84] The law grants peace-officer powers to private jailers but denies them the power to award or take away gain time; that decision is left to sheriffs. It limits contracts to three years, and requires the contractor to assume all liability and to buy enough insurance to cover itself, as determined by the Risk Management Division of the General Services Department. Counties are required to inspect both private and public jails at least two times a year. If these inspections uncover apparent violations of statute, the district attorney must sue the sheriff, jail administrator, or contractor. Finally, the New Mexico law provides for termination of contracts on 90 days notice, for cause—which may include failure to meet minimum standards or other deficiencies that seriously affect the operation of the jail.[85]

Volunteers of America Regional Corrections Center

Corrections has a long history of volunteers who come into institutions or who work with offenders and ex-offenders in the community. Volunteers of America (VOA) has been involved in corrections since its founding in 1896.[86] It was not until September 1984, however, that VOA contracted to assume total operation of a jail.

The Volunteers of America Regional Corrections Center, in Roseville, Minnesota, a suburb of St. Paul, has 40 beds, of which about 25 at a time were occupied in 1985.[87] It has a staff of 17 full-time, 3 part-time, and 12 volunteer workers. All the inmates are women serving sentences of up to one year.[88] The VOA leases its facility—a former juvenile detention center—from Ramsey County, and receives prisoners from county, state, and federal courts.[89] Two other counties also place prisoners at the VOA facility, under separate contracts,[90] and some prerelease prisoners are received from the federal Bureau of Prisons.

Pricor Incorporated: Two Jails

Pricor Incorporated is a private corrections firm headquartered in Nashville, Tennessee, where it spun off from CCA early in the latter's development. Like CCA and Wackenhut, Pricor issues public shares of common stock and operates on a national level.

While Pricor lately has been focusing on juvenile facilities, it also operates adult preparole facilities (described above) and jails. One jail contract is for the Tuscaloosa Metropolitan Minimum Security Detention Facility, a 150-bed jail, where Pricor books all arrestees and holds just the minimum security cases for the city and county of Tuscaloosa, Alabama, and for the city of Northport. A second contract is for the Greene County Jail, in Greeneville, Tennessee, a 160-bed jail for all county arrestees and detainees.

Butler County Prison

On October 1, 1985, Butler County, Pennsylvania, turned over management of its county prison (and jail) to Buckingham Security Limited, under a two-year contract. It thus became one of the first two jails (along with CCA/Bay County) to transfer from public to private management. The contract specified that Buckingham was to be responsible for management and operating costs, while Butler County was responsible for capital improvements, medical expenses, and jail employee labor costs.[91] The contract was later renewed for one more year, then allowed to expire without renewal when a new county commission was elected following an intense campaign against the prison contract. More on that development shortly.

Buckingham Security was incorporated in Connecticut by Peter Savin, a Hartford builder, and Joseph and Charles Fenton.[92] Buckingham had previously planned to build a 720-bed prison in Pennsylvania to hold protective custody cases from several states. These prisoners require special resources inside a normal prison, where they must be segregated from the general prison population. In a regional facility, however, they can be served more efficiently, due to economies of scale and greater homogeneity of population. That plan, however, foundered on the shoals of siting problems, liability issues, and a one-year moratorium on prison privatization imposed by the Pennsylvania legislature. The moratorium did not affect the preexisting contract with Butler County.

Charles Fenton, who had served as the warden of maximum security penitentiaries in Marion, Illinois, and Lewisburg, Pennsylvania, during a 23-year career with the federal prison system, became warden of the Butler County Prison under the contract.

The prison, or jail, is a high-security facility holding both pretrial and postconviction county prisoners, with some state and federal offenders as well. All are adults, both male and female.

The capacity of the prison at the start of the contract was about 100.[93] Buckingham increased the total capacity by over 10 percent in the first year, without additional staff, and another 50 percent increase was anticipated soon thereafter.[94] The facility was rehabilitated with inmate labor under Buckingham's supervision, thereby reducing the county's capital improvement costs. Previously, inmates performed no work of any sort.

The contract was monitored by a county employee. Disciplinary protocol was outlined in the contract. However, since the jail officers were still county employees, there was less of an issue of private delegation than is the case under some other contracts.[95] In contrast to prior Butler County custom, under the contractor's management police no longer were allowed to bring their firearms with them into the jail.[96]

A professional system of key control, head counts, security system checks, cell inspections, and classification, admission, and release procedures was established at the jail for the first time.[97] Buckingham ended the county practice whereby officers and other staff did not venture into living areas, passageways, and recreation yards while inmates were there.[98]

An interesting feature of this contract is that up until the day before it was to go into effect, Buckingham had intended to fire the entire staff of unionized county employees and replace them with workers of its own choosing and in its own employ. However, the union obtained an eleventh-hour court ruling that required the company to retain the county workers. The resulting contract adjustment left Buckingham in the strange if not unique position of being a private management company supervising public employees who remained on the county payroll.

In view of the rocky start, the ensuing hostile atmosphere, and the long-standing and vehement opposition to private contracting on the part of the union leadership, one might have expected all-out internal warfare. Surprisingly, however, labor relations at Butler Prison were in some ways better after the contract than they were before. Every year since the prison workers first unionized under AFSCME, negotiations with the county had ended in impasse followed by arbitration. Under Buckingham's management, the workers achieved their first labor contract with the county. The employees gained higher pay, while management was allowed to redefine job responsibilities and to eliminate much costly overtime and part-time work.[99] Although union opposition remained vehement, employee morale was high. During the first few years after Buckingham assumed management, no employee left, in contrast to a turnover of three or four per year previously.

In a first-year report, Buckingham summarized its accomplishments as follows:

> The County Commissioners have saved money and are confident that the prison for the first time is under competent, professional management. The union for the first time in history has a signed contract with the county. Employees have better working conditions, higher pay and greater pride. The sheriff has fewer hassles and less expense. The prison board is confident that they have a smoothly running prison, functioning in accord with local, state and federal laws. Inmates have brighter, cleaner, safer and more peaceful living conditions. New programs have been instituted that have positively impacted on work release, health, education, cleanliness, physical fitness, work and recreation.[100]

While Buckingham might be expected to toot its own horn, this assessment was confirmed by county officials. In a letter to Warden Fenton dated November 13, 1986, the Chairman of the County Commission, Richard M. Patterson, said:

> Less than one year ago, we had a great deal of concern about the Butler County Prison. It occupied our time almost daily. Control was in question. Both the employees and the prisoners were in a serious state of turmoil. Court action was involved, and the public was agitated by negative media comment.
>
> Within three months, due only to the professionalism of Buckingham Securit[y], the whole matter has made a one-hundred-eighty degree turn, and all is quiet and all is under control, including the cost.[101]

Not everyone was happy with the contract, however. The union (AFSCME) was opposed from the beginning and was already organized throughout the state in support of a legislative moratorium on prison privatization. At the next election, they gave their full support, in money and campaign labor, to two candidates for County Commission who promised, if elected, to put the jail once again under direct county management. The union disagreed with the contractor, and County Commission members and candidates disagreed among themselves, as to whether the contract was saving the county money. According to accounts from all sides, however, it was labor and county politics even more than economics that drove the conflict.[102] This became the major issue of the campaign and the two union-backed candidates were elected, defeating and replacing two incumbents who supported the contract with Buckingham.

I have given extra attention to this contract because it reflects the intensity of the debate surrounding private prisons. Most of the rest of this book will be devoted to identifying and examining the issues and arguments involved in that debate.

3

Issues and Arguments in the Debate over Private Prisons

This chapter gives a concise overview of arguments on both sides of the controversy over private prisons. It identifies the issues and lists in summary form a series of claims and counterclaims that will be examined in detail in the remainder of the book. The chapter is intended as a reference tool; many readers may prefer to skim through it and proceed quickly to the more complete discussions of each issue that begin with the next chapter. However, readers who want to see a conceptual framework defining and organizing the issues, and a comprehensive but condensed guide to arguments on both sides of each issue, will find that here.

Private Prison Issues[1]

Privately contracted prisons raise many philosophical, empirical, and policy questions. These cover at least the following range of issues:

1. propriety		6. security	
2. cost		7. liability	
3. quality		8. accountability	
4. quantity		9. corruption	
5. flexibility		10. dependence	

1. Questions of *propriety* may be philosophical, political, or legal. Is it proper for imprisonment to be administered by anyone other than government officials and employees? How might private delegation of authority affect the legitimation of prisons in the eyes of inmates or the public? Is the "profit motive" more or less compatible with doing justice than are the motives to be found within state bureaucracies, employee unions, or nonprofit agencies? Should prison contracts permit the private exercise of quasi-judicial authority (i.e., classification, discipline, allocation of gain time)?

2. Is *cost* as likely to be reduced with the privatization of corrections as it has been with some other public services? Or does experience with privatization in other areas suggest that the net costs may actually be higher in the long run, as a result of "lowballing" or due to the added costs of supervision and of the contracting process itself? Can the process of contracting help clarify the true costs of both public and private service delivery in corrections?

3. Will privatization increase the *quality* of imprisonment due to innovations by private companies? Or will commercial companies cut corners to save costs and thereby lower quality? What are the advantages and disadvantages of government control versus competition as a quality control mechanism? Can the advantages of competition be obtained without involvement of the private sector? How can the contracting process be used to specify and clarify standards?

4. How might privatization affect the *quantity* of imprisonment? Will it merely help meet an independently determined demand, or will commercial companies lobby to increase the demand?

5. Will private contracts bring with them the greater *flexibility* characteristic of small businesses and entrepreneurs? Do they reduce red tape and avoid the perpetuation of agencies and programs commonly found in government? Can the private sector more accurately anticipate and more rapidly respond to the correctional needs of government? Or will contracts bring with them their own form of rigidity, such as restrictions on what can be expected or demanded? Do contracts encourage short-term, over long-term, planning?

6. Can *security* be ensured in private prisons? What are the legal limits to the delegation of authority to use deadly force? How does

the training of government correctional personnel compare to that of the staff of private companies? What steps can be taken to prevent, ensure against, or deal with a possible disruption of private prison operations due to strikes or bankruptcy?

7. Does a private prison contract simply extend and add to the *liability* of government, or does it defray and reduce liability costs through insurance and increased incentives to avoid expensive lawsuits?

8. Is *accountability* decreased because private prisons are less accessible to public scrutiny, or increased because the private sector is more vulnerable than the state to legal controls? Do contracts diffuse responsibility, or do they increase it by providing another mechanism of control over prison managers? How accountable are correctional institutions and personnel under current arrangements?

9. Would the potential for *corruption* in running prisons be higher, lower, or merely different in form under contractual arrangements? Can close monitoring, along with competition and market processes, keep the bidding for and the granting of contracts honest, or is collusion inevitable? How do the possible forms of corruption under public-private management differ from those under purely public systems? Which forms are easier to control?

10. How can government protect itself from merely substituting a private monopoly for a public monopoly? Should the government retain some correctional capacity in its own hands in order to forestall *dependence* on a private provider? Should it contract only to multiple providers? Or does the possibility of competition at some time in the future limit the potential for abuse by a solitary contractor?

Arguments for and against Private Prison Contracting

In the chapters that follow, each of the issues defined above will be examined closely. Generally, the format of those chapters will be one in which an issue is raised as a negative or critical question posed by opponents of private prisons, followed by a response on the positive side. Here, that order is reversed, with arguments favorable to contracting for management of prisons followed by a separate set of arguments in opposition. The arguments have been abstracted and adapted from general literature on privatization as well as from discussions specific to prisons.[2]

Arguments for Contracting

1. Propriety

   a. Contracting enhances justice by making prison supply more responsive to changes in demand, both upward and downward.
   b. Contractual wardens have an incentive to govern inmates fairly in order to enhance their legitimation, induce co-operation, lower costs, and ensure renewal of contracts.
   c. Contracting does not jeopardize due process; private and public wardens are equally subject to the rule of law and accountable to the same constitutional standards.
   d. Contracting, in conjunction with governmental monitoring, adds a new layer of independent review of correctional decisions and actions, thus improving due process.
   e. Contracting can help clarify the purposes of imprisonment and the rules and procedures that define due process.
   f. Contracting for operating prisons is compatible with federal law and the laws of many states; specific enabling legislation has been passed in some states.

2. Cost

   a. Contracting allows prisons to be financed, sited, and constructed more quickly and cheaply than government prisons; also, private firms are more apt to design for efficient operation.
   b. Contracting across jurisdictions permits economies of scale.
   c. Contracting may reduce overly generous public employee pensions and benefits.
   d. Contracting typically indexes fee increases to the Consumer Price Index, while government costs have been shown to rise faster than the general level of inflation.
   e. Contracting discourages waste because prodigality cuts into profits.

    f. Contracting counteracts the motivation of budget-based government agencies to continually grow in size and to maximize their budgets.

    g. Contracting makes true costs highly visible, allowing them to be analyzed, compared, and adjusted.

    h. Contracting avoids cumbersome and rigid government procurement procedures; vendors can purchase more quickly, maintain lower inventories, and negotiate better prices and values.

    i. Contracting, through more effective personnel management, better working conditions, and less overcrowding, may increase employee morale and productivity while lowering absenteeism and turnover.

3. *Quality*

    a. Contracting provides an alternative yardstick against which to measure government service; it allows for comparisons.

    b. Contracting motivates both governmental and private prisons to compete on quality as well as cost.

    c. Contracting, by creating an alternative, raises standards for the government as well as for private vendors.

    d. Contracting adds new expertise and specialized skills.

    e. Contracting promotes creativity and enthusiasm by bringing in "new blood" and new ideas more often than is possible under civil service.

    f. Contracting promotes quality and high standards by forcing officials and the public to evaluate expenditures carefully, rather than masking costs through overcrowding and substandard conditions.

    g. Contracting will expand the political constituency concerned about legislative reforms of the correctional system.

    h. Contracting could hardly do worse than some current (public) prisons, in terms of quality.

4. *Quantity*

    a. Contractors can help alleviate today's capacity crisis by building new prisons faster than the government can.

    b. Contracting will allow quicker response in the future to meet changing needs or to correct mistakes resulting from inaccurate predictions or faulty policies.

    c. Contracting facilitates the distribution of inmates across agencies or jurisdictions, thereby maintaining occupancy rates at an efficient level (i.e., near capacity but not overcrowded).

    d. Contracting helps limit the size of government.

5. *Flexibility*

    a. Contracting allows greater flexibility, which promotes innovation, experimentation, and other changes in programs, including expansion, contraction, and termination.

    b. Contracting can avoid capital budget limits through leasing, or spread capital costs over time through lease-purchasing.

    c. Contracting reduces the levels of bureaucracy (red tape) involved in management decisions.

    d. Contracting reduces some of the political pressures that interfere with good management.

    e. Contracting avoids civil service and other government (and sometimes union) restrictions that interfere with efficient personnel management (i.e., hiring, firing, promotion, and salary setting; assignment of duties, work schedules, vacations, and leaves; adequate staffing to avoid excessive overtime).

    f. Contracting reduces the tendency toward bureaucratic self-perpetuation.

    g. Contracting promotes specialization to deal with special-needs prisoners (protective custody, AIDS patients, and so forth).

    h. Contracting relieves public administrators of daily hassles, allowing them to plan, set policy, and supervise.

6. *Security*

    a. Contracting may enhance public and inmate safety through increased staff training and professionalism.

    b. Contracted corrections officers are less likely to go on strike because they are more vulnerable to termination.

7. *Liability*

    a. Contracting may decrease the risks for which government remains liable, through higher quality performance and through indemnification and insurance.

8. *Accountability*

    a. Contracting increases accountability because market mechanisms of control are added to those of the political process.

    b. Contracting increases accountability because it is easier for the government to monitor and control a contractor than to monitor and control itself.

    c. Contracting promotes the development and use of objective performance measures.

    d. Contracting can help enforce adherence to procedures and limit or control discretion in the discipline of inmates.

    e. Contracted prisons will be highly visible and accountable, in contrast to state prisons which, at least historically, have been ignored by the public and given (until recently) "hands-off" treatment by the courts.

    f. Contractors are forced to be more responsive to the attitudes and needs of local communities when siting a prison.

    g. Contracting can require prisons to be certified as meeting the standards of the American Correctional Association.

    h. Contracting motivates vendors to serve as watchdogs over their competitors.

    i. Contracting will encourage much broader interest, involvement, and participation in corrections by people outside of government.

    j. Contracting provides a surgical solution when bad management has become entrenched and resistant to reform.

9. *Corruption*

    a. Contracting gives managers more of a vested interest in the reputation of their institution.

    b. Contracting pits the profit motive against other, less benign motives that can operate among those whose job it is to punish criminals.

10. *Dependence*
    a. Contracting can increase the number of suppliers, thus reducing dependence and vulnerability to strikes, slowdowns, or bad management.

Arguments against Contracting

1. *Propriety*
    a. Contracting for imprisonment involves an improper delegation to private hands of coercive power and authority.
    b. Contracting may put profit motives ahead of the public interest, inmate interests, or the purposes of imprisonment.
    c. Contracting prisons raises legal questions about the potential use of deadly force.
    d. Contracting creates conflicts of interest that can interfere with due process for inmates.
    e. Contracting may face legal obstacles in some jurisdictions.
    f. Contracting threatens the jobs and benefits of public employees; it is antilabor.
    g. Contracting may threaten corrections officers' sense of authority and status, both inside and outside the prison.

2. *Cost*
    a. Contracting is more expensive because it adds a profit margin to all other costs.
    b. Contracting creates the special costs of contracting: initiating, negotiating, and managing contracts, and monitoring contractor performance.
    c. Contracting may cost more in the long run as a result of "lowballing"—initial low bids followed by unjustifiable price raises in subsequent contracts.
    d. Contracting may cost more in the long run if high capital costs inhibit market entry and restrict competition.
    e. Contracting lacks effective competition in "follow-on" contracts, which are commonplace.
    f. Contracting costs the government extra for the termination, unemployment, and retraining of displaced government workers.

   g. Contracts with cost-plus-fixed-fee provisions provide no incentive for efficiency.

   h. Contracting may have a higher initial marginal cost than would expanding government services.

3. *Quality*

   a. Contracting may reduce quality through the pressure to cut corners economically.

   b. Contracting may "skim the cream" by removing the "best" prisoners and leaving the government prisons with the "worst," which will spuriously make the private prisons look better by comparison.

   c. Contracting will decrease the professionalism of rank and file prison employees because they will be underpaid and insecure and thus not able to develop a career orientation.

4. *Quantity*

   a. Contracting creates incentives to lobby for laws and public policies that serve special interests rather than the public interest; in particular, private prison companies may lobby for more imprisonment.

   b. Contracting, simply by expanding capacity and making imprisonment more feasible and efficient, may unduly expand the use of imprisonment and weaken the search for alternatives.

   c. Contracting on a per prisoner, per diem basis gives private wardens an incentive to hold prisoners as long as possible.

   d. Contracting creates a kind of underground government, thus adding to total government size.

5. *Flexibility*

   a. Contracting may limit flexibility by refusal to go beyond the terms of contract without renegotiation.

   b. Contracting may be stopped in advance, or suddenly reversed in midstream, by adverse public reaction, legal challenges, partisan politics, or organized opposition by interest groups, including public employee unions.

c. Contracting reduces ability to coordinate with other public agencies (police, sheriff, probation, parole, transportation, maintenance, and the like).

6. *Security*

   a. Contracting may jeopardize public and inmate safety through inadequate staff levels or training.
   b. Contracting may limit the ability of the government to respond to emergencies, such as strikes, riots, fires, or escapes.
   c. Contracting increases the risk of strikes, which may not be illegal for contractor personnel.
   d. Contracting may cause high employee turnover at transition.

7. *Liability*

   a. Contracting will not allow the government to escape liability.
   b. Contracting may cost the government more by increasing its liability exposure.
   c. Contracting shifts risk away from the government, which is the party best able to bear it.

8. *Accountability*

   a. Contracting reduces accountability because private actors are insulated from the public and not subject to the same political controls as are government actors.
   b. Contracting diffuses responsibility; government and private actors can each blame the other.
   c. Contracting may encourage the government to neglect or avoid its ultimate responsibility for prisons; supervision may slacken.
   d. Contracting reduces accountability because contracts are difficult to write and enforce.

9. *Corruption*

   a. Contracting brings new opportunities for corruption (i.e., political spoils, conflict of interest, bribes, kickbacks).

10. *Dependence*
  a. Contracting lowers the government's own capacity to provide services, which makes it dependent on contractors.
  b. Contracting carries the risk of bankruptcy by the vendor.
  c. Contracting may involve exclusive franchises that simply replace public monopolies with private monopolies.

4

The Propriety of Proprietary Prisons

The most strongly expressed, and least critically examined, objections to private prisons are those that are presented as statements of "principle." Some of the government's most vehement critics, especially when it comes to running prisons, nonetheless—for reasons of principle—are championing the government as the only suitable manager of these institutions. The ACLU, for example, regards imprisonment as among the "functions which *rightfully belong* to government." [1] The officially recorded policy of the ACLU states:

> The delegation of control and custody of prisoners to private entities, in and of itself, raises serious constitutional concerns. Because the deprivation of physical freedom is one of the most severe interferences with liberty that the State can impose, and because of civil liberties concern created by private management . . . the power to deprive another of his/her freedom cannot be delegated to private entities. [2]

Sandy Rabinowitz, Director of the Houston office of the ACLU, declares that "the whole concept [of private prisons] is really frightening." [3]

Mark Cuniff, Executive Director of the National Association of Criminal Justice Planners, says: "We're talking about taking away people's liberty, and I have questions about the propriety of anyone but the state doing that." [4] These organizations, like many critics of private prisons, raise a troublesome question but make no effort to explore possible answers. It is simply taken for granted that if the power in question is strong enough, only the state may legitimately apply it.

John DiIulio, Jr., a political scientist at Princeton and a brilliant analyst of prisons, is one critic who has carried the propriety objection beyond the level of intuitive reaction and into the realm of more serious thought. Writing in *Public Interest* and elsewhere, DiIulio identifies the central question as a normative one: Who *should* govern prisons?[5] In a thoughtful answer, DiIulio begins by accepting for the sake of argument that private prisons could do everything that prisons are supposed to do, and do so better and cheaper than government prisons. Even then, DiIulio insists, private prisons would be undesirable, as a matter of principle. With admirable clarity and consistency, DiIulio points out that the issue of motive (whether profit or other) is irrelevant, as is the issue of scope. The private administration of even one halfway house, he says, would raise the matter of principle just as sharply as the private ownership and operation of every prison in the country.[6] It is not clear why DiIulio stops there. The final extension of this argument would seem to be that even specific aspects of the care and custody of prisoners—such as food service, health care, and treatment programs—must also be provided directly by government.

While DiIulio does not take his argument to its limits, he does insist that proponents of private prisons should be prepared to extend their position to encompass private police, judges, juries, and executioners.[7] Indeed, DiIulio asks them to go so far as to explain why we should not turn over to private contractors the process of selecting a president, supposing for the sake of argument that professionals could do a much more competent job of it than can the general electorate.[8] These might be fair questions to ask of those who advocate total privatization, divestiture of all government authority, and dismantlement of the state. However, where the issue is contracting part of one particular government function (and delegation of relevant authority), it is not necessary to defend the privatization of all functions or delegation of every authority.

It must be made clear that contractually managed prisons are still government prisons. They do not exist on their own authority.

A case might be made for truly private prisons independent of government authority, but no one arguing for prison *contracting* is attempting to make *that* case. In the current argument, the choice is only between (a) direct governmental provision through salaried employees versus (b) governmental procurement through contract.

Those who govern prisons at the facility level (administrators and correctional officers) derive their authority and legitimacy only indirectly from the electoral process. Unlike DiIulio's presidential analogy, none of these actors is elected; they are all hired. Their legitimacy depends on an uncorrupted chain of accountability leading back to those who are elected and who set policies and issue orders in the name of the people. Our elected leaders exercise very little direct power; rather, they issue instructions and directives that are carried out by subordinates. The bigger and more centralized the state or government becomes, the longer the chains down which authority is transmitted and the greater the power that is exercised by those at the ends of the chains. The integrity of each link in a particular chain is therefore very important. However, it is false to assume that the integrity of a chain of civil servants is necessarily superior to a contractual chain.

Compare the chains of authority in the following two examples: (1) an elected county commission chooses a private jail vendor in an open, competitive process at a public meeting, using publicly announced criteria developed by the commission; and (2) an elected mayor appoints a friend and financial supporter to run the jail as a public employee. These examples, which are not unrealistic, make it clear that public employee jailers are not necessarily chosen through processes that are more open, democratic, or inherently honest than the methods used to select contractual jailers.

DiIulio argues that, all other things held equal, something which he calls "the public interest" or "the common good" requires that prisons be run directly by government employees.[9] He does not identify any specific public interest that can be shown to be ill-served by contracting. Rather, he presents an apparently analytic truth—a tautology. Seemingly as a matter of definition, only government employees, not contractors, can be public servants—i.e., can serve "the public interest." DiIulio does not use the phrase "government employees." He simply refers to "government."

However, government cannot act without recruiting individual actors; the relevant distinction here is between two kinds of governmental recruitment: employment versus contract.

DiIulio asks, rhetorically, whether the government's responsibility to govern "ends at the prison gate," as if a contract could cause it to do so.[10] He concludes that "we are most likely to improve our country's prisons and jails if we approach them not as a private enterprise to be administered in the pursuit of profit, but as a public trust to be administered on behalf of the community and in the name of civility and justice."[11] This thesis, however, is based on an erroneous assumption. Contracting does not constitute abdication of responsibility, and it is not necessary to choose between contracting, on the one hand, and civility, justice, and fulfillment of the public trust, on the other.

The Derivation and Delegation of Authority to Imprison[12]

How can it be proper for anyone other than the state to imprison criminals? Perhaps the place to start is by asking what makes the punishment of lawbreakers proper for the state itself. By what right does the state imprison?

In the classical liberal (or in modern terms, libertarian) tradition on which the American system of government is founded, all rights are individual, not collective. The state is artificial and has no authority, legitimate power, or rights of its own other than those transferred to it by individuals.

Why does this transfer take place? In the instance of criminal justice, John Locke argued that individuals in the state of nature have the right to punish those who aggress against them. However, there will always be disagreement over interpretations and applications of natural law; people cannot be unbiased in judging their own cases; and the victims of crimes may lack the power to punish. For these reasons, said Locke, people contract to form a state and completely give over to it the authority to bring malefactors to justice. Locke's contractarian view of government can be used either to justify or to challenge governmental monopoly of the legitimate use of force. On the one hand, Locke gives pragmatic reasons for limiting to government the power to judge and punish. On the other hand, Locke insists that this authority does not originate with the state, but is granted to it. Moreover, that grant is a conditional one. Citizens reserve the right to revoke any of the powers of the state, or indeed, the entire charter of the state, if necessary.

Robert Nozick, like Locke, sees the right to punish as one held by individuals in a state of nature. He also insists that no collective rights or entitlements emerge beyond those held by individuals. Thus, the right to punish is not exclusive or unique to the state. Is it, however, *special* to the state in some way? Is there an argument for individuals turning over their punishment power to a *state* rather than to some private agency?

In *Anarchy, State and Utopia*, Nozick answers as follows. Punishment, to be just, can be administered only once (or up to the amount deserved); anyone who punishes will thus preempt others in their exercise of this right. When persons authorize an agent to act for them, they confer their own entitlements on that agent. The more clients on whose behalf a protection agency acts, the fewer others whose exercise of the right to punish has been preempted or displaced. Therefore, a dominant protection agency (a state) has a higher degree of entitlement to punish, in the sense that it preempts the fewest others.

Whatever reasons may exist for placing the power to punish in the hands of the state, the major point is that it must be transferred; it does not originate with the state. The power and authority of the state to imprison, like all its powers and authority, are derived from the consent of the governed and may with similar consent be delegated further. Because the authority does not originate with the state, it does not attach inherently or uniquely to it, and can be passed along to private agencies.

Anarchists go further. They argue that people may delegate their rights, including the right to punish offenders, directly to private agents acting on their behalf. Here, I defend only the weaker (libertarian but not anarchist) claim: any legitimate governmental authority may be further delegated, through the government, to private agents. This assumes the existence of a legitimate and representative government so that the chain of authority is unbroken from its original source—the people.

In short, the state does not *own* the right to punish. It merely *administers* it in trust, on behalf of the people and under the rule of law. There is no reason why subsidiary trustees cannot be designated, as long as they, too, are ultimately accountable to the people and subject to the same provisions of law that direct the state.

Legitimation of Authority

In any prison, someone will need authority to use force, including potentially deadly force in emergencies. Questions of legitimacy in the use of that force, however, cannot be resolved simply by declaring that for state employees some use of force is legitimate, while for contracted agents none is.

In a system characterized by rule of law, state and private agencies alike are bound by the law. For actors within either type of agency, it is the law, not the civil status of the actor, that determines whether any particular exercise of force is legitimate. The law may specify that those authorized to use force in certain situations should be licensed or deputized and adequately trained for this purpose, but they need not be state employees.

The distinction between a contractual relation and salaried state employment, in terms of the derivation of authority, may be more apparent than real. The authority of a corrections officer, for example, derives from the fact that he or she is functioning not just on behalf of the state, but within the scope of the law. Consider the case of state-employed prison guards who engage in clear-cut, extreme brutality. We do not say that their acts are authorized or legitimate, or even that they are acting at that moment as agents of the state. In fact, we deny it, in spite of uniforms and all the other trappings of their positions. We say that they have overstepped their jurisdiction and behaved in an unauthorized and unlawful fashion. The state may or may not accept some accountability or liability for their acts, but that is a separate issue. The point here is that the authority or legitimacy of a position does not automatically transfer to the actions of the incumbents.

There is, in effect, an implicit contract between a state and its agents that makes the authority of the latter conditional on the proper performance of their jobs. This conditional authority can be bestowed on contractual agents of the state just as it is on civil servants. Where contractually employed agents, such as corrections officers, have identifiable counterparts among state-salaried agents, there is no reason why their authority should not be regarded as equivalent. Thus, the boundaries of authority for contracted state agents should be no less clear than those for state employees; they could be even clearer if they are spelled out in the contract.

What about authority inside the prison itself? Would private prisons lack authority and legitimacy in the eyes of inmates?

Legitimation constitutes one of the most effective methods of cutting the cost of exercising power in a wide range of social organization[13]; prisons are no exception. Since legitimation is generally granted in exchange for the fair exercise of power, a profit-seeking prison has a vested interest in being perceived by inmates as just and impartial in the application of rules. Commercial prisons, unlike the state, cannot indefinitely absorb or pass along to taxpayers the cost of riots, high insurance rates, extensive litigation by maltreated prisoners, cancellations of poorly performed or controversial contracts, or even a wave of adverse publicity. Thus, the self-interest of a for-profit prison company is more likely to increase, than to decrease, its concern with fairness. Moreover, the state is more likely to renew a contract with an organization that has a good record of governance than with a contractor that generates numerous complaints and appeals from inmates. In short, economic self-interest can motivate good governance as well as good management.

Symbols vs. Substance

Many critics of private prisons are extremely concerned about matters of symbolism. For example, Ira Robbins, Professor of Law at American University, asks:

> When it enters a judgment of conviction and imposes a sentence, a court exercises its authority, both actually and symbolically. Does it weaken that authority, however—as well as the integrity of a system of *justice*—when an inmate looks at his keeper's uniform and, instead of encountering an emblem that reads, "Federal Bu-

reau of Prisons" or "State Department of Corrections," he faces one that says "Acme Corrections Company"?[14]

I suspect that prisoners care more about practical than philosophical distinctions. They care more about how officers treat them than about what insignia grace their uniforms. To the extent that they are treated with fairness and justice, inmates will be more inclined to legitimate their keepers' authority and to cooperate with them.

DiIulio, too, shares this concern with the symbols of authority: "The badge of the arresting policeman, the robes of the judge, and the state patch on the uniform of the corrections officer are symbols of the inherently public nature of crime and punishment." [15] It is true that symbols are important to perceptions of legitimacy. However, perception is affected by substance as well as by symbol. In fact, substance is ultimately the biggest part of what creates, sustains, or undermines a symbol. "Pinkerton" and "Brinks" are private trademarks that symbolize the public virtues of honesty, reliability, and accountability as well as security, law, and order. "City Hall," while it obviously refers to a public institution, is a phrase that, for many people, symbolizes corrupt but overwhelming power in the service of private ends (as in, "You can't fight City Hall").

There is no government monopoly on probity and integrity. The symbols of government and the symbols of business enterprises are functionally similar in this respect: they each represent the reputations of the organizations behind them. Since reputations are ultimately founded on deeds, the degree to which any symbol— whether of government or of business—is honorific or legitimizing will be determined, over time, by the quality of what stands behind the symbol.

If it were symbols, rather than substance, that we were worried about, we could find plenty of them in a contractual situation. A contract itself is a powerful symbol of legally enforceable obligations and responsibilities. For private prisons, a license could be required, and hung on the gate if that would make people feel better. The vendor's employees could be ceremoniously deputized and sworn. They could be given official-looking uniforms and badges, for that matter.

Michael Walzer is another who argues that administering criminal justice is an enterprise that is largely symbolic and therefore requires not just technical expertise, but the application of social values. For this reason, says Walzer, criminal justice should always be in the hands of "representatives of the people": "Police and prison guards are our representatives, whose activities we have authorized. The policeman's uniform symbolizes his representative character." [16] Most public employees, however, including police and corrections officers, are neither politically appointed nor democratically elected. They are hired, and cannot be said to "represent" the public by virtue of their selection. Rather, they represent by virtue of their function; that's their job. How they do their job determines how well they represent the public. Moreover, the values that criminal justice workers are supposed to administer are codified in law. They are not the personal value preferences of either public officials or employees, whether elected, appointed, or hired through civil service procedures. The important question, then, is whether relevant legal values will be served more faithfully by public employees or by contractual agents. This is not a question of principle; it is an empirical question.

The great concern with symbolism on the part of those who question the propriety of private prisons indicates that their argument is not substantive. Essentially, it is theological,[17] or rather, theocratic. Substantively, however, what we are ultimately trying to symbolize is legal authority, not government employment. Employment is merely one method of conveying or delegating legal authority; contract is another.

Contracting and Sovereignty

Are there any theoretical limits as to which functions and powers (or as to how much of any one of them) government can delegate? Operating prisons, which is an exercise of executive, and perhaps quasi-judicial, power, is widely recognized as one of the basic functions of government. However, it is only one among many that have been carried out through the use of private agents. David M. Lawrence, Professor of Public Law and Government at the

University of North Carolina, notes that many delegations of executive and judicial powers are well established:

> Important judicial and executive powers have been delegated, in some cases for decades or even centuries, without the validity of the delegation being questioned. The power of arrest has been delegated to railway police, to humane society agents, and to bail bondsmen. The power to seize and sell property has been delegated to certain lienholders. The power to destroy buildings, without personal liability, in order to stop the spread of fire has been delegated to anyone at the scene of a fire. The power to adjudicate grievances between employees and employers has been delegated to private arbitrators. And the authority to determine which law schools' graduates may sit for the bar examination has been delegated to the American Bar Association. Only the last of these has been challenged on delegation grounds, and the challenges consistently have been refuted.[18]

Laurin Wollan points out that the perception that criminal justice is inherently and exclusively a function of the state is strongest when it is least closely examined. Moreover, it makes a big difference whether the question is asked broadly ("who should be responsible for the welfare of prisoners?") or narrowly ("can a private company provide prisoners with better food at lower cost?").[19]

When criminal justice is broken down into specific activities, or into functions and subfunctions, it is no longer so clear that any of these tasks must be the exclusive province of the state. Wollan presents a typology in which criminal justice is divided into 22 functions across 6 categories, and he gives examples of privatization for each of these functions. In many cases, private performance of discrete functions has been going on for some time with little or no controversy. Specific aspects of criminal justice that already have experienced varying degrees of privatization include:

Community security and prevention

Initial detection and accusation

Investigation and evaluation of evidence

Victim services

Bail services

Bounty hunting

Legal aid and representation

Prosecution

Presentence investigation and sentencing recommendations

Transport of prisoners

Incarceration

Prison services (food, medical, education, and so forth)

Reintegration (i.e., halfway houses)

Community corrections programs

Alternative sentencing supervision

Probation services

Other functions widely regarded as "governmental" have also been privately delegated or contracted. National defense is clearly an essential governmental function. Yet not only does private enterprise produce the full range of materiel for the armed services, it participates directly in our defense. The Distant Early Warning System, which warns of attack by missiles or aircraft over the Arctic, is manned and operated by a private contractor.[20] Police protection, fire protection, even the entire management and administration of some cities have been provided under contract. Private courts adjudicate many civil cases. Private prosecutors have operated to some extent in California and to a considerable extent in England. Even capital punishment is sometimes administered by private contractors in the United States today. It is hard to find any specific governmental function or power, the administration of which has not been delegated at least in some part at some time to private agents.

If there is no *qualitative* limit to delegation—no type of function or power that can never be delegated in any degree—is there perhaps some *quantitative* limit? The question here is not *what* function can be delegated, but *how much* of it.

The concept of sovereignty places a theoretical limit on the delegation of state power. While there is no limit to the number or type of functions that the state may delegate to private parties, there is a limit to the amount of power that can be ceded. The power to coerce is part of what defines the state. It can give up any amount of that power, but if it gives up too much, it ceases to be sovereign; if it gives up all of it, it ceases to be a state. The "far end" of that limit is the point at which the state loses actual sovereignty, at least over a particular function; at the "near end," the state begins to lose effective control.

Correctional law expert William Collins, drawing from a leading treatise on municipal corporation law, concludes that delegation becomes "excessive" when the government gives away so much power as to compromise its ability to act in the public interest in a certain area.[21] In operational terms, this would mean loss of control over basic policy or ultimate supervisory authority, rather than over ministerial matters. "The more the contract makes the private provider simply the administrative extension of the . . . government, and leaves ultimate authority in the hands of government officials, the more likely the contract will satisfy judicial scrutiny."[22]

With respect to the operation of prisons and jails, Collins believes that it would be excessive delegation to relinquish control over admission or release (including granting or denial of good time). He is less certain about questions of classification (i.e., custody level), which affect the conditions, but not the fact, of confinement. Note, however, that to pass the sovereignty test it is not necessary that private prison officials be excluded entirely from decisions and actions relating to discipline or to release dates; only that they not be given final control in those areas. So long as the government retains final authority and the power of review over disciplinary actions or good time—decisions that affect the liberty of prisoners—delegation of responsibility for these functions would not be "excessive" because sovereignty will not have been lost.

In addition to preventing erosion of its sovereignty, there is another, and much more important, reason for the state to retain final (not exclusive or total) authority over decisions affecting prisoners' liberty. In the political philosophy of liberal, or libertarian, constitutional government, the rights of individuals are more important even than the sovereignty of the state. From this perspective, the strongest argument for placing in private hands something less than final authority over prisoners is not that this will preserve state sovereignty, but that such a restriction will help to preserve due process.

Issues of Due Process

Certain aspects of prison administration have a quasi-judicial character. Examples would include imposing solitary confinement or other disciplinary actions, making or contributing to parole decisions, allocating "good time" sanctions that affect the date of release, and classification procedures that significantly affect the conditions of confinement. Discretionary decision-making in these areas, whether done by public or by private prison staff, clearly requires some elements of due process. Moreover, even where prison decision-making is administrative rather than judicial, the coercive environment in which it occurs can still make the question of due process relevant.

The best approach to the question of delegation is to view it as just one aspect of the broader issue of due process, within the general problem of power. The central issue in due process is not *who* exercises power or *how much* power is delegated, but *how* it is exercised and what safeguards exist to prevent it from being abused.

A Due Process Theory of Constitutional Delegation

In his comprehensive review of delegation issues, David Lawrence has noted that the ability of the federal government to delegate power is both broad and clear. "Since *Carter v. Carter Coal Co.*, decided a half-century ago, the federal courts have consistently allowed delegations of federal power to private actors. . . . Private exercise of federally delegated power is no longer a federal constitutional issue. Nor is the private exercise of governmental power delegated by state or local governments a federal constitutional issue. . . ." [23]

Among court decisions at the state level, Professor Lawrence finds no clear or consistent doctrine to distinguish constitutional from unconstitutional delegation. As a step toward producing such a doctrine, he suggests that the closest approach to a coherent

principle or standard against which to judge a potential delegation
of governmental power is the test of due process:

> In summary, a due process basis for reviewing private delegations
> permits a court to approach and resolve the problem in terms of
> the essential danger that such delegations present: that govern-
> mental power may be used to further private rather than public
> interests. A court can address the danger directly to determine
> whether it exists in a particular instance and then test the mecha-
> nisms available to protect against the danger. This approach, well
> within the traditions of due process, not only permits handling the
> basic dangers raised by private delegations, it has the further ad-
> vantage of being more likely to force a court to address those con-
> cerns directly and to articulate the considerations behind its
> decision.[24]

Judicial constraint on the delegation of power to financially interested *private* parties is not essentially different from judicial
constraint on the exercise of power by financially interested *public*
officials.[25] Both rest on due process concerns, not on a theory of
delegation that distinguishes private actors as a class from public
actors as a class. An objection to a private delegation cannot be
based solely on the assumption that a private actor will, by definition, have conflicting interests, financial or otherwise. Nor can
one assume that a comparable public actor will have fewer conflicting interests. Due process procedures are designed to prevent
conflicting interests or other biases from interfering in either case.

Due process is grounded on a justifiable lack of trust toward
those who exercise power. Neither business nor government is
inherently deserving of trust; it has to be earned. Moreover, trust
is not enough; power must be limited by procedural safeguards
even when it is in the hands of those whom (at the moment) we
do happen to trust. Differences between government and business,
insofar as they relate to questions of due process, are not just
exaggerated by opponents of privatization, but distorted so as to
portray business as inherently less trustworthy than government.

In my view, government and business are equally untrustworthy,
but *given comparable procedural safeguards* there is no aspect of
the administration of a prison that can be entrusted to government
employees but not to private contractors. By comparable procedural safeguards, I do not mean that the specific mechanisms of

accountability must be exactly the same for government and private operations, only that the degree and standards of accountability should be comparable between the two. There is nothing intrinsic to the natures of business and government that requires higher standards of accountability for one than for the other.

Contracting Contributes to Due Process

Contracting can make positive contributions to due process. One of the strengths of contracting is that it forces us to make visible and to treat as problematic some important issues of authority and due process that we might otherwise ignore or take for granted. Due process requires preset rules and rigorous adherence to them. It is universalistic, not individualistic: discretion, individualization, and "creativity" in punishment are detrimental to due process. Contractual arrangements offer an excellent means of limiting and controlling discretion, of clarifying rules, and of enforcing adherence to procedures.

In a recent note in the *Yale Law Journal*, David Wecht argues that private prisons may increase prisoners' due process protections by forcing courts to move away from their historical pattern of deference to prison administrators.[26] While courts actually began to abandon their "hands-off" approach to prison administration long before the recent emergence of contracted prisons, Wecht's note argues that court supervision will now be accelerated as a result of the longstanding suspicion of courts toward delegation of power to private, for-profit entities. In order to ensure that conflicting private interests do not interfere with either prisoners' rights or the public interest, courts will insist on strong procedural safeguards. These might include strict legislative and contractual standards; training and certification requirements for prison staff; independent, state review of policies and of discretionary or adjudicatory decision-making; and greater liability to lawsuits.

Unfortunately, Wecht dismisses too lightly a warning that courts, on equal-protection grounds, must apply the same standards of due process to government as to private prisons.[27] Instead, he argues that private prisons should be held to higher standards and scrutinized more closely. Public actors, in Wecht's view, presumably are not greatly influenced by private incentives that might conflict with public interests. But government employees no less than others have self-interests that can conflict with the rights of prisoners. It will not do to say or imply that public prisons are run by civil servants who have no profit motives and therefore can be trusted not to compromise prisoners' rights, health, or safety.

Equal Protection of Due Process

Being suspicious of authority in the hands of commercial prison managers is an example of having the right attitude for the wrong reasons. It is not because these managers pursue profit that we should be vigilant, but because they wield power. A constructive response to this suspicion would be to require as part of a contract that commercial prisons codify the rules that they will enforce, specify the criteria and procedures by which they will make disciplinary decisions, and submit to review by a supervisory state agency. In short, the requirements of due process should be built into the conditions of the contract. But this is no different from the attitude we should have toward the state itself, and toward its employees.

Since due process is an important problem for all prisons, we should not design solutions that apply only to private prisons. To do so distracts attention from the problem in public institutions. Our focus should be on the procedures that will best protect the due process rights of inmates regardless of whether they are applied by government employees or by contracted agents. The procedures that will do this best will probably be the same or similar in either case. It should not be assumed *a priori* that one system or the other requires more stringent safeguards.

It is also no solution to propose, as some have, that only those decisions having implications for due process must be left in government hands.[28] The whole point of having procedures is to reduce our reliance on being in "the right hands." And the whole point of constitutional guarantees of due process is that decisions affecting life, liberty, or property cannot simply be entrusted to agents of the government. Whether prisons are run directly by the "iron fist" or respond also to the "invisible hand" is less important than a rule that, either way, those hands should be bound by the same requirements of due process.

Evaluating, sanctioning, and controlling inmate behavior are integral parts of every aspect of a prison program; they cannot be handled by a separate and distant staff. Trying to contract for the overall management of a prison by a private company, while restricting exclusively to government all decisions and actions that require due process protections, would be futile. Worse yet, formally defining "administration" as the business of the private company and "rights protection" as the business of the state would discourage contractors from maintaining an attitude of full responsibility. While protection of due process is ultimately guaranteed by the state, it should be made a responsibility of contractors as well. Each contract should establish a system of supervision whereby the state can monitor the discretionary decisions of the contractor, and whereby inmates can appeal what they view as unfair treatment.

In a comprehensive review of the delegation doctrine as it may affect private prisons, Ira Robbins observes: "State courts generally invalidate statutes and administrative regulations that delegate adjudicative power to private parties when there is no provision for judicial review of the private adjudications. When there is provision for such review, however, the delegation is upheld." [29] Thus, courts probably will accept arrangements in which classification decisions, disciplinary sanctions, good time determination, and other quasi-judicial decisions are first made by private prison officials and then reviewed by or made subject to appeal before government authorities and courts. [30]

One essential element of due process is the provision of mechanisms for independent review and appeal. It is important that the reviewing agent be disinterested, or at least not influenced by the same interests as the agent whose initial decisions are being reviewed. A warden who reviews the judgments and decisions of his officers, has some independence, but not a great deal. A Disciplinary Hearing Officer from a central office is somewhat more independent, but still remains part of a common administrative structure. In a contract situation, initial decisions made by the contractor may be reviewable and reversible by a government monitor as well as subject to challenge in court. In this way, contracting adds another layer of independent review, which enhances due process.

Recognizing the importance of independent review to the protection of due process, some corrections systems provide for an ombudsman to hear and act on inmate grievances. Ideal characteristics for an ombudsman are independence, impartiality, expertise in government, universal accessibility, and power only to recommend and to publicize.[31] In Connecticut, a private research institute provides the ombudsman for the state's correctional system. The Connecticut ombudsman's function is to serve as an informal check against the power of the state.

If it is acceptable for Connecticut to have initial decisions made by state employees, subject to informal but influential review by a private agency, it should be at least as acceptable for a contracted prison to have initial decisions made by people who are not on the government payroll, subject to formal review by the state and in accordance with rules and procedures that are also subject to state review. It should not be necessary to require that the whole process, including initial decisions, be left in the hands of state employees. Indeed, it would seem that impartiality is increased when a government agency reviews decisions that have been made by a private agent rather than by another government agency or, worse, by a subdivision of the agency itself.

If due process is satisfied in a *government* prison by the existence of channels of independent external review of decisions, then due process will also be satisfied if initial decisions by the staff of a *private* prison are subject to independent external review. In neither case does due process require that the prison's staff be excluded from the decision-making process.

Inmate Discipline and Good Time Decisions

Critics of private prisons fear that due process, particularly as it affects discipline and allocation of good time, will be trampled in the pursuit of profit. Most of all, they fear that private wardens will try to retain custody of their charges as long as possible to maximize their per diem revenues. The Legal Director of the Indiana Civil Liberties Union predicts:

> Private prison operators would not only want to reduce costs, but to enhance revenues by maintaining their facilities at capacity and

by creating new demands for their services. Inevitably, private prison officials would have a role, even the key role, in making classification decisions, parole recommendations, awarding good time credits and meting out disciplinary sanctions. It will be only too easy for them to abuse these powers in order to increase the length of incarceration and their own income.[32]

Three observations are needed to put this fear in its proper perspective. First, a private penitentiary has a financial incentive to hang on to prisoners only if nonreplacement is assumed. Under conditions existing today and projected well into the future, that is not a rational supposition. As regards good time policies and decisions, overcrowding actually has an unbiasing effect on a private prison, but a biasing effect on a government prison. In a private prison, there is no economic interest either for or against denial of good time if systemwide overcrowding guarantees replacement of inmates. In contrast, overcrowding gives the state system a material bias toward early release through liberal use of good time, in order to avoid the possibility of expensive court-ordered reforms or massive fines. Second, the argument that private prisons will have an incentive toward unfair and improper denial of good time assumes that such decisions will confer only benefits and carry no costs; no commercial company with a competent legal staff would make so unrealistic an assumption. Third, it should be noted that only a small proportion of disciplinary cases (often less than 10 percent) result in revocation of a prisoner's good time credits; the majority involve other sanctions.[33] In those cases where significant prisoners' rights are at issue, due process can be protected by provisions for appeal to higher authority.

In his Model Contract and Model Statute proposals to the American Bar Association, Professor Robbins argues that officers in private prisons should have only the most limited possible role in the disciplinary process: the role of a complaining witness before a state judicial officer.[34] Robbins believes that all discretionary decisions potentially affecting a liberty interest must be reserved, both by statute and by contract, to state officials. Such decisions would include classification; transfers; formulating rules of conduct; any disciplinary action; allocation of sentence credits; parole recommendations; calculating sentence credits and dates of release or parole eligibility; assigning, supervising, or rewarding inmate work; and determining eligibility for furlough and work release.[35]

The basic premise behind Robbins' stance is that private employees are inherently biased in ways that government employees are not. In brief, no private corrections officer should be involved in discretionary decision-making that affects an inmate's liberty, because the officer's employer has a material interest in the outcome of those decisions. Commenting on discipline, Robbins describes this interest as both monetary and institutional. The monetary interest is an alleged "pecuniary interest in increasing— or at least, not decreasing—each inmate's stay," while the institutional interest is an alleged "institutional bias in favor of disciplining prisoners." [36] To support the latter charge, Robbins simply asserts that: "A decision to deny certain privileges or services, for example, would reduce the operating costs of the company and would promote its administrative convenience. . . . Moreover, any exercise of nonreviewable discretion by the company would be cheaper than complying with due process constraints." [37]

Aside from the fact that no one has ever proposed that private prison contractors should be allowed to exercise *nonreviewable* discretion, Robbins' assertions can be countered along several lines. First, the daily actions and decisions of employees everywhere are guided largely by personal motives, interests, and incentives that are often quite different from, and may even conflict with, those of the employing organization. This is equally true of both private and public employees. Employees are supposed to follow official organizational policies and rules, which can be examined for potential biases, but departures from official policy are more likely to be influenced by personal incentives, such as convenience, than by some general consideration of the interests of the company (or state).

Second, private organizations are not unique in their potential for conflicts of interest. Public organizations also have self-interests that may bias and distort the decisions of workers and administrators. We cannot avoid such biases by allowing only public employees to make important decisions. As mentioned earlier, overcrowded government facilities operating under limited budgets are under great pressure to release offenders early regardless of the merits of individual cases. This is a type of pecuniary bias, and it is clear that government officials such as sheriffs, wardens, and parole board members respond to it. In addition, nonpecuniary as well as pecuniary biases are found in all organizations, whether public or private. For example, saving face and maintaining personal authority can influence both private and public corrections officers in disciplinary matters.

Third, in neither type of organization do potentially biasing incentives operate in only one direction. In the case of private prisons, the alleged pecuniary incentive toward *delaying* release in order to maximize revenue is counteracted by a second pecuniary bias toward *early* release in order to avoid prisoner litigation. A third pecuniary "bias" favors *neither* early *nor* late release in order to maintain a reputation for fairness and integrity, which helps to secure and renew contracts and cuts the costs of conflict with inmates. Thus, even a private warden who fit Robbins' stereotypic caricature of someone who cares only about the bottom line would not inherently be biased in any one consistent direction. Will the cost-calculating warden revoke a prisoner's good time to gain a little "extra" per diem revenue? Or will he bribe inmates with liberal grants of good time credit in order to buy their cooperation and to avoid the expense of the extra paperwork required by disciplinary proceedings? Or will he decide that it is least costly in the long run to govern firmly but fairly and consistently?

The most fundamental fallacy in Robbins' argument is that it rests on the false assumption that due process requires purity of heart on the part of those who make decisions. If due process awaits the appearance of mortals who are certain to be impartial and objective, then due process will wait forever. The whole point of due process is to substitute reliance on procedures for reliance on motives or character to guarantee fair treatment. We must insist on procedures that will enhance due process regardless of whether they are administered by public or by private employees, each with their varying mix of occupational, personal, and institutional biases.

The single most important element of such procedures is the provision of a mechanism for independent review so that decisions can be evaluated by someone whose biases will probably be different from those of the original decision maker. An independent layer of review is preferable to concentrating decision-making power among persons whom we presume to be impartial. Therefore, rather than requiring government officials to make all discretionary decisions in a contracted prison, the initial decision-making authority should be ceded to the private officials responsible for running the prison. These decisions, in turn, should be subject to independent review by the government.

Take the case of the Hamilton County prison run by Corrections Corporation of America. There, the County Superintendent of Corrections serves as an onsite monitor and also makes all decisions regarding gain time, discipline, and work assignments. Professor Robbins, presumably, would be satisfied with this arrangement because these decisions are left entirely in government hands. I am not satisfied, because what I see is a situation in which the Superintendent acts as Disciplinary Hearing Officer, Warden, and Secretary of Corrections all rolled into one. He is the first, last, and only discretionary decision-making official. There is no internal or external independent review, unless a case goes to court. Due process, and therefore justice, would be enhanced in this prison if initial decisions were made by CCA employees, subject to review by the Superintendent. Professor Robbins' Model Contract and Statute would preclude this potential enhancement of justice through privatization.

Inmate Classification

Classification of inmates according to the degree of security or supervision they require, which determines where and with whom a prisoner will be housed within a facility, can have a major effect on the conditions of confinement.   Classification decisions must be made not only at the time of entry, but throughout an inmate's sentence as behavior or circumstances change. Logically, the closer the decision makers are to the actual operations of the institution, the more information they will have on which to base their classifications. This suggests that classification decisions are best made by those who actually run an institution.

Critics worry that private prisons will make classification decisions in accordance with their own agendas, not in the best interests of prisoners or of the public. It is not at all clear, however, that these separate concerns are truly in conflict.

From any standpoint, classification decisions should be based on accurate predictions. Accuracy is not something that serves one set of interests better than another. The causes of justice, order, economy, and inmate welfare are all served best when prisoners are subjected to the minimum degree of control sufficient to ensure security. In the public system, the highest status, largest budgets, and biggest staffs attach to maximum security institutions. There is thus an incentive to overclassify inmates (i.e., a bias toward higher security designations). In addition, most states overclassify inmates because higher security space is often all that is available.[38] The economic cost of overclassification is not borne directly by those who do the classifying, but passed along to taxpayers. More-over, while oversecurity increases economic costs, it decreases po-litical costs by minimizing the risk of escapes or loss of control. Public officials are more vulnerable and sensitive to political costs than to economic costs and thus tend to overclassify.

In a private prison, on the other hand, there is a financial in-centive to treat cases at the lowest possible level of security, so that more prisoners can be held under lighter supervision or in facilities less costly to construct and administer. Nonetheless, there are restraints against carrying the downward classification too far. Escapes, violence, lawsuits, and other consequences of inadequate security carry both direct financial costs and indirect public rela-tions costs in the form of lost contracts due to a poor reputation. Thus, while private vendors have some incentives to engage in underclassification, they also have countervailing disincentives.

It is not necessary here to decide whether classification biases are more likely to occur in private or in governmental prisons. The major point is that they can occur in either type. The implication of this for due process is the same as in the case of discipline. Review procedures and other checks and balances are neither more nor less needed in private prisons than they are in prisons run by government employees.

The Profit Motive vs. Other Motives

Before we look at motives, we should note one point of logic at the outset. Strictly speaking, the motivation of those who apply a punishment is not relevant either to the justice or to the effectiveness of the punishment. Of course, for punishment to be a moral enterprise, it must be meted out for the right reasons. This, however, is a stricture that applies more to those who determine and decree the punishment than to those who carry it out—to legislative and judicial more than to executive agents. The immediate agents of punishment may be humans with motives virtuous or venal, or robots with no motives at all; that does not affect the requirements of justice. Still, the matter of motives—or rather, one particular motive—seems to be of such great importance to so many opponents of proprietary prisons that it must be dealt with. These critics believe that "criminal justice and profits don't mix." The ACLU especially has complained repeatedly that "the profit motive is incompatible with doing justice."

If it is legitimate to examine the motives of interested parties, then to be consistent we ought to examine the motives of *all* parties, including state agencies, public employee unions, prison reform groups, and "public interest" groups.[39] All these parties, like private vendors, have motives that reflect self-interest as well as altruism, and agendas that are hidden as well as overt. For example, the ACLU's National Prison Project, by making the point that more efficient prisons will mean more imprisonment, may be as much opposed to prisons *per se* as to running them like a business. The ACLU does not object to the profits that are made from the private administration of community correctional programs that serve as *alternatives* to prison.

A consistent objection to the existence of vested interests in punishment would have to scrutinize the public sector as well as the private. Is it wrong for state employees to have a financial stake in the existence of a prison system? Is it wrong for their unions to "profit" by extracting compulsory dues from those employees? Is it wrong for a state prison bureaucracy to seek growth (more personnel, bigger budgets, new investment in human and physical capital) through seizing the profits of others (taxation) rather than through reinvestment of its own profits? Are the sanctions of the state diminished or tainted when they are administered by public employees organized to maximize their personal benefits? If not, would those sanctions be compromised if they were administered by professionals who make an honest profit? Admittedly, I have posed these questions in prejudicial language, but I have done so to make a point. The notion that any activity becomes suspect if it is carried out for profit, as compared to salary and other benefits, is simply an expression of prejudice.

Of various possible motivations for serving as an agent of punishment, the profit motive is among the most benign. Compare, for example, some alternative motives: enjoyment of power, arrogance, self-righteousness, zealotry, machismo, malice, cruelty, sadism, vengefulness, adventurism, aggression, hostility, hatred, anger, resentment, prejudice, or displacement. No one has proposed that all criminal sanctions be administered by unpaid volunteers motivated by pure love of justice. If someone does propose it, watch out! Great injustices are often done in the name of noble-sounding values. The history of corrections, from the penitentiary to the juvenile court, is a chronicle of good intentions that produced bad results.[40] The clear lesson from this history, drawn by criminologists of all political persuasions, is that criminal justice policies and practices must be judged by their consequences, not by their motives. In particular, declarations of "public service" should not be taken at face value.[41] Instead, public service should be judged as an outcome, regardless of whether the motivating force behind it is probity, power, or profit.

Replacing "public servants" with "profit seekers" in the management of prisons will not trade those whose motives are noble for those whose motives are base. Rather, it will replace actors whose motives we suspect too little with actors whose motives we might suspect too much. Still, that is a step in the right direction when we consider the high cost of relying on good intentions in the past.

Constraining (Everyone's) Self-Interest

But won't a commercial institution be "driven by profit" and, as a result, be tempted to put its own welfare ahead of the welfare of inmates, the needs of the state, or the interests of justice? This concern is legitimate, but it is at least partially misplaced when it is portrayed as a problem unique to commercial enterprises. Actually, the problem exists for public as well as private, for nonprofit as well as profit-making organizations. If justice and the profit motive really were incompatible, then justice would be doomed, because in one form or another the profit motive is universal. Like the rest of society, politicians, government bureaucrats, and other agents of the state are motivated by self-interest. The field of public choice, a hybrid of economics and political science, is founded on this insight, and one of its founders, James Buchanan, recently received a Nobel Prize for his extensive research and theory in this area.

Consider the case of prosecutors. One does not have to be cynical to understand that prosecutors, like other people, are motivated by self-interest and not purely by love of justice. Job security, prestige, and power are among the incentives of prosecutors. Many have political ambitions. They are rewarded along these lines according to their conviction rate. Although justice is served best through careful review of cases and the prosecution of lawbreakers on the most deserved charge, conviction rates are maximized by generous plea bargaining and by pursuing the most and the easiest cases. It is this structure of incentives, rather than caseload, that explains the prevalence of plea bargaining.[42]

Suppose now that prosecution were privately contracted. The profit motive of a commercial prosecutor would be at least as defensible, morally, as the mixed motives of a public prosecutor. More importantly, however, the profit motive has the advantage of being more controllable. We cannot easily structure and manipulate the complex incentives of public prosecutors. In contrast, if we wish to encourage a commercial prosecutor to concentrate on making the charge fit the crime, rather than on the quantity or rate of convictions, we simply structure this incentive into the fee. The fee can be set by an agency authorized to reflect society's concerns (and accountable for doing so) and can vary according to charge of conviction. To discourage wrongful prosecution or improper charges, fines could be imposed on commercial prosecutors whose convictions are overturned on review or appeal.

This proposal is sketchy at best, but it illustrates the point that the profit motive is subject to creative public management in a simpler fashion and to a greater degree than are the motives and incentives operating in public bureaucracies.[43]

Among the most universal of motives is one that could be called the "convenience motive"—the desire to behave in ways that maximize one's own convenience. Compared to the profit motive, the convenience motive has few societal benefits; it is much more asocial and self-interested. Not only individuals, but institutions, too—from hospitals and universities to courts and prisons[44]—tend to operate according to their own convenience unless they are motivated to do otherwise. For public or nonprofit institutions, this motivation takes the form of political pressure. For private, profit-making institutions, the motivation can take economic as well as political forms, because market mechanisms of discipline and supervision are added to those of the state apparatus. Shaped by market mechanisms, the profit motive can act as a powerful constraint on the convenience motive. Businesses must often sacrifice their own convenience if that will increase their profit. Businessmen understand that to sustain any competitive enterprise it is generally necessary to satisfy some needs other than one's own.

Competition does not just contain costs; it advances other goals as well. When it is possible for a commercial company to take business away from a competitor (including the state) by showing that it can do a better job, then that company becomes a self-motivated watchdog over other companies (and over the state). Such a company will have an interest in critically evaluating the quality of its competitors' services and an interest in improving its own.

In the case of prisons, the existence of competition, even potential competition, will make the public less tolerant of facilities that are crowded, costly, dirty, dangerous, inhumane, ineffective, and prone to riots and lawsuits. Indeed, the fact that these conditions have existed for so long in monopolistic state prisons is a big part of what makes private prisons seem attractive. The possibility of an alternative will make the public, the courts, and the government justifiably more demanding in their expectations.

Without competition, the state has had a monopoly over both service and supervision, over both doing justice and seeing that it is done properly. With competition, there will be a proliferation of agencies having a direct stake in both, without detracting from the state's role as the final arbiter of justice.

For these reasons, among others, the profit motive is not necessarily in conflict with the pursuit of justice; it can, in fact, be conducive to it.

5

Issues of Cost and Efficiency

Among claims made for the superiority of proprietary prisons, the most frequent and most salient—but not necessarily the strongest—is that they will be less expensive, or at least more efficient. So far, very little systematic empirical evidence exists either for or against this premise. As a result, both advocates and critics of proprietary prisons base their contentions on theoretical (or often ideological) grounds and on analogies to privatization in other areas. Those arguments will be reviewed here, along with all the empirical evidence available at this time.

The relative cost and efficiency merits of public and proprietary prisons can be examined within three areas: finance, construction, and operation. Greatest attention here will be given to the area of operation.

Private Financing and Lease-Purchase Arrangements

State and local governments are faced with the need to finance $5 to $10 billion in new prison construction. The traditional method of financing is through general obligation bonds. These bonds are secure, and government can generally borrow at slightly lower interest rates than private enterprise. This, however, is assuming that it can borrow at all. Some jurisdictions have borrowed to the point that they have very low credit ratings. Others have legal debt ceilings. And increasing numbers of voters are reluctant to authorize further borrowing.

Lease-purchase arrangements and private financing offer government the opportunity to pay for new prison space out of annually appropriated operating budgets. While lease-purchase arrangements are long-term in outlook, they include nonappropriation clauses allowing the government to terminate the lease. The main purpose of these clauses is to avoid classifying the expenditures as debt. But governments are not likely to terminate their leases, especially as their equity in the property increases.

Private financing, even when it is through a nonprofit corporation or authority that can sell tax-exempt revenue bonds, generally carries a slightly higher interest rate. However, it avoids the cost of a referendum, has lower transaction costs, and is much faster than the issuance of general obligation bonds. This greater speed can save many months worth of inflation in the cost of the eventual construction. California, for example, has reported needing about $1.3 billion for new prison construction. Assuming a 5 percent inflation rate, an 8-month to 10-month delay associated with a general obligation bond would result in a $43 to $54 million increase in total construction costs.[1]

Private financing and lease-purchase deals are options for government to consider, but they are not by any means a simple solution to the high cost of financing new jails and prisons. The issues involved are very complex and the relative advantages of different financing schemes depend on a jurisdiction's credit rating and can shift rapidly with changes in interest rates and tax laws.[2] Moreover, governments will want to consider other factors besides cost. For example, a straight lease—the most expensive option— might be preferred because it offers flexibility in meeting a temporary need.

Recent tax reforms have made private financing less attractive to investors by eliminating tax write-offs for accelerated depreciation. However, depreciation is still allowed if the facility is both owned and operated privately. Thus, there may be a trend toward this form and away from private financing by itself.[3]

The "Bypassing" of Voters

Avoiding debt limitations and capital-budget restrictions—the reputed advantages of lease-purchasing—raise several political

questions. Where voters have turned down bonds or passed propositions restricting debt, private financing may be seen as no more
than a scheme to spend taxpayer's money without direct voter
approval. Similarly, an off-the-balance-sheet technique such as
lease-purchasing, may enable a municipality to acquire a new jail
or prison without the appearance of long-term obligation or capital
expenditures. Under this arrangement, some people claim that
"it's the brokers, architects, builders and banks—not the taxpayers—who will make out like bandits."[4]

On the issue of imprisonment, many government officials view
the public as inconsistent. In opinion polls and letters to the editor,
citizens demand stiffer sentences for lawbreakers, yet bond referenda to pay for new jails often fail. Rather than inconsistency,
however, this may reflect dissatisfaction with current government
performance in constructing and operating prisons. The public may
sense that it does not get full value for its correctional dollar. It
wants more and better imprisonment but does not want to pay a
lot more for it. This is not necessarily irrational. Indeed, it is a
reasonable reaction to dissatisfaction under conditions of monopoly. Only where competition and comparison demonstrate the true
price of a product does it become irrational to demand more without being willing to pay what it takes.

Even if a majority of the public did not want more prisons, that
would not settle the question. We live in a representative republic,
not a direct democracy, and under constitutional rule of law, not
direct majority rule. Where the crime rate is high and our laws
call for imprisonment of serious offenders, we must provide space
for them. Where courts declare overcrowding and other conditions
to be unconstitutional, we must expand jail space and make the
conditions acceptable. Thus, a fiscally strained government in a
high-crime area or facing court orders may be forced to "find ways
around" a prison-expansion referendum. Such a government is not
necessarily behaving in a high-handed fashion; it may simply be
living up to its responsibilities.

In any case, while a referendum may be the last word on one
particular type of financing, it does not preclude other forms, nor
is it the last word on the issue of construction. Indeed, it is not
always clear just what it means when voters defeat referenda on
the issuance of new bonds to finance prison construction. The

results may simply reflect public apathy and confusion. Relatively few voters bother to cast ballots on these issues, often allowing a well organized and financed opposition campaign to prevail.

James Jacobs studied one prison bond referendum that was narrowly defeated in New York State.[5] He found strong and organized opposition among a small number of groups, combined with general public apathy and low voter participation. According to Jacobs, voting in favor of the bond, when examined by area, correlated positively with the crime rate; thus the bond was supported strongly in politically liberal but high crime New York City, and rejected strongly in politically conservative but low crime upstate New York. To some extent, the split probably reflected the general pattern of upstaters not wanting to pay for New York City's problems, but Jacobs was not wholly satisfied with that explanation.[6] He concluded that the vote was the result of confusion and apathy, not conscious rejection of prison expansion as a policy.

Opinion polls consistently show strong public support for more spending on criminal justice. An ABC News poll in 1982 found that 69 percent of a national sample would approve of building more prisons and 62 percent said they still would approve even if this meant their taxes would go up as a result. In a Gallup poll the same year, these figures were 57 percent and 49 percent, respectively.[7] Thus, a failed prison construction referendum may reflect objections that are specific to the issuance of bonds and the expansion of public debt, not to the expansion of the prison system. In any case, with lease-purchasing, voters still have the option of objecting, if they wish to, through their elected representatives.

Construction

Private companies have demonstrated repeatedly that they can locate, finance, design, and construct prisons more rapidly than the government can. Corrections Corporation of America reports its construction costs to be about 80 percent of what the government pays for construction.[8] CCA notes that it can build not only faster, thereby saving inflation costs, but also at a lower immediate cost, since construction contractors charge the government more.[9] A few examples illustrate these points clearly.

In 1975, the Attorney General of Pennsylvania ruled that even hard-core delinquents must not be incarcerated in facilities with adult offenders. Faced with the need to relocate all affected juveniles immediately, and lacking suitable facilities, the state turned to RCA Services Corporation, with which they already had a contract for educational programs for delinquents. In 10 days, RCA set up the Weaversville Intensive Treatment Unit, a heavy security facility with 20 beds and 30 staff members.

In the Pennsylvania case, RCA was able to convert buildings already owned by the state; other contractors have built their own or remodeled existing private structures, such as motels, to make them secure.[10] While a spokesman for the Federal Bureau of Prisons states that it takes two or three years to site and build their prisons[11] and other sources report that it takes five years or more to build secure facilities,[12] some private contractors have been able to design, finance, and build prisons in six months.[13]

In Houston, Texas, a privately owned, 68,000 square-foot detention facility for 350 illegal aliens was financed and built in just seven months, to be operated under contract to the Immigration and Naturalization Service. T. Don Hutto and G. E. Vick describe the process:

> INS's request for proposal required a response within 30 days from the date of advertisement, complete with plans of the proposed facility. Work on programming and site acquisition began immediately. Site criteria were established and feasibility studies conducted in a matter of days. . . . Preliminary drawings and specs were completed in two weeks and ready for contractor review and pricing. . . . After the contract was awarded, the project was fast-tracked with construction drawings completed in the sequence required for each building system.[14]

In Laredo, a 150-bed detention facility for adult and juvenile males and females was built and opened by a private company within eight months of signing a contract with the INS.[15]

When Wackenhut signed the contract to provide a new detention facility for the INS in Aurora, Colorado, it paid for the facility up front. Design and construction, from the signing of the contract to the opening of the institution, took five months.[16] In another contract, Wackenhut took just 90 days to perform a $1.4 million renovation of an eight-story building, hire and train 150 local staff, and open what at that time was the largest (619-bed) private detention facility in the country.[17]

Time savings such as these are almost impossible to achieve in the public sector if normal bureaucratic procedures are followed.

Operation

Salaries account for about 80 percent of most prisons' operating expenses.[18] Starting salaries for corrections officers are generally low, however, so cutting salaries may not be the best method of reducing labor costs. Although there are occasional stories of lower wages,[19] contractors generally pay salaries comparable to government, especially when they take over the operation of an existing facility.

According to CCA, more effective personnel management can cut costs without cutting salaries.[20] Adequate and appropriate staffing, better working conditions, and more efficient procedures improve productivity and morale, decrease absenteeism and turnover, and reduce expensive reliance on overtime. For example, police chiefs around Bay County say that after CCA took over management of the jail there, booking time was cut in half as a result of streamlined procedures.[21]

CCA reports that it achieves savings in the key area of security personnel through efficient scheduling and facility design, and through strategic use of electronic surveillance systems. These management and capital investments have enabled CCA to reduce labor costs to about 60 percent of operating costs.[22] A building design or work schedule that eliminates one post can save over $100,000 a year in salaries and fringe benefits, since it requires more than 5 staff positions to fill a post 24 hours a day.[23]

Red tape and other restrictions endemic to the civil service system impede efficient personnel management in the public sector. E. S. Savas gives an extreme example from New York City:

> Inefficient staffing was legitimized by a state law that called for an equal number of police officers on duty on each shift, despite the fact that crime statistics showed few criminals working in the small hours of the morning. Because of this legislated inefficiency, if more police were needed for assignment to evening duty, when most street

crimes occur, more would also have to be hired and assigned when
there was little work for them to do.[24]

When the Eckerd Foundation took over operation of the Okeechobee School for Boys, it eliminated what an independent study
referred to as "a convoluted personnel bureaucracy."[25] Under the
state personnel system, facilities "cannot add, delete, reclassify,
exceed 10% above the minimum pay range, or carry out other
personnel functions on a local level." State administrators found
the personnel process time consuming and frustrating. In contrast,
under Eckerd, the Superintendent at Okeechobee "has the latitude
to hire, fire, and exceed the minimum salary, as long as he stays
within the budget." Positions can be added or reclassified with a
telephone call to get concurrence from Foundation headquarters.
Dismissals are formalized, with an appeal mechanism, but there
is no union.

The existence of a union of county employees at the Butler
County Prison in Pennsylvania did not prevent Buckingham, a
private management company, from instituting personnel reforms.
All prior full-time employees retained their jobs (as the result of
a court order) and received pay hikes, but management was able
to redefine job responsibilities and work schedules in order to
reduce overtime and eliminate part-time, nonunion positions.[26] At
first the union insisted, like the police in New York City, that every
shift had to have an equal number of staff, regardless of need; in
a later agreement, however, differential staffing was instituted.[27]
Other new personnel efficiencies covered work assignments, ver-
ification of worker presence, and more systematic provisions for
sick and vacation relief. Turnover fell from three or four employees
annually under the county, to zero during Buckingham's first
year.[28]

Skepticism Regarding Cost Savings

Critics of privatization challenge the assertion that prisons can be
run more efficiently and less expensively by private companies.
For example, John Hanrahan, a leading opponent of private contracting of public services, asserts: "One basic item that should

make contracting-out more expensive, all other things being equal, is that contractors exist to make a profit, while governmental units have no such motivation."[29] By specifying "all other things being equal," Hanrahan makes his argument tautological. To escape the tautology, he would have to show that the profit motive adds more to expenses than it subtracts and also that it does more to increase expenses than do comparable incentives characteristic of nonprofit organizations. In a competitive environment, profit margins must be kept as low as possible, as part of the process of keeping total costs down. Among current prison contractors, RCA makes a profit of 5 percent at Weaversville, while Behavioral Systems Southwest runs its detention centers with a profit margin of 8 percent.[30] Naturally, if "all other things" were equal, these two contractors would have costs that were excessive by 5 percent and 8 percent, respectively. By the same token, however, other costs need only be lower by 5 percent or 8 percent for these contractors to compensate for their profits.

Another critic, John Donahue, argues that the scope for cost savings in running prisons is very limited. Imprisonment is such a simple, basic arrangement, he says, that there is little room for improvement in efficiency. "Prisoners must be sheltered, fed, cared for when sick, protected from each other, and prevented from escaping. These do not appear to be the type of tasks that allow for major innovations in technique."[31] John DiIulio also argues that so much of running a prison is either a fixed cost or judicially mandated that it is hard to imagine that there is any room for greater efficiency by the private sector.[32]

If this argument were correct, there would also be little room for variation in *public* prisons, either in performance or in cost. Yet, as DiIulio himself points out, prisons vary greatly in both performance and cost, with no simple relationship between the two.[33] Since there *is* variation, it *must* be true that there is *room* for variation.

Reasons to Expect Cost Savings

Peter Drucker suggests that public service institutions tend to be both inefficient and ineffective, not simply because they are public rather than private, but because of the way they are financed.[34] Profit-and-loss incentives differ fundamentally from budget-driven bureaucratic incentives. Entrepreneurs are competitively motivated to provide maximum satisfaction at minimum cost. In contrast, bureaucrats are rewarded not so much for efficiency, but in direct proportion to the size and total budget of their agencies.[35]

Bureaucratic organizations increase in size and budgetary resources on the basis of promises, intentions, and efforts, not strictly on results. Because they depend for support on their ability to appeal to a broad constituency, they must be all things to all people and alienate no one.[36] This compromises their effectiveness because they cannot concentrate their efforts successfully.

Economies of Scale

Economies of scale vary greatly by the type of service and by the size and nature of the area being served. However, as Robert W. Poole, Jr., points out, "The one arrangement *least likely* to be most efficient is for all the services to be provided at the scale defined by the size of the [political jurisdiction]."[37] For example, nearly all cities need jail facilities, but a multi-city contract might meet the needs of small cities, while a large city can operate more efficiently by using multiple contractors to meet its varied needs (e.g., high and low security, male and female inmates, juveniles and adults, detoxification units).

Private contractors should be able to realize significant economies of scale by contracting across jurisdictions. When a private prison rents to a secondary contracting jurisdiction space that is unused by the primary contracting jurisdiction, all parties concerned benefit. The company can keep its unit costs low by running closer to capacity. The secondary contracting jurisdiction benefits because it can rent space rather than build it. The primary contracting jurisdiction benefits because the company can charge the primary jurisdiction a lower fee and share with it the higher fee charged to the secondary jurisdiction.

Economies of scale could also be achieved by governmental units contracting directly with each other, rather than through private contractors. Interjurisdictional prisons and jails have been widely advocated, but cooperation between governments has been hard to achieve. Private contracting may help overcome some of the political, fiscal, and administrative obstacles to establishing regional, interjurisdictional facilities.[38] Such facilities offer a potentially more efficient means of accommodating low prevalence cases, exceptional needs cases, and other special categories of detainees.

Wastefulness in Public and Private Sectors

Waste and extravagance can be found in both the public and the private sectors, though they tend to take different forms in each. Business is better known for padded expense accounts, expensive perquisites like company aircraft, and lavish offices (though these are found at the upper levels of government bureaucracies also). Private use of company or agency cars is common in both sectors.

Dereliction of duty, tardiness, absenteeism, and abuse of sick leave are probably less prevalent in private industry, where management controls are stronger.

Employee theft occurs in both sectors, but only in very large corporations (which are occasionally the targets of elaborate embezzlement schemes) is it as common as it is in government.[39] Personal use of telephones and mail privileges and other types of petty pilferage are so common in government that they are hardly even perceived as theft, except for occasional abuses so flagrant as to be scandalous.

The form of waste that is most characteristically governmental (though it would be more accurate to identify it as "budget-based" rather than "governmental") is the deliberate splurging that occurs toward the end of each fiscal year. It is universally understood among bureaucracies that to end the year with a surplus is to invite a reduction in the next year's budget. Most certainly, it weakens the case for an increase.

In sum, while various forms of waste can be found in either sector, prodigality is probably much greater in the public sector.

Public vs. Private Retirement Benefits

In 1983, the President's Private Sector Survey of Cost Control (the Grace Commission) reported the results of its efforts to identify sources of waste and inefficiency in the federal government. They found that the largest single source was retirement programs. Historically, government had to compensate its employees for lower salaries by offering them greater security, both before and after retirement. However, when the Federal Salary Reform Act of 1962 mandated "comparability" of salaries, this trade-off was undermined, to the benefit of government workers and the detriment of taxpayers. Today's federal blue-collar workers are better paid than their private counterparts and their retirement arrangements are two to three times as generous.[40] Federal employees also take two-thirds more sick pay than do those in the private sector.[41] Assuming that the bulk of correctional workers are blue-collar and that state and local (like federal) retirement systems and other benefits are also relatively generous, the findings of the Grace Commission suggest that there is room for savings in the overhead and indirect costs of prisons.

Inflation and Contracting

Another potential cost advantage of contracting is in controlling the effects of inflation. Prison contracts, if they are not renegotiated annually, typically include a provision constraining the vendor to limit fee increases according to inflation, as measured by the Consumer Price Index (CPI). In contrast, growth in government costs usually outpaces the general level of inflation, and government costs in the corrections area have been rising particularly fast.[42] Economist Harry W. Miley, Jr., found that from 1974 to 1984, the per inmate costs of the South Carolina Department of Correction increased by an annual average of 11.4 percent while the CPI increased an average of 7.7 percent a year.[43]

Purchasing

Government agencies require bureaucratic controls (red tape) to regulate their purchasing procedures because they lack the more automatic restraints of a profit-oriented firm. With their greater latitude, private prisons can shop more effectively and obtain better prices. Because they can purchase more quickly, they can maintain lower inventories.

An American Correctional Association report on the private operation of the Okeechobee School for Boys illustrates the difference between public and private purchasing arrangements:

> Purchasing practices constitute an additional bureaucracy at the State level. In addition to Department of Health and Rehabilitative Services policies and procedures, there is a Department of General Services—Division of Purchasing—Bureau of Institutions which is responsible for training school purchasing. This Bureau has a schedule for purchasing commodities needed in an institution. Consequently, the facility's Business Manager and Purchasing Agent have to plan ahead for at least six months and forecast the quantity needed for every item in those categories. Once a purchase order is issued by the Department of General Services it cannot be canceled by an institution for any reason without going back to General Services with complete written justification.
>
> The Foundation, in contrast and with minimum interference, gave complete latitude to Okeechobee to purchase needed commodities. There is little delay in receiving goods, and no six-month lead time.[44]

In Hamilton County, Tennessee, the county had to go through a formal bidding process every week for prison kitchen supplies. After a private operator took over all prison purchasing, the county was able to eliminate two buyer positions.[45]

Property Management

The Grace Commission's comparison of public versus private property management is also instructive and relevant to the issue of prisons. The Government Services Administration employs 5,000 people to manage 8,600 buildings worth $9 billion, at a cost of $125 million. In contrast, a large life insurance company requires only 300 managers for 10,000 buildings worth $8 billion, at a cost of only $9 million.[46] In other words, the private company manages more buildings (of nearly comparable value), with far fewer managers, at a small fraction of the cost of government management. It therefore seems reasonable to suppose that the management of prison property would also be more efficient in private hands.

Experience with Contracting for Specific Prison Services

Virtually every aspect of operating a prison—such as food service, medical service and counseling, educational and vocational training, recreation, maintenance, security, industrial programs, and so on—is already subject to outside contracting. In addition, many states and the federal government now contract out the majority of their community corrections programs. If correctional administrators say that it is cheaper for them to farm out these various aspects of corrections separately, that may not prove, but it certainly does suggest, that it could also be cheaper to administer an entire subsystem, such as a prison, under private contract.

Camille and George Camp's comprehensive national survey of correctional agencies identified 52 agencies that had contracts with the private sector in 38 states plus the District of Columbia.[47] Those contracts encompassed 32 varieties of service, covering "literally every aspect of institutional operations."[48] Fifty agencies reported a total of about $200 million in contracts.[49] Looking only at their largest contracts, 22 agencies reported saving $9.5 million in all, that is, they spent 26 percent less than they would have if they had provided those services themselves. On the other hand, six agencies spent 17 percent more on their largest contracts than they would have if they had provided the services themselves, for a total loss of $800,000.[50]

Since the aforementioned figures pertain only to the largest contracts (excluding construction or architect fees), the total value of savings due to private contracts is not known. However, we do know that three-quarters of the agencies reported some—at times considerable—savings. Moreover, at least some of the money-losing contracts were a response to court orders or some other motivation to upgrade services[51] and thus not primarily designed to save money.[52] Reviewing the cost implications of their survey in a later article, the Camps concluded:

"Contracting with the private sector has proven to be cost-effective most of the time." [53]

Cost Inferences from Privatization of Other Public Services

All public services—not just corrections—either have direct counterparts in the private sector, or can be broken down into components, each of which has a commercial analogue. Not counting the postal service, the jobs of one-quarter of all federal employees are identical to jobs in private business and industry. The Office of Management and Budget has estimated that $1.7 billion a year could be saved by contracting this work to the private sector.[54] Therefore, the literature on privatization of other public services is relevant to the question of whether we should anticipate cost savings in the privatization of corrections.

The contracting process has been shown to save the government money even when the government, after study, decides *not* to contract out. Circular A–76 of the Office of Management and Budget specifies the procedures for federal agencies to follow in determining whether some of the goods and services they produce could be more efficiently procured under contract. The first step is to write a clear Performance Work Statement defining the activity in question. The agency then analyzes its current method of carrying out that activity in-house and determines what changes would be necessary to make it as efficient as possible. The estimated cost of a reorganized in-house operation is then compared with the estimated cost of contracting the activity to a commercial firm. About 45 percent of these comparisons favor the in-house operation, but the government agency wins either way by achieving greater efficiency. In 1984, OMB reported that almost 1,700 cost studies conducted since 1979 showed an average savings of 20 percent over previous costs, "regardless of whether Federal employees or contractors won the competition."[55]

Other empirical research has shown economic benefits in the privatization of such diverse services as solid-waste collection, electric power, fire protection, transportation, postal service, health care, education, social services, protective services, and a number

TABLE 5.1.   Operating Costs, Per Capita, at Okeechobee and Dozier
Schools for Boys

	1981–82 (Before)	1982–83 (Transition)	1983–84 (After)
Dozier	$12,155	$13,604 (+ 10.7%)	$17,215 (+ 41.6%)
Okeechobee	$10,853	$11,310 (+ 4.2%)	$14,617 (+ 34.7%)
Differential		6.5%	6.9%

Source: Adapted from American Correctional Association, Private Sector Operation of a
Correctional Institution (Washington, D.C.: U.S. Dept. of Justice, National Institute of Corrections, April 1985), p. 69.

of others.[56] Obviously, imprisonment differs from other public
services in important respects, but not necessarily in ways that
relate to efficiency and cost. Evidence of successful private delivery
of other services is cause enough to anticipate that it also would
be feasible for corrections.

Okeechobee—An Early Cost Comparison

In a report sponsored by the National Institute of Corrections, the
American Correctional Association compared Florida's privately
run Okeechobee School for Boys with the state-run Arthur G.
Dozier School for Boys. Table 5.1 is adapted from that report.[57]

In the ACA report, the dollar figures given in Table 5.1 were
interpreted as showing that Okeechobee did not become more
efficient under private management. While Okeechobee continued
to operate at a lower per capita cost under the Eckerd Foundation,
just as it did under state management, it did not show any decrease.
At Okeechobee, the per capita operating cost increased from
$10,853 to $14,617, while at Dozier it went from $12,155 to
$17,215.

A very different interpretation, however, is actually more consistent with Table 5.1 than is the ACA study's conclusion that
savings were not achieved because costs were not reduced. The
three fiscal years shown in the table are the years before, during,
and after the takeover of Okeechobee by Eckerd. The "promise"

of Jack Eckerd (which was more like a boast or a bet) was not that his foundation could decrease costs over time, but that it could run the school for less than the state could.[58] An early claim of 10 percent in achievable savings was reduced to a prediction of 5 percent before the agency solicited bids, so the lower target of 5 percent seems fair to use as Eckerd's test.

Costs are ordinarily expected to increase through time as a result of inflation, so the proper design for a before-and-after study is to compare the *rates of increase* under the two different types of management. A lower rate of increase found in a before-and-after comparison is most correctly interpreted as a cost saving. To then attribute such a saving to private management would require an assumption that Okeechobee in state hands would have increased in costs at the same rate that Dozier did in state hands.

This is a logical assumption, and there is some empirical support for it. Dozier's major cost increase was for additional staff, hired in response to the recommendations of a 1981 legislative study of the state's training schools.[59] In 1981, Okeechobee's client/staff ratio (1.7) was higher than Dozier's (1.6).[60] It is thus reasonable to assume that the state would have upgraded the staff at Okeechobee at least as much as it did Dozier, at a comparable percentage increase in cost.

As shown in Table 5.1, costs at Okeechobee during Eckerd's first year increased 4.2 percent—6.5 percentage points below Dozier's increase of 10.7 percent. The difference, 6.5 percent, is an estimate of the increase in Okeechobee costs that would have occurred under state management but was avoided by the change to private management. This compares quite favorably to Eckerd's claim to be able to run the school for "5 percent less" (than it would cost the state to run it during the same year). In other words, Jack Eckerd's boast was fulfilled, at least in the short run.

On the other hand, Okeechobee's cost control advantage across two years (6.9 percentage points) was not very much greater than its advantage across one year (6.5 percentage points). Additional data would be needed to determine whether Eckerd's efficiencies were temporary or continuing. Both Okeechobee and Dozier changed in important ways across these three years.[61] Such changes make comparisons from one year to the next very difficult.

Despite these problems, many simple cost comparisons between public and private facilities can be cited. Most of the comparisons are favorable to private management, while a few favor government.

Simple Cost Comparisons Favorable to Private Management

In a 1982 census of juvenile facilities, the average cost to house one resident for one year in a private facility was $21,256; in a public facility it was $22,009. However, there was great variation by state in costs and in the relative cost advantages of private versus public facilities. Public facility costs were higher in 30 states and private facility costs were higher in 17 states. Much of the cost advantage of private facilities was probably due to their open environments. While 90 percent of the private facilities had open environments, this was true for only 61 percent of the public facilities. The average daily cost per inmate for all public facilities was $60, a little higher than the cost of $58 for private facilities. However, the cost for "open" public facilities was $53 and for those with an "institutional" environment it was $62. Thus, cost was associated more with type of environment than with type of management.

One privately run juvenile facility that has an institutional rather than an open environment is RCA's Intensive Treatment Unit at Weaversville, Pennsylvania. While expensive, this program is comparable or a little lower in cost than equivalent state programs. Its per diem of $130 is about 11 percent less than the $141 and $152 costs at two comparison state facilities.[62] RCA's staff salaries at Weaversville are often lower than equivalent state positions and their medical and pension benefits are more modest.[63] In 1983, Pennsylvania allocated $912,819 for Weaversville. RCA came in under budget, with expenses for that year of $868,449, of which $59,761 was their proprietary fee.[64]

At the Marion Adjustment Center, the Kentucky Corrections Cabinet reports that U.S. Corrections Corporation's cost is about 25 percent higher than the cost of state-operated minimum security facilities, but comparable to the cost of contracts for community

corrections, which is how the Cabinet defines the facility.[65] Another source compares the USCC fee of $25 per day with a state
cost of $21. This would be 19 percent higher, but it includes $1
million for remodeling.[66] The state cost probably does not include
financing, construction, and other capitalization. A third source,
however, compares the USCC per diem fee of $25 in 1986 with
1983–84 costs of $22.74 and $26.83 at two similar state-operated
institutions.[67] Allowing for inflation from 1983–84 to 1986, the
USCC fee would be lower than state costs.

Facilities of the Immigration and Naturalization Service (INS)
are generally cited as less expensive when in the hands of private
operators. In 1984, Behavioral Systems Southwest (BSS) charged
the INS, for its Pasadena facility, about half of what the INS was
paying the Los Angeles County Jail two years before.[68] Another
source compared a BSS per diem of $14 to INS costs of $40 to $50
(producing savings of 65 to 72 percent).[69] CCA's per diem charge
of $23.84 in 1984 compared to an INS cost of $34.85 a (32 percent
savings).[70] While these comparisons can be countered with others
that favor government operators (see below), the INS has reported
an overall savings, across contracts, of about 6 percent.[71]

In addition to its INS contracts, Behavioral Systems Southwest
also operates six minimum security reentry facilities. As reported
in *Money* magazine: "The firm charges $14 to $33.50 a day per
detainee, or 15% less than it costs California to run similar programs. The difference is mostly labor costs. While starting correctional officers at a state-run prison usually earn slightly more
than $2,000 a month, Behavioral Systems' monitors—they don't
carry firearms or wear uniforms—make about half that."[72] The
comparison between prison guards and halfway house monitors,
however, may not be appropriate. Also, the implication that cost
savings require salary cuts for similar work does not hold up when
training and duties are held constant. For example, when CCA
takes over a facility previously run by the government, where
comparison of function is more appropriate, it generally raises the
salaries of employees who stay on.

Santa Fe County, New Mexico, spent $94 a day to run its jail
before CCA took over in 1986. CCA costs in 1987 were $45 a day
(52 percent lower). New Mexico Attorney General Paul Bardacke
attributed the lower cost to better use of the facility.[73] The jail was

originally overbuilt and rarely more than half full, but CCA has subcontracted space not used by the county to other jurisdictions. While Santa Fe County's budget for the jail under its own operation was $1.5 million a year, its payment to CCA came to $858,678 a year for the population size at the time of takeover. Assuming an arbitrary 12 percent increase in population, that would rise to about $975,771 in a year. The contract with CCA sets a ceiling price of $1.3 million a year during the three-year life of the contract.[74] At the end of the first year, Dr. Patricio Larragoite, Chairman of the Santa Fe County Commission, reported savings of $400,000 under the contract and projected a total of $1.5 million in savings over the three-year period.[75]

In Florida, CCA's final bid of $24.50 per diem to operate the Bay County Jail was 12 percent lower than the sheriff's final bid of $27.80.[76] As an added benefit, CCA's figure (unlike the sheriff's) included $700,000 in renovations. When CCA and the sheriff each projected their total jail costs for the following year, CCA's estimate of $2.5 million was 22 percent lower than the sheriff's estimate of $3.2 million.[77] The sheriff's true costs were probably understated in his final bid. According to County Commissioner John Hutt, the sheriff's proposed budget prior to county negotiations with CCA worked out to about $48 per inmate day. During county negotiations with CCA, however, the sheriff presented about six different revised budgets, in which he shifted costs from the corrections budget to the law enforcement budget.[78] His final figure, however, was still higher than CCA's. In addition, CCA initiated a work program that provided the county with $660,000 worth of labor in one year.[79]

Volunteers of America in 1985 charged Ramsey County, Minnesota $57 a day for fully confined inmates[80] in its women's detention center. This was 29 to 37 percent less than the $80 to $90 estimated cost if Hennepin County (Ramsey County's prior, public contractor) were to build new space for them.[81]

In Ohio, the Corinthian Corporation proposed to build a jail for Summit County or Cuyahoga County. The 100-bed, $3.5 million facility would hold minimum security cases only: misdemeanants or nonviolent first offenders. The corporation's proposed charge of $50 a day would be lower than the $57 per diem cost of the current Cuyahoga County jail or the $70 charged by Lake

County to hold prisoners for other jurisdictions. Those facilities, however, probably handle a broader range of offender than the Corinthian Corporation expected to house. The $44 to $50 sliding scale at the Warrenville Workhouse might reflect the public cost for a comparable population.[82]

A three-county group in New Mexico negotiated with a private company, Southwest Detention Facilities, to build and operate a regional prison. The company offered to do this for $54 per inmate day, 31 percent less than the counties' costs of $78 a day.[83]

During its first year of operating the Butler County Prison, Buckingham Security saved the county $100,000 in overhead by eliminating 15 part-time, nonunion jobs, while retaining 21 full-time, unionized county workers and reorganizing work schedules. The cost of running the jail was reduced from $700,000 to $600,000. Of that, $270,000 was for costs the county pays directly—capital improvements, medical expenses, and jail (county) employee salaries. The remaining $330,000 was Buckingham's management fee, which covers food service, utilities, maintenance, management salaries, and a profit of 5 to 10 percent.[84]

Simple Cost Comparisons Favorable to Government Management

Just as some INS facilities, like those cited above, did better financially under private management, similar facilities showed lower costs under the aegis of the government. In 1985, the per diem cost at privately operated INS facilities was $37.26 as an unweighted average across five sites; the cost at publicly operated INS facilities was $31.89 as an unweighted average across six sites for which there were data.[85] However, as noted by the Pennsylvania Legislative Budget and Finance Committee, which reported these figures, there is so much variation among INS facilities by location, size, security, and services that comparing average expenditures is not very meaningful. The range among the government-run facilities was $17.65 to $68.14. Among the privates, the range was $17.76 to $88.69. A Massachusetts legislative report cited these comparative figures to emphasize the point that such comparisons are practically useless.[86]

Norman Carlson, Director of the Federal Bureau of Prisons from 1970 to 1987, informed Congress that the privately operated Hidden Valley Ranch charged $92 per diem to hold Youth Corrections Act offenders. At the Bureau's three other facilities holding YCA offenders, he said, the cost was $55 per inmate day (40 percent less). Even so, Carlson regarded Hidden Valley as "cost-effective" because it provided flexibility during a period of transition as the Youth Corrections Act expired.[87] Data on Hidden Valley are conflicting, however. Another source reports that Bureau of Prisons records showed payments to the contractor of about $76 per inmate day. This was described by the contractor as "about what it would cost the government to do the job itself."[88]

California plans to contract for several minimum security facilities to hold parole violators. The estimated cost of $16,000 to $20,000 per year per inmate would be one-third to two-thirds higher than the $12,000 figure for low-security state prisons.[89] State officials caution, however, that these figures may not be properly comparable.[90]

The State of Alabama in 1985 decided not to contract after its own Stanton Correctional Facility for juveniles was compared with Florida's privately managed Eckerd Youth Development Center at Okeechobee. The study showed that "privatization of correctional facilities in Alabama would significantly raise costs, not reduce them."[91] The annual cost difference was $2,694 per inmate (or $7.38 per diem).

Problems with Simple Cost Comparisons

Simple comparisons like those presented above can be used to support opposite conclusions: that proprietary prisons are less expensive—or more expensive—than their governmental counterparts. The key word here, and a source of confusion, is "counterpart." Researchers who compare institutions must face the fact that facilities vary widely on a great many factors that affect costs; so much so that most simple comparisons of per diem rates are not very meaningful.

Region or location of a facility affects wage rates, property values, construction costs, and the price of food, fuel, utilities and many other costs.

The age of a facility affects maintenance, depreciation, and costs related to efficiency of design. If buildings are still being financed, the speed at which the debt is being retired has a substantial impact on per diem costs, just as housing costs vary by length of mortgage.

Construction costs and the purchase or rental of land may be included in some budgets or per diem figures and not in others.

Population size, homogeneity of inmates, and security level and custody needs of inmates all affect costs. So, too, does the match between the physical design of a facility and the nature of its population. For example, a facility that must be built, staffed, and programmed to accommodate a mixture of security levels may not be as efficient as one that is designed for a more narrow population and purpose.

Processing costs vary by sentence length and turnover. Treatment costs are a function of the range of services and programs offered.

The foregoing are a few of the many factors that make one correctional facility inherently more expensive than another. Unless these items are explicitly taken into account, it is not very useful to compare the per diem cost of a private facility to its governmental "counterpart."[92]

Simple comparisons also suffer from being insufficiently thorough. A complete analysis of the cost of a prison should include construction, depreciation, debt servicing, rent or rent equivalence, taxes paid or foregone, overhead, indirect costs, and many other complexities. The official budgets of government-run prisons generally do not include all of these components.

One of the inherent difficulties in comparing costs of government and private services is that the usual mechanism for reporting government expenditures—the budget—is not as thorough or as accurate as the cost-accounting mechanisms that are used by contractors, who want to be sure that they recover all of their outlay. As a result, government is often unaware of the true costs of its own services. In a 1971 study of refuse collection in New York City, E. S. Savas showed that the full cost was 48 percent greater than what was shown in the city's budget.[93] In a later analysis across cities nationwide, Savas found that the true cost of municipal refuse collection averaged 30 percent higher than what was shown in the city budget.[94] An independent study of 18 Connecticut cities also found actual costs of collection to exceed the budget figures by an average of 30 percent (with a range up to 256 percent).[95]

In contrast, Savas found that cities that contracted for their refuse collection were able to set user fees fairly close to actual costs, while cities with municipal collection charged user fees that had no relation to real expenditures. His conclusion: "Cities with contract collection know how much the service costs; cities with municipal collection do not." [96]

There is reason to believe that government is often just as ignorant of the true costs of corrections as it is of the costs of refuse collection.

Hidden Costs of Corrections

Generally, reports of government correctional costs are taken from a single budget, either of a facility or of the agency in charge of the facility. These budgets vary a great deal in terms of what components they include. It is probably fair to say, however, that no agency or facility budget shows all of the direct and indirect costs of corrections.

Costs that do not appear in an agency's budget can be referred to, for convenience, as "hidden costs." This does not imply that they are deliberately concealed; only that they are not readily apparent or easily discernable. Most will come from the budgets of other government agencies, where they will probably not be identified as expenditures on corrections.[97] For example, litigation and liability costs are generally taken from the budget of the state or county attorney; fringe benefits and pensions often come out of some general fund rather than the budgets of particular agencies or facilities. Services provided by other agencies should be (but rarely are) prorated into the budgets of correctional agencies, and services provided centrally by a correctional agency should be prorated into the budgets of individual facilities. Facility budgets commonly list only operating costs, omitting land purchase, construction, financing, depreciation, and other capital outlays.

The problem with hidden costs is not merely that they are underestimated in comparisons; they are also harder to control. When costs are out of sight, they are often out of the minds of the people who incur them and of the people who might want to curtail them. Legislative budget review committees will lack the information necessary to evaluate competently the reasonableness of requests for funds. Outsiders (and even insiders) will find it hard if not impossible to do realistic cost-effectiveness analyses. Program managers lose at least some incentive to hold down costs when they do not get direct and accurate feedback. For example, if fringe benefits come from a separate budget, correctional managers and workers are not encouraged to view pensions, health insurance, and so forth as a trade-off against salary, or against other expenses (like equipment) that affect working conditions.

A list of cost components frequently missing from the budget of a correctional agency or facility would include at least the following:

1. Capital costs: land purchases, construction, major equipment, depreciation or amortization.
2. Finance costs: service and interest on bonds.
3. Employment benefits: longevity bonuses, pensions, insurance.
4. External administrative overhead: prorated share of the expenses of centralized executive offices (governor, mayor, and so forth) or administrative offices (e.g., personnel services, central purchasing, data processing, general services administration).
5. External oversight costs: inspections, program monitoring, administrative or judicial reviews and appeals of decisions, auditing and other comptroller services.
6. Legal service costs: counsel, litigation, and other legal services occasioned by the activities of the correctional agency or facility in question but charged to other budgets (includes publicly funded litigation costs of inmate plaintiffs or defendants as well as defense of the institution or agency and its political jurisdiction).
7. General liability costs: successful legal claims, punitive damages, fines, court costs, general liability insurance premiums or costs of administering a self-insurance plan.

8. Property insurance costs: premiums or self-insurance costs for fire, theft, and casualty protection (or risk-cost of uninsured losses).
9. Staff training costs: when provided at cost or subsidized by another agency.
10. Transportation costs: transportation services, vehicles, vehicle maintenance, fuel, parts, and related costs may be provided by other departments.
11. Food costs: other government agencies may provide surplus food or subsidies.
12. Interagency personnel costs: personnel may be borrowed from other agencies for either routine purposes or emergencies.
13. Treatment or program costs: other agencies may provide hospitalization, medical and mental health care, education services or programs (including vocational education or job training), recreation, counseling, or other treatment programs and services.
14. Opportunity costs: taxes or rent foregone from alternative uses of land or buildings.
15. Unemployment and workmen's compensation costs.

When asked to provide a per prisoner figure for the cost of running their facilities, most corrections agencies simply divide the operating budget by the average daily population. This, as noted above, may leave out many hidden expenses. In the absence of information that indicates a more thorough accounting, it would be reasonable to add 35 percent to most figures reported by public agencies as an estimate of their real costs.[98]

In 1985, George and Camille Camp asked state correctional agencies to report their average daily cost per prisoner.[99] The 42 states that responded reported an average cost of $38.87 (and a range of $20.27 to $84.72). They were then asked to give an estimate of the total cost of correctional confinement and care taking into account expenditures by other agencies. These estimates ranged from $22.02 to $100, with an average of $44.11. The average estimated total cost was 13.5 percent higher than the average reported agency cost. The estimates of other agencies' costs may have been anything from informed appraisals to outright guesses.

Six states did not answer the second part of the question, one reported a total cost six cents higher than the agency cost, implying an uncanny degree of accuracy, and eleven states indicated that there were no outside costs of corrections, which seems very unlikely.

Even the estimated total costs in this study did not include construction and financing. The Camps suggest that a "more accurate, yet conservative estimate is a 20 percent addition in expenditures above those in the correctional agency's budget. In some systems, other than correctional agency expenditures for corrections may account for up to 35 percent more in prisoner expenditures."[100] The Camps' data, however, show a 45 percent addition for Colorado, a 104 percent addition for Ohio, and a 128 percent addition for New Hampshire. A study by the Correctional Association of New York found that the real cost of housing inmates in New York City jails was 54 percent higher than the figure used by the Correction Department.[101]

Agencies or facilities that do not pay pensions and fringe benefits out of their own budgets are probably underestimating their expenses by 25 to 30 percent. The Camps found that salary accounts for an average of 80 percent of correctional budgets and that retirement and other fringe benefits "frequently amount to one third of salary expenses."[102] A broader study by the U.S. Chamber of Commerce reported that government spends an average of 31 percent of payrolls for pensions (compared to 13 percent for private enterprise).[103] Adding current retirement contributions to reported cost figures may not be sufficient, however. Government pension systems are often underfunded, because they are subject to less stringent (and less fiscally sound) funding requirements than private pension systems must meet.[104] Since pension obligations eventually must be honored, part of their cost has simply been delayed, and thus hidden in another way as well.

Hidden Costs of Contracting

A private contractor's charges will also underestimate the total cost of corrections, albeit to a lesser degree. While we can have some confidence that a contractor's per diem will reflect all of the costs to the private vendor, plus a margin for profit, we cannot be sure that it will contain all of the costs to the government purchaser.

A contractor's fee will include (1) items that are visible in both public and private operations; (2) costs that are not visible in a public agency's budget but are explicitly factored into a contractor's bill; and (3) costs that are special to contracting or to the private sector, but which can be included in the fee to government. Beyond those costs that can be explicitly incorporated in a contractor's fee, there will be some costs to government that cannot be passed to the contractor, to be charged back as part of the fee. An example would be the cost of preparing Requests for Proposals (RFPs) and evaluating the responding proposals. In addition, some costs may remain with the government because it is more efficient for the government to perform the service itself than to purchase it from a contractor.

Those costs to the government that are not included in the contract are the "hidden costs" of contractual corrections. That is, they are hidden in the sense that they do not appear in the per diem costs reported by the contractor. Thus, while contracting makes costs *more visible*, it does not by itself reveal *all* costs. Expenditures that the government retains, however, will be more easily identified as a result of the contracting process. For example, when asked how much it costs to run their jail, most county officials, looking at their jail budget, will not think to include any part of the cost of running the county hospital. If, however, they have a contract specifying that the county is responsible for the bills of hospitalized inmates, they are more likely to include this component in their cost computations.

Other government costs that are generally ignored also may be uncovered through examination of contractors' costs. For example, the ACA study of Okeechobee notes that Eckerd must pay over $175,000 for insurance and spend $250,000 of allocated funds on overhead, which the report incorrectly refers to as "costs that Dozier does not have."[105] But the state of Florida *does* have overhead and self-insurance costs in running Dozier, Okeechobee's sister school. These costs should (but do not) appear in the budget for that facility.

One paper critical of private prisons contends that among the hidden expenses of proprietary jails are the costs of emergency situations, such as escapes, riots, fires, natural disasters, public health problems, employee strikes, or bankruptcy.[106] These emergencies also occur in public prisons[107]; we do not know yet whether private jails will be more or less likely than their public counterparts to incur catastrophic costs. However, the risk-cost will probably be more rather than less visible in private prisons. Contracts generally specify the liability of contractors for costs like these and require that the private company insure itself against them and indemnify the government. Contractors therefore must take these costs into account explicitly when they bid for contracts or renewals.

The contracting process itself—including the cost of soliciting, evaluating, drawing up, monitoring, renegotiating, and terminating contracts—is said by critics of contracting to add to the total cost of services. The federal government uses 4 percent of the total contract cost as the incurred expense for contract administration, though the American Federation of State, County, and Municipal Employees feels this figure is "often too low."[108]

Monitoring costs may or may not be hidden, depending on the provisions of the contract. In any case, these costs will accrue to the government, since if they are charged by contract to the private provider they will then be calculated into the provider's fee. This procedure forces the government to identify and make explicit the cost of an activity that exists in one form or another with or without a contract.

Most discussions of monitoring treat it as a new cost, attributable only to proprietary prisons. However, all public correctional facilities have, or should have, at least some provisions for monitoring, supervision, or inspection. Monitoring is no less important for public facilities than for private ones. The Council of State Governments and the Urban Institute, in their study of private prisons, focused on this subject:

> It can also be argued that states should monitor their own state-operated facilities as carefully as they do a contracted institution and, therefore, monitoring expenses should be about the same for both modes of operation.[109]

Thus, only differential costs—not all of the cost of monitoring a private prison—should be attributable to the contracting process.

Assuming that it costs money to monitor both public and private correctional facilities, then the question is whether the degree of monitoring required by a private facility is more or less expensive than the degree of monitoring needed in a public jail. For example, it would be more expensive if a private facility required the hiring of new or specially trained monitors, different from those that monitor public facilities. It also would be more expensive if monitoring a private facility required the keeping of duplicate records whereas a public facility maintained only one set of centralized records. On the other hand, monitoring a private contractor might be less expensive if the contractor kept better records, or had a more sophisticated and efficient information management system. It also would be less expensive if private facilities passed their inspections more often the first time around, thereby eliminating repeat inspections.

Another kind of indirect or hidden cost of proprietary corrections may occur if contractors pay some of their workers wages that are below the level of subsistence. In this case, an apparent savings in lower per diem fees may have to be balanced by a "hidden" government cost in the form of added welfare payments. Similarly, some of the apparent savings from lower fringe benefits may be spurious. Contractor contributions to social security and company retirement plans will be included in the fee charged to the government. However, if those contributions are not adequate, they may eventually be added to government costs in the form of post-retirement welfare benefits.[110]

"Hidden Rebates" from Contracting

Some of the costs of running a private prison, although they are charged to the government as part of the company's fee, eventually return to the government in some form of tax. These could be referred to as "hidden rebates." Hidden rebates are expenses paid through a private contractor that return to the government as revenue.

For example, business taxes, property taxes, sales taxes, FICA (social security) and workmen's compensation contributions, unemployment taxes, telephone and utility taxes, fees for water, sewage, and waste disposal, inspection fees, and license fees are all costs of business incorporated in a contractor's fee, but they all return to the government as revenue. So do taxes on the profits of a private prison.

If the government contracts for the operation of a prison, the hidden rebates described above would have to be subtracted from the contractor's fee to calculate the true net cost to the government.

Hamilton County: A Relatively Thorough Cost Analysis

Correctional officials will find it very difficult to identify and estimate interagency costs. A county auditor, however, is in a good position to do so. The analysis that follows is based on the work of Hamilton County (Tennessee) Auditor Bill McGriff.[111]

On October 15, 1984, Corrections Corporation of America assumed management of the Hamilton County Penal Farm, a 350-bed minimum to medium security county prison holding convicted county misdemeanants, state felons, and some pretrial detainees under the jurisdiction of Hamilton County at Chattanooga. The cost of the contract is renegotiated by the county every year. For that purpose, Bill McGriff prepares an annual analysis estimating and comparing the total cost to the county of: (a) reassuming direct county operation of the prison, versus (b) continuing to contract with CCA for the operation of the facility.

Costs under County Management

The question facing the county each year is whether they could run their prison for less than the fee that the contractor is requesting for the upcoming fiscal year. Since fiscal year 1983–84 was the last year in which the county managed the prison itself, and many things have changed, it is necessary to identify and annually reestimate component costs, rather than relying on outdated budget figures.

McGriff based his analysis on several assumptions:

1. Staffing would remain the same as CCA's, with certain adjustments, if the county took back the facility.

2. Prison employee salaries would have increased since fiscal year 1983–84 by the same amount as the salaries of other county employees.
3. Nonsalary expenses would have increased at a rate equal to inflation as measured by the Consumer Price Index (CPI) plus, where appropriate, a rate equal to the increase in the prisoner population.
4. The county would have incurred no extraordinary expenses, such as a lawsuit settlement beyond the level of insurance coverage.
5. The county would issue $1.6 million in bonds at 7 percent for 15 years to pay CCA for the new facilities they built at the Penal Farm.

These assumptions were designed to be conservative, i.e., to underestimate costs to the county if it had retained, or if it took back, management of the prison.

The assumption that county staffing would be the same as the contractor's is realistic for purposes of pricing a *resumption* of control. However, it could well underestimate what the staff size might have grown to under *continued* county management, since one of the goals of contracting is to achieve greater staffing efficiency.

Assumption 2 had to be modified in fiscal year 1986–87 because a county wage study indicated that prison employees, among others, had been underpaid by the county. If the county took back the prison, it would have to pay salaries responsive to the wage study, whether higher or lower than CCA's. Furthermore, the personnel department indicated that since corrections officers at the prison must have the same certification and receive the same training as the sheriff's jail officers, they should be paid accordingly. Jail officer trainees with six months' experience were paid at grade 8, while the entry level for prison officers prior to the contract was at grade 4. On the other hand, the county had a policy of not upgrading a position more than two grades in one year, which might or might not have applied to the prison officers, who had already been out of the county system for a year. To be conservative, McGriff upgraded their positions only two grades. This is a significant underestimate, since it is reasonable to suppose that corrections officers returning to the county system (especially those with experience) would be paid no less than entry-level jail employees. Note that underestimation of salaries also implies underestimation of fringe benefits. Together, these two categories constitute close to half of total costs.

Assumption 3, by using the CPI, probably underestimates inflation in other county costs. Since World War II, the cost of services provided by the government has tended to rise substantially faster than the CPI,[112] and correctional costs have recently been rising even faster than other government costs.

Assumption 4, that no extraordinary (i.e., unforeseeable or incalculable) expenses would occur, is a necessary supposition almost by definition. However, since sooner or later such expenses are bound to arise, the assumption has the effect of underestimating the potential costs of county management. Under contractual management, the contractor serves as a buffer for many such potential costs.

In computing the total costs of the prison under county management, McGriff included the following components:

Hamilton County Penal Farm Component Costs	
Salaries & wages	Fringe benefits
Consumable maintenance supplies	Maintenance & garbage
Utilities	Insurance
Medicine & personal care	County hospital care
Food & kitchen supplies	Depreciation
Uniforms	Interest expense
Capital outlay (equipment)	Other direct costs
Other operating expenses	Other indirect costs

The costs listed in the column on the left are those that would ordinarily be found in any prison budget. The costs listed on the right are often taken from other budgets and not accounted for in the budget of the facility being examined.[113] As Hamilton County Auditor, however, McGriff was in a position to be unusually thorough in identifying the indirect and interagency costs as well as the regular budget line-item costs of operating the Penal Farm.

Several of the items in the right-hand column need some elaboration.

For maintenance and garbage, McGriff at first used a figure provided by the public works administrator. However, when he had his own people check out actual costs, counting the number of pickups and identifying costs not billed back to the facility, he found that the real cost was about twice that amount.[114]

Insurance includes both property and liability insurance.[115] McGriff made a conservative estimate of the cost of insurance for the prison, based on county insurance covering both its jail and its sheriff's department. The cost of the (estimated) jail portion of that coverage was used to estimate the cost of covering the Penal Farm.

The Workhouse Records Clerk keeps records on time served by prisoners. Her salary is separate from the Penal Farm's budget.

County hospital care would not come from the Penal Farm's budget in any case. Since the county defines all prisoners as indigents, any hospitalization is paid for out of the $3 million annual contribution the county makes for indigent care to Erlanger Medical Center, the joint city/county hospital. McGriff pulled Erlanger hospital costs for Penal Farm prisoners from this total, separate from the costs for jail inmates.

Depreciation and interest costs are calculated for all construction at the prison prior to the contract. In addition, if the county terminates the contract, it must reimburse CCA for the $1.6 million in renovations and additions invested by the contractor during its first year of operation. To estimate the cost of this reimbursement, McGriff assumed a bond rate of 7 percent and a depreciation period of 40 years.

The categories labeled "other direct costs" and "other indirect costs" are listed below.

Other Direct Costs	Other Indirect Costs
Personnel	County Commission
Accounting	County Executive
Financial management	County Auditor
Data processing	County Attorney
Purchasing	Finance Administrator
County Physician	
Human Services Administrator	

"Other direct costs" include activities of those central offices that routinely perform services for all county agencies: personnel, accounting, financial management, data processing, and purchasing. Some portion of the activities of these offices would be directed toward the Penal Farm. The County Physician was (at that time) a doctor who worked part-time for the county. All he did for Hamilton County was to treat prisoners at the jail and the prison.[116] The Human Services Administrator is the head of the county's Human Services division.[117] Since the prison falls under this division, the services of the Administrator and her secretary are "direct" rather than "indirect" costs.

"Other indirect costs" are those incurred by the activities of other county officials at the executive level. These officials, and their staffs, must spend some portion of their time dealing with matters pertaining to the Penal Farm. The matters requiring their attention may be occasional, periodic, or seemingly constant, but they are distinct from the direct, routine dispensations included in "other direct services."

All these interagency costs come from budgets other than those of the Penal Farm. Thus, each item must be prorated to calculate what proportion of these monies goes toward the existence and operation of the prison. As described below, the prorated amounts were based on county expenditures (obligations) and other data for fiscal year 1985–86.

For personnel, McGriff assumed that time and costs would distribute in a manner equal to the number of Penal Farm employees expressed as a percentage of total county employees. This is certainly conservative. If correctional workers have higher turnover than other county employees (which is often the case) or if their recruitment requires a more extensive background investigation (which is less often the case than it should be), then the assumption of equal effort per worker from the personnel department would be false. The prorated personnel costs would be underestimated.

The County Physician (at that time) attended only to prisoners, so his salary and fringes were split between the Jail and the Penal Farm. When total Penal Farm prisoner days for fiscal year 1985–86 were added to jail prisoner days, the prison accounted for 54 percent of the total. Under the assumption that jail and prison inmates have equal daily needs for a doctor's services, the auditor prorated 54 percent of the physician's salary and fringes to the Penal Farm.

The attentions (and salary and fringes) of the Human Services Administrator and her secretary were prorated to the Penal Farm at 34 percent. This is equal to the county's total Penal Farm obligations, expressed as a percentage of the county's total human services obligations.[118]

All other direct and indirect costs were prorated at a rate equal to total Penal Farm obligations as a percentage of the county's total general fund obligations. This technique assumes that the ratio of external costs to internal costs was no greater at the prison than in the average county operation. As in the case of personnel, such an assumption is quite conservative. For example, auditing and purchasing for the prison were more difficult than for other county operations, and thus are underestimated by the prorating technique. As a case in point, the county had to go through a formal bidding process every week for prison kitchen supplies. After the contractor took over all prison purchasing, the county was able to eliminate two buyer positions. Also, it is a good bet that when the prison was under direct county administration, it caused more headaches per dollar of internal spending, and required more time from some county executives, than did the average county operation. The County Attorney, for example, probably spent more time on prison matters than on many other county matters, prior to contracting. County commissioners everywhere cite the county jail or prison as a disproportionate source of their problems, particularly when they are uninsured against personal liability in the case of lawsuits.

Based on the calculations and estimation procedures described above, Table 5.2 presents McGriff's estimated costs to the county if it were to resume management of the prison for fiscal year 1986–87. Table 5.2 shows a conservatively estimated total cost of $3,413,741 for fiscal year 1986–87, if the prison were under direct county management.

Items 1–9 in Table 5.2 are those costs that appeared as line items in the Penal Farm budget when it was under county operation. Items 10–18 are expenses that would not appear in the Penal Farm budget under county administration; rather, they would be charged to other budgets. Note that the total cost shown in Table

TABLE 5.2.   Hamilton County Penal Farm Estimated Total Cost if
Operated by County, FY 86–87

1. Salaries & wages	$1,239,380
2. Fringe benefits	320,491
3. Food & kitchen supplies	404,966
4. Medicine & personal care	28,694
5. Utilities	198,587
6. Consumable maintenance supplies	56,532
7. Uniforms	61,237
8. Equipment	45,506
9. Other operating expenses	108,045
Subtotal: operating budget items	$2,463,438
10. Maintenance & garage	70,195
11. Insurance	41,885
12. Clerk of workhouse records	16,238
13. County hospital care	238,886
14. Depreciation on pre-CCA construction	57,500
15. Interest on pre-CCA construction	74,878
16. Amortized purchase of CCA addition	152,000
17. Other direct costs[a]	204,888
18. Other indirect costs[b]	93,833
Total cost for year	$3,413,741
Prisoner days (avg. daily pop. = 364)	132,788
Cost per prisoner day	$25.71

[a]Other direct costs: personnel, accounting, financial management, data processing, purchasing,
County Physician, Human Services Administrator.

[b]Other indirect costs: County Commission, County Executive, County Auditor, County Attorney, Finance Administrator.

5.2 is 38.6 percent higher than the subtotal, which includes only
prison budget line items. In my earlier discussion of hidden costs,
based on other studies, I suggested adding 35 percent to most
prison budgets as a conservative estimate of indirect costs. If Hamilton County, like many other jurisdictions, had charged "fringe
benefits" to a general budget, the total would have been 74 percent
higher than the subtotal.

At an estimated total cost per prisoner day of $25.71, Hamilton
County would be fairly frugal. A 1986 survey showed a reported
cost of $30.26 per prisoner day for 10 jails in the East South Central
region (Alabama, Kentucky, Mississippi, Tennessee).[119] In 1983–

TABLE 5.3.   Hamilton County Penal Farm Estimated Cost of
Operation Under Contract to Corrections Corporation of
America, FY 86–87

Total payments to CCA ($21.82 avg. per diem)	$2,897,685
Superintendent's budget (monitoring)	67,783
Continuing, noncontracted county costs[a]	387,502
"Hidden costs"[b]	23,458
Subtotal	$3,376,428
Less "hidden rebates"[c]	($64,000)
Total	$3,312,428
Total prisoner days (avg. daily pop. = 364)	132,788
Cost per prisoner day	$24.95

[a]Clerk of Workhouse Records, county hospital care, depreciation on pre-CCA construction,
and interest on pre-CCA construction (itens 12–15 from Table 5.2).

[b]Other indirect costs of county management (item 18 from Table 5.2), reduced by 75 percent
(auditor's estimate) under CCA management.

[c]Local sales, property, and business taxes.

84, the reported cost per prisoner day across all of Tennessee's
state adult confinement facilities was $30.17.[120] Although this last
figure includes capital as well as operating expenditures, it is probably not as inclusive of other costs as is the Hamilton County
estimate, and it was calculated three years earlier.

Clearly, then, Hamilton County's estimated costs were low relative to those of other government-run facilities in the region.
Therefore, Hamilton County provides a fairly severe test of a
private contractor's ability to lower government costs.

Costs under Contracting

After estimating costs under county management, total prison and
related costs to the county under contractual management can be
calculated rather clearly, simply, and thoroughly. The fee per prisoner day is fixed by contract and the number of prisoners, while
not predictable in advance, is known precisely for any past or
current period. Table 5.3 calculates what it cost the county to run
the Penal Farm under contract during fiscal year 1986–87.

Payments to CCA averaged $21.82 per diem, rather than the
contracted $22, because of an agreement by which the contractor

charged a lower fee for offenders convicted of drunk driving. These offenders serve their time on weekends. Beyond its payments to CCA, the county incurs other costs, which are included in Table 5.3 and described below.

Tennessee law calls for a Director of Corrections (also referred to as superintendent) in counties with correctional facilities. Prior to the contract, the warden of the Penal Farm doubled as superintendent. The former warden now serves only as superintendent, while an officer of CCA serves as warden. The superintendent acts as contract monitor for the county. He has an office at the facility plus an office downtown. He spends about two-thirds of his day at the facility and the other third downtown. He has a secretary and some other expenses. The superintendent has final say on disciplinary matters, "good time" allocation, and release decisions.

At least part of the superintendent's budget represents new expense to the county under contracting, since a monitoring function has been added and a previously combined role has been split into two paid positions. On the other hand, it is not just new cost; a new function (independent monitoring) has been added, which the county did not have before. In keeping with McGriff's conservative methodology (underestimating costs under county operation and overestimating costs under contracting), the superintendent's entire budget is included in Table 5.3, even though some of his time is spent on correctional matters other than the prison, such as electronic monitoring, community corrections, and community service programs.

In addition to the superintendent, some other correctional expenses continue to be paid by the county directly, rather than through the contract. In Table 5.3, these also have been added to the cost of the contract, in the line labeled "Continuing, noncontracted county costs." They all relate to the prison and were discussed in connection with Table 5.2. Some of these costs would be the same under county operation (Table 5.2) or under contracting (Table 5.3)—specifically: the salary of the Clerk of Workhouse Records, county hospital care for prisoners, and depreciation and interest on construction prior to the contract (items 12–15 in Table 5.2).

Some other costs, referred to in Table 5.3 as "hidden costs" of contracting, are basically the same as the "other indirect costs"

TABLE 5.4.   Hamilton County Penal Farm Costs under County
vs. Contract to Corrections Corporation of America, FY 85–86,
86–87, 87–88

	1985–86	1986–87	1987–88
County operation	$2,853,513	$3,413,741	$3,642,464
(per diem)	($25.05)	($25.71)	($27.49)
CCA contract	$2,746,073	$3,312,428	$3,346,300
(per diem)	($24.10)	($24.95)	($25.25)
Savings	$ 107,440	$ 101,313	$ 296,164
(as %)	(3.8%)	(3.0%)	(8.1%)
Prisoner days	113,928	132,788	132,514
(avg. pop.)	(312)	(364)	(363)

(item 18) in Table 5.2, but at a lower level. The prison continues
to demand some attention by county executives. However,
McGriff estimated that county officials now spend at most one
quarter of the time they used to on prison matters, so this cost
estimate was reduced accordingly.

The "hidden costs" under contracting are offset by what are
referred to in Table 5.3 as "hidden rebates" from contracting:
every year CCA pays about $64,000 back into the community in
local sales, property, and business taxes that would not have existed
without the contract.

Comparison of Costs

Table 5.4 compares, for three fiscal years, the total costs to Hamilton County when the prison was managed under contract, with
the total costs (as estimated by the methods described above) that
would have occurred if the county had resumed management itself.

Fiscal year 1985–86 was the first full fiscal year under the contract. CCA's fee that year was $21 per diem. The higher per diem
in the table is based on total county costs under the contract, not
just the payments to the contractor. In fiscal year 1986–87, the fee
was raised to $22, where it remained the following year.

Table 5.4 shows savings to the county of *at least* 3.8 percent the
first year, 3.0 percent the second year, and 8.1 percent the third
year. The savings dipped a little when the contractor first raised

its fee; however, a considerable increase was evident the following year, when CCA held (or was held) to the same fee while the county's estimated costs increased.

Recalling the conservative nature of the county cost estimates, the savings should be described as *certainly more than* those identified in Table 5.4. For example, consider the effects of McGriff's assumption 2 (regarding county salaries) on the figures for fiscal year 1986–87, where savings were lowest. If McGriff had estimated the average pay of prison guards as *equal* to that of novice jail guards, rather than two grades lower, this would still have been a low estimate. However, it would have added $148,676 to estimated county costs, and the estimate of savings for that year would have been 7 percent, rather than 3 percent. This adjustment would not affect the estimate for the previous fiscal year, 1985–86 (see earlier discussion of assumption 2), but the $148,676 increase in county salaries would continue during fiscal year 1987–88, so the estimated savings for that year would be 12 percent rather than 8 percent.[121]

There still remain several other downward biases in the estimates of county costs and therefore in the estimates of savings. These biases, however, such as the underestimation of governmental inflation, the assumption of no unforeseen expenses, and the conservative prorating techniques for "other direct costs" and "other indirect costs," are known only as to their direction; it is too difficult to estimate their magnitude. Making a subjective allowance for their existence, however, a reasonable and still cautious estimate of real savings over the three years would range from 5 to 15 percent per year.

In discussions before the County Commission, McGriff has repeatedly emphasized the very conservative nature of his estimates of the costs of county operation. Where he could not get figures in which he had confidence, he either left costs out or used assumptions that he thought would err on the low side. Because of McGriff's consistently understated assessments of the costs of county operation, we can have confidence at least in the direction (if not the absolute size) of his findings. It is clear that Hamilton County saves money by operating its prison under a private contract. The savings are at least in the range of 3 to 8 percent, and more probably in the range of 5 to 15 percent.

When the County Commission reevaluates the contract every

year, it takes into consideration some costs and benefits that McGriff was not able to quantify. For example, CCA carries $5 million in liability insurance. In the event of a successful lawsuit, an indemnification clause in the contract could save the county (and perhaps the commissioners personally) a considerable, but unpredictable, amount of money. Also, the commission believes that CCA provides better management and more professional training than previously existed and spares county officials many of the daily hassles involved in running a prison. The additional staff training, new inmate classification system, computer records management system, and other improvements provided by the contractor would have cost the county money to have achieved on its own. Grand jury reports have all been positive since the contract began, thus eliminating the time and expense required of the county to correct the sorts of problems identified by earlier grand juries.

Two benefits in particular make the facility and its operation under contract not truly comparable to the alternative county version. These are: the physical improvements made by the contractor, and the added service gained by splitting the superintendent function from the warden function.

The county benefited from $1.6 million in new construction that was handled by the contractor. The cost for this is factored into both sides of the analysis. However, if the county had overseen the construction itself (i.e., had there been no contract), it almost certainly would have cost more. Inmate housing constructed by the county in 1981, for example, cost approximately $65 per square foot. The contractor's cost to construct inmate housing in 1985 was $48.62 per square foot. Thus, for the amount of money that was put toward construction, the county would not have been able to add as much space to the prison without the contract.

In addition to the new construction, the contractor invested capital and labor in repair and preventive maintenance of every aspect of the physical plant, including plumbing, heating, and electrical systems that the county had allowed to deteriorate. The cost for this work was included in the contractor's fee, but the analysis does not include any estimate of what the extra repair and maintenance would have cost under county administration.

The contract added human as well as physical capital. Under

the contract, the county has two full-time managers (each with a secretary) performing three functions: warden, superintendent, and monitor. Without the contract, the county would have only one person (with one secretary) to perform as both warden and superintendent, and it would have no monitor. It should be emphasized that monitoring is not just an added cost; it is an added benefit as well.[122]

The county has also added quality as well as quantity to its human capital. The warden under CCA is a man with much more experience than the county would have been able to attract on its own. Moreover, each CCA facility has behind it the quite considerable experience and expertise of the top corporate officers in Nashville.

Thus, the prison operation that Hamilton County has under its contract is not the same as what it would have if it took the operation back, or if it had never contracted. It gets more (and better)[123] for less money by contracting.

Conclusion

Private prisons will not necessarily be less expensive than those owned and run directly by the government. A very safe generalization from the broader literature on contracting for public services is that often it saves money, but sometimes it does not. It is too soon to say much more than that for prisons, but there are many theoretical reasons, and the beginning of some empirical evidence, to support the proposition that private prisons can offer to government at least the potential for gains in efficiency.

Whether or not proprietary prisons are less expensive than those run by the government, their greatest economic benefit may be that they make more visible the true costs of correctional facilities. As stated in a report to the National Institute of Justice:

> Government accounting systems are generally incapable of isolating the full costs of a public activity or service. For a specific function such as prison security or standards compliance, the direct costs are usually buried in the expenditure records of several agencies, and the indirect costs are particularly elusive. One of the advantages typically ascribed to contracting in other fields is its ability to reveal the true cost of public service. Corrections is no exception. Under

a contract system, the costs of confining particular numbers of clients under specified conditions will be clearly visible and more difficult to avoid through crowding and substandard conditions. While corrections authorities might welcome the opportunity to demonstrate clearly that more prisoners require more resources, it remains unclear whether legislators and voters will be prepared to accept the real costs of confinement practices that meet professional standards.[124]

Correctional authorities should welcome the chance to reveal the true costs of uncrowded, properly run prisons and jails. Voters and legislators can then make realistic choices. To get this information, however, as well as to provide the maximum range of choices, there must be competition and information from the private market.

6

Issues of Quality

Critics' Predictions of Poor Quality

Even if private prisons do prove to be less expensive, critics charge that this can come only at the cost of sacrifices in quality. Indeed, responsiveness to economic incentives, which proponents see as essential to competition on both cost and quality, is regarded by many opponents as the natural enemy of value. Achieving economy at the expense of quality is commonly referred to as "corner cutting."

Corner Cutting

Critics contend that corner cutting is an almost inevitable consequence of the pursuit of profits. "It's impossible to make a profit and not cut those corners," declares Stefan Presser, a Houston ACLU attorney.[1] Corner cutting by private prisons, it is charged, will mean poor food and less of it, fewer services, and cheaper labor with lower professionalism and less training. John Donahue insists that "private firms will be unable to reduce labor costs without debasing the quality of the work force and, with it, the conditions of confinement for prisoners."[2] Barry Steinhardt, Executive Director of the ACLU of Pennsylvania, predicts: "Since the object of private prison operators will be to maximize profit, companies will inevitably look to reduced services and unacceptably low standards."[3]

Those who would be affected most adversely by reduced labor costs—unionized public employees—maintain that cutting back on wages, benefits, or number of workers will yield dire consequences:

> [Private prisons will have] fewer correctional officers . . . more escapes, more inmate attacks . . . more riots. [Staff will be forced to work] longer correctional careers [with] more heart attacks, more alcoholism, more nervous breakdowns—in short, more death. Lower salaries [will] mean greater turnover; less qualified personnel; less job commitment; and in many cases, exploited workers. . . . [A]s the companies cut corners to bolster the bottom line, law and morality will fall by the wayside. . . . [4]

That may be an extreme expression of the thesis, but it captures the essence of the argument: private companies, by their very nature, must put cost before quality and therefore quality will suffer.

Concern with quality is certainly called for in the field of imprisonment, and it is true that excessive concern with costs can jeopardize quality. However, whether competition and profit-seeking lead to corner cutting or to improved quality will depend less on the intrinsic nature of private business than on the nature of government's oversight and regulation of the contracting process. If government becomes caught up in the lowest bidder syndrome, competition for business and the need for profit may indeed cause a reduction in standards. For this reason, concern with cost savings should not outweigh considerations of quality when evaluating programs or proposals.

Experience with competitive contracting in other contexts has shown that market forces can be used to assure quality as well as cost containment. However, to enhance this effect it is generally necessary to pay a premium, in the form of a somewhat higher than perfectly competitive price. Thus, prison contract proposals should be compared on a *cost-benefit* basis, and not on cost alone. For example, when the Immigration and Naturalization Service evaluates proposals and bids for its contracted facilities, it uses a weighting scheme that gives greater weight to quality than to cost. [5]

"You get what you pay for" is a message that both government planners and taxpayers need to hear. But that message can be a promise as well as a threat. The real question is not whether private enterprise will be motivated to produce whatever is demanded (and paid for), but whether it is able to meet demands for higher quality.

Cream Skimming

A frequent objection to contracting for any public service, including prison management, is that contractors, instead of *producing* quality, will simply take it for themselves. "Skimming the cream" refers to the possibility that private prisons may be able to decide which cases they will accept, or that the government will place only less problematic cases with a contractor, retaining the more difficult cases itself. A 1986 textbook portrays skimming as characteristic of prison privatization:

> Most privatization plans call for skimming off the best of the worst—the nonserious offenders who can be efficiently processed. Thus, the correctional enterprise faces the possibility of having to manage only the most costly, most intractable offenders on a reduced budget, and with the worsened fiscal and personnel situations that would result from such a development.[6]

There has indeed been selectivity in some of the contracts for secure confinement facilities. The INS reserves its own facilities for more difficult cases and screens for escape risks those aliens placed in the privately contracted Pasadena and San Diego facilities.[7] For the Marion Adjustment Center in Kentucky, a contractual prerelease center, the state allegedly selects only its best prisoners out of a desire for the contract to succeed.[8] Tom Keohane, warden at Eclectic Communications' juvenile facility, reported that their contract with the U.S. Bureau of Prisons (now expired) effectively allowed them to reject inmates they considered likely to cause trouble.[9] In a proposal that never became reality, the Corinthian Corporation of Beria, Ohio, offered to build a 100-bed minimum security jail to receive only misdemeanants or nonviolent first offenders. A local county official complained that Corinthian's charges, while less than those of other jails in the area, were still high for that type of prisoner.[10]

Not all contracts are oriented toward minor offenders. Most of the existing county jail contracts obligate the vendor to take whatever offenders the sheriff brings in for detention, from the mildest misdemeanants to the most dangerous felons. When CCA officials offered to take over the entire Tennessee prison system, they did not want just the cream. In Pennsylvania, the Weaversville Intensive Treatment Unit receives many of the state's most serious juvenile offenders and has little control over its referrals.[11] At Okeechobee, in Florida, the Eckerd Foundation incarcerates predominantly hard-core, serious felony delinquents, with a complicating mix of severely disturbed and first-time offenders. When cream skimming does occur in private prisons, it will usually be because the contracting agency or jurisdiction wants it that way, not because companies are unwilling to provide a full range of custody and security.

In the government's own prison system, "cream-skimming" goes on all the time, except that it is called "offender classification." When it occurs entirely within a single system, it is seen as a legitimate management tool designed to enhance security, efficiency, effectiveness, and other ends. Ernest van den Haag has argued persuasively that prisons could be built and run much less expensively if security classifications were more sharply defined.[12] Though they might balk at some of van den Haag's proposals for "no-security" prisons, most correctional officials would agree in principle that it is wasteful to confine inmates in prisons that have much higher security than they need.

In practice, offender classification operates with uncertain success. Predictions of offender behavior are unreliable, there are few clearly established standards for classification, and the classification of particular inmates can change at any time. Despite extensive classification efforts in prisons today, facilities at all levels, from the most to the least secure, are not homogenous in their populations. They each have the full range of offender "types."[13] Hence, "cream skimming" may not be as easy to demonstrate in practice as it is to discuss in principle.

The crucial flaw in the charge that privatization will "skim the profitable cream and leave the losses to the government" is that it ignores the fact that all imprisonment is paid for by the government. Assuming an informed governmental purchaser, the only way that a contracted prison can keep its contract, let alone make a profit, is by operating at a lower cost than the government could operate that same prison, with the same prisoners. This is true whether the facility and its inmates are "cream" or "milk." Even if a prison also generates revenue through a prison industry, work crews, work-release programs, or businesslike management of the commissary, this will bring a profit to the contractor only to the extent that the contractor can do these things more efficiently than could the government. Otherwise, the government has the option of running the prison itself and keeping the "profit"—i.e., the excess payment that it would have made to the contractor. The only way that "cream skimming" could constitute a relative loss to the government would be if the government failed to maintain effective competition between contractors, or between itself and contractors. If this occurs, the government will waste money whether contractors take the cream, the milk, or a homogenized mixture. So long as profit is the result of a gain in efficiency, rather than the result of inattention, corruption, or other dereliction of duty on the part of government in the contracting process, it will be a gain to taxpayers as well as to the contractor.

To illustrate how different this positive view of "cream skimming" is from that of the critics of privatization, consider the following statement by John DiIulio, to which I have added comments in brackets that offer the positive interpretation:

> [I]f extensive privatization does occur, it is likely to create a two-tiered correctional system [that's a gain of one tier more than there is now] in which managers on the public tier have an unwelcome monopoly on [or rather, competitive superiority in] the worst facilities and the most hard-to-handle inmates. Public prison managers will then govern facilities where costs, staff turnover, and violence run high [but not as high as if they were contracted] while productive inmate activity and staff morale run low [but not as low as if they were contracted].[14]

As this illustrates, the important question is not who gets to run the easy facilities or who has to run the tough ones; the question is who can run which ones better.

Why should it be supposed that private enterprise will be interested only in the "cream" of corrections? This would, of course, be true in a tautological sense, if "cream" were defined as whatever part of corrections is profitable to a contractor. Suppose, however, that cream and milk are defined on other grounds, such as difficulty of management. The profit motive attaches a premium to hard work and risk-taking, but that premium is double-edged. Prisons and prisoners that are hard to manage will be expensive whether they are in contractors' hands or in the government's. What counts is the differential. If it is profitable for private companies to handle troublesome inmates, they will be motivated to do so. If this population can be handled more efficiently by the government, outside contracting would not be feasible. That is a rational solution and should not be referred to, pejoratively, as "cream skimming."

Assuming that, indeed, government is better at running the difficult and expensive facilities while the private sector is better at running the easy and less expensive ones, the critics of privatization have one legitimate point concerning "cream skimming": direct comparison of such apples and oranges makes the private sector look good and the government look bad. As DiIulio points out:

> Where facilities are modern, staff is abundant, populations are small, and offenders are not hard-core, both public and private agencies have run safe, clean, cost-effective institutions. Most inmates, however, are confined [by government managers] in places where facilities are huge, the physical plant is in disrepair, trained personnel are lacking or hard to retain, and populations are large, racially polarized, and dangerous.[15]

This, however, is a basic methodological point about proper comparisons, not a valid argument against contracting per se.

"Dumping," the opposite of skimming, may occur if a state tries to use a contractual facility to selectively rid itself of its most difficult cases.[16] Both skimming and dumping will cause problems only to the extent that they are noncontractual manipulations of one party by the other. Such practices can be avoided by identifying as clearly as possible in the contract the nature of the intended population and the respective powers of selection on each side.

Related to skimming, but less controversial, is the prospect that contractors could be used to handle specific categories of prisoners. Protective custody cases, medical cases, the aged or handicapped, youthful offenders, and females require separation from the rest of the adult, male prison population and often have special treatment needs. Protective custody cases, for example, total about 7 percent of all prisoners, or around 35,000 cases nationally, but require a disproportionate share of resources. Courts often rule that the conditions under which they are held, involving solitary confinement purely for purposes of segregation rather than punishment, constitute cruel and unusual punishment.[17] Since these cases are few as a proportion of any one public facility, greater economies of scale could be achieved if they were contracted to a private facility, particularly one that served multiple jurisdictions. Many prison officials view this particular form of prison privatization more favorably than other forms. With specialized populations, it is easier to see that a contract can be mutually advantageous to the government and the contractor.

Hence, these proposals are not characterized as either "skimming" or "dumping."

Mud Slinging

Speaking of "dumping," this seems as good a place as any to examine a couple of the more unsavory charges that critics of private prisons have directed at certain members of the industry. These accusations are important not so much because of the substantive issues they raise as because they reveal the ideological intensity to which the debate over private prisons sometimes rises (or sinks).

The ACLU and some other critics frequently repeat a story about an entrepreneur who planned to "build a prison on a toxic dump purchased for $1."[18] Apparently the ACLU, if it cannot defeat private prisons by other means, is prepared to smear them with toxic waste—or at least, with toxic waste stories that mislead through innuendo.

The truth is that for $1, Beaver County, Pennsylvania, transferred to Buckingham Security Limited 60 acres of land as part of an agreement in which, at a cost to itself of $350,000, Buckingham would clean up, completely remove, and safely dispose of some toxic industrial chemicals contained in a shallow, monitored storage pit in the woods at the *back* of the land, and build a prison on the *front* of the land (not "*on*" or even significantly near the former dump site).[19]

The clearly intended point of the story, as presented by the ACLU, is that only a greedy private company could have such dirty hands. However, if the ACLU and others want to make the general point that penology and pollution don't mix, they could find a better target than a private company that wanted to *clean up* a toxic waste site in order to replace it with a prison.[20]

Another story uncritically repeated for its shock value, and to imply that private wardens will not run humane institutions, is the story of "axe-handle Charlie." Charles Fenton, co-founder of Buckingham Security Limited, had a long career in the Federal Bureau of Prisons, including terms as warden at three major prisons. Several critical sources have referred to an incident in his career when Fenton was Warden of the penitentiary at Lewisburg, Pennsylvania.

The facts of the case (*Picariello v. Fenton*) are readily available.[21] Warned that he was about to receive two busloads of unusually dangerous offenders from the Atlanta penitentiary and that most of the prisoners had succeeded in removing their shackles during their trip in the enclosed rear of the bus, Warden Fenton had good reason to be prepared for the possibility of a serious disturbance. When he and his men met the bus, they were equipped with riot batons and pick handles, these being among the riot gear approved by the Federal Bureau of Prisons. The pick handles were used only as a show of force and to constrain, not hit, certain offenders. Some who refused to cooperate during processing were pointed at or touched lightly with the handles to designate them for removal to a separate room where they had to lie on the floor. If they attempted to rise, they were held down with a pick handle.

Private prison critics have repeated many times a distorted version of this story in which a jury is said to have found Fenton liable in a "brutality case" in which inmates were allegedly "beaten with axe handles while shackled and handcuffed."[22] In reality, the court and jury found that no inmates were beaten, with axe handles or anything else, while in restraint or otherwise. In fact, the plaintiffs did not even claim that they had been "beaten" in the usual sense of the word; rather, that they were "terrorized" and subjected to "assault and battery" in the legal sense of "offensive touching." The U.S. District Court, in its review of the case, found that no one was beaten or terrorized or offensively touched, that escorting and restraining the prisoners had involved only "privileged contact," and that all of Warden Fenton's actions had been reasonable, except for one. The action found by the court to be "not reasonable" (but also "not extreme and outrageous") was the decision to keep one plaintiff's handcuffs on while he was in his cell, for three days. The court awarded this plaintiff $200 as full and fair compensation for his discomfort.

These two stories represent extreme examples of attempts to discredit private prison companies and to imply that they cannot be trusted to run decent, humane institutions. I have discussed them at some length here because of the frequency with which they are repeated and because of the danger that dramatic stories like these might foreclose a fair test of whether private companies can, in fact, run high-quality prisons. These particular stories happen to be misleading. Sooner or later, however, some scandalous or horrifying stories about private prisons probably will be proven true. This will happen not because the prisons are private, but because corrections is a dangerous and difficult business where it is easy to make mistakes. And when things go wrong in a prison the results can be calamitous.

Much of the rest of this chapter will, of necessity, rely on anecdotal evidence regarding the quality of performance by private prisons. As illustrated above, this type of evidence needs to be viewed with caution.

General Goals and Standards

Most people, including legislators, judges, and criminal justice administrators as well as the general public, are ambivalent and inconsistent in their views of criminal justice. They mix together utilitarian and nonutilitarian considerations. They want prisons to be places of rehabilitation, deterrence, incapacitation, and retribution all at once. They offer little consensus on priorities, to resolve the inevitable conflicts among their many goals and expectations. Consequently, it will not be any easier to evaluate private prisons than it has been to evaluate their public counterparts, let alone to compare the two.

These observations about conflicting goals, however, indicate one of the most important contributions that private prisons can make to the enhancement of quality. Without a contracting process, an agency may never face up to the question of just what its purposes and goals are. It may even remain deliberately vague or ambiguous about its activities in order to satisfy conflicting demands placed upon it. In contrast, jurisdictions concerned about their contractors' fulfillment of contractual obligations will need to clarify and specify their goals and performance measures. Every jurisdiction has laws, regulations, and policies that apply to the administration of prisons. These can be incorporated into contracts simply by reference (though the laws would probably apply even without reference in the contract). In addition, contracts can be used to spell out standards, regulations, and performance measures beyond those that apply to all prisons in that jurisdiction.

ACA Standards

In a study for the National Institute of Justice (NIJ), the Council of State Governments and the Urban Institute report that private prison contracts often include a requirement to adhere to standards developed by the American Correctional Association (ACA) and to seek accreditation by the Commission on Accreditation for Corrections, which uses the ACA standards.[23] In some cases, the adherence to ACA standards was proposed by the contractor, rather than requested by the government agency. Generally, ACA standards go beyond what is required locally; where they are incompatible, or less stringent, the local regulations take precedence.

As noted in the report to NIJ,[24] ACA standards cover such areas as:

Security and control	Work programs
Food service	Educational programs
Sanitation and hygiene	Recreational activities
Medical and health care	Library services
Inmate rules and discipline	Records
Inmate rights	Personnel issues

Missing from this list, but very important to the ACA, are standards that relate to crowding, such as the size of cells and recreation areas or the total floor space per inmate.

The ACA standards all refer to internal conditions, such as

standards of security and decency, rather than to external results, such as rehabilitation or crime control. They are concerned primarily with process rather than with outcome and they emphasize nonutilitarian, rather than utilitarian, criteria. In short, they relate to the "quality of confinement" and the "quality of life" in prisons, in terms of criteria important to prisoners, their keepers, and the public: security, order, safety, space, sanitation, food, recreation, work, discipline, and programming.

As of early 1987, Corrections Corporation of America had secured accreditation of two of its nine facilities and was preparing to apply for accreditation of the remaining seven. As CCA pointed out, this ratio compared favorably to the one-fifth of state and federal facilities and less than 1 percent of local jails that are accredited.[25] In fairness to the Federal Bureau of Prisons, it should be noted that 38 of their 47 institutions were accredited for three-year terms as of 1986.[26] However, within the category of state and local facilities, accreditation is clearly an unusual event.

By mid–1989, CCA had achieved accreditation at six facilities and was pursuing accreditation at others.[27] When their Bay County jail facility was accredited, the ACA's regional administrator for standards and accreditation reported that CCA had received one of the highest ratings of any such facility.[28] Wackenhut Corrections Corporation received accreditation of its INS detention facility in Aurora, Colorado, in August 1989.[29]

The private sector already plays a major role in the supply and accreditation of health services in prisons. Doyle H. Moore, founder of Prison Health Services, which supplies the services of nurses, doctors, psychiatrists, and dentists, points out that "[o]f the nation's 3,900 jails, only 160 are accredited by the National Commission on Correctional Healthcare and we provide the health services at 31 of them."[30] The company guarantees to get its clients accredited within one year or pay a penalty. In 1985, Prison Health Services did not have to pay any of the $1 million it faced in potential penalty fees.[31]

Accreditation, while a useful measure of quality, is not always reliable. As John DiIulio[32] and Stephen Gettinger[33] point out, even accredited public prisons are sometimes crowded, dirty, violent, or deficient in work or other programs, so there is no guarantee that private prisons will be free of these problems even when they are accredited. Still, it is likely that accredited institutions, as a group, will tend to be of higher quality than most others, so accreditation status is still useful as a single (albeit not definitive) indicator of quality.[34] Moreover, accreditation must be renewed every three years, so the longer a facility's history of accreditation, the more reliable that is as an indicator.

American Correctional Association standards generally exceed constitutional minima, and many are more stringent than those specified in state statutes. In turn, the standards of private prison companies sometimes exceed those of the ACA. Staff training is an example.

Training

The ACA calls for a minimum of 120 hours training for new staff. CCA requires "at least 160 hours of training for new correctional officers, a minimum of 40 hours of additional training each year, and at least 24 hours of training per year for management personnel."[35]

As a comparison, new federal Bureau of Prison staff also undergo 4 weeks (160 hours) of formal training and a minimum of 40 hours training each year.[36] The Immigration and Naturalization Service trains its officers for 6 weeks (240 hours) at the Federal Law Enforcement Training Center.[37] The intensive training of federal correctional officers, however, may not be typical of the larger number of state and local correctional workers.[38]

Florida is unusual in the amount of training it requires of correctional officers: 360 hours. CCA testified in support of changing the law to apply to private as well as to public corrections officers.[39] On the other hand, perhaps reflecting different standards for juvenile as opposed to adult corrections, Florida's contract for private operation of the Okeechobee School for Boys requires only a minimum of 40 hours preservice training, and 40 hours per year in-service training for all direct child-care employees.[40]

Corrections officers at the privately owned Marion Adjustment Center "receive the same training as their state-employed counterparts."[41] At Silverdale Detention Center, however, because CCA is seeking accreditation, the private guards "have received more training than did the county guards."[42]

The most important training, however, may not be the formal, classroom type. Nor do most prison jobs require higher education, and therefore a more expensive labor pool. What an effective officer needs is on-the-job training in the "simple, paramilitary routine of numbering, counting, checking, looking, monitoring inmate movement, frisking convicts, searching cells, and so on."[43] In short, officers must be trained in how to run things "by the book."

To support their warnings about lack of training in the private sector, some critics have pointed to the case of Danner, Inc., a one-time private provider of detention space to the INS. Danner did not train its employees in security and emergency procedures or in the use of firearms. During an escape attempt, one prisoner was accidentally shot and killed by a Danner guard. While this case indicates the importance of training, it is not a fair representation of correctional contractors. Danner's primary function was to provide transportation for spare parts and shipping crews in the port of Houston. As a secondary activity, it supplied security watchmen for ships.[44] Lacking training and proper facilities, Danner should not have been involved at all in providing detention, even on a one-time emergency basis. There is a lesson here, but it does not necessarily generalize to companies whose primary business is incarceration. Danner, not incidentally, is no longer in business. The same cannot be said for the many public institutions of confinement where even worse things have happened.

Training is important to the staff of any prison, public or private. Indeed, it is too important to be taken for granted in either type of facility. Contracts for private prisons certainly should require that corrections officers be at least as well trained as their public counterparts. But if contracts call for higher training levels, it merely invites the question, "Why don't we expect this of our public employees also?" Raising expectations is, after all, a major purpose of competition, and either side may have something to learn from the other.[45]

Turnover

Even the best training program will be diminished in its contribution to quality if staff turnover is very high. Not only is training an ongoing process, but there is no substitute for experience, which accumulates over time in an efficient, stable work force.

Unfortunately, high turnover is endemic to corrections, from top to bottom. Among sheriffs and top administrators in departments of corrections, there is potential for discontinuity at every election. In 1987, the average length of service among directors of adult correctional agencies was 3.6 years.[46] John DiIulio, an insightful student of prison governance, believes that this problem of fluctuating executive leadership "is largely responsible for the fact that prisons have been ill-managed, under-managed, or not managed at all."[47]

Among the line staff, turnover in corrections has historically been very high. The figure most commonly cited for turnover among correctional officers is a national average of about 30 percent. A recent textbook, for example, says: "Turnover is high, about 28 percent nationally, and absenteeism runs as much as 15 percent in some prisons."[48] The National Manpower Survey of state correctional institutions found that workers resigned voluntarily at an average annual rate of 19 percent and were hired at a rate of 32 percent. At institutions with 25 to 74 employees, the resignation rate was the highest—an average of 28 percent—and the hiring rate averaged 47 percent.[49] A more recent source cites a national average turnover rate of 18 percent a year among correctional officers in adult state systems, but does not indicate whether this is a quit or hiring rate.[50]

It is not clear yet whether private prisons will be able to reduce staff turnover significantly or reliably. In an occupation with low pay and extreme stress, the turnover problem may be intractable. One of the early secure facility contracts showed at least a short-term negative impact on turnover. Severe problems of transition caused a turnover rate that was already exceptionally high among the state employees to almost double during the first year after the private takeover. This contract, at the Okeechobee School for Boys, will be discussed in some detail later in this chapter.

Corrections Corporation of America has reported a facility staff turnover rate of about 15 percent overall, though it is sometimes higher during the first year of a contract.[51] CCA had its highest turnover at Silverdale, the prison in Hamilton County, Tennessee. Three years after that contract went into effect, less than half of the original staff remained.[52]

Staff turnover is likely to be a problem for private prisons, just as it is for others. It is too soon to predict whether it will be higher or lower, and in any case it will probably vary so much over time and across facilities as to make generalization difficult even when more data are available. Rates of turnover will be useful in future research to comparatively evaluate governmental and private prisons. Of course, the meaning of a turnover rate is not self-evident; it must be interpreted according to information about its cause. However, turnover is at least relatively easy to measure and it is one of several factors that can be used to evaluate prison quality.

Credentials

Private companies can bring to corrections experience and expertise that would not otherwise be available to government, particularly at lower levels. Many of the officers of proprietary prison companies are veterans of state and federal corrections systems; others have expertise in management, business, finance, construction, and the law. As Richard Crane, then a Vice President at CCA, put it:

> If anyone should be using the "no experience" argument it should be us. Our over 160 years of correctional experience among top management is surely better than any you will find in most state corrections systems.[53]

Among the current or recent executive officers at CCA are two who were former state directors or commissioners of corrections, one of whom is a past president of the American Correctional Association and recipient of the E. R. Cass Correctional Achievement Award. Three are former state prison wardens. Three hold doctorates in law; one of these, a specialist in correctional law, is the former Chief Counsel for the Louisiana Department of Corrections and a legal issues trainer for the National Institute of Corrections. Several other officers hold degrees in criminal justice or business. One is an architect, another a Certified Public Accountant. The company's board includes a former Chairman of the U.S. Board of Parole.

CCA's competitors, large and small, also have personnel with training and experience. These would include: Wackenhut, the largest provider of private security in the country; Pricor, whose officers include one who worked 15 years as a state prison budget director[54] and another who is a former Commissioner of Finance and Administration and Commissioner of General Services for the State of Tennessee; Buckingham Security Limited, one of whose co-founders was once warden at the tough Lewisburg and Marion federal prisons during a 23-year federal corrections career; Behavioral Systems Southwest, whose two chief officers had long careers in the California Department of Corrections; Eclectic Communications, Inc., whose warden at Hidden Valley Ranch worked 27 years in the federal prison system, including stints as Warden at maximum security institutions.[55]

Private corrections companies will not necessarily have strong correctional experience and training among their initial executive officers. U.S. Corrections Corporation, for example, was founded by two men with no corrections experience (they hired that expertise when they got their first contract). However, the contracting process does give a jurisdiction a higher degree of control over selecting correctional authorities on the basis of experience than often occurs in the political processes of election and appointment. Sheriffs, for example, are often elected without prior experience in law enforcement, let alone in running a jail. A small city or county has little chance of hiring directly the high level of competence, training, and experience it can obtain through contracting.

Ironically, the extensive prior experience of private corrections officials is sometimes used against them. Critics ask, rhetorically, what these people can do in the private sector that they couldn't do in the public sector. Or critics search through the records to find some problem faced by private corrections officials when they were in government service. In both cases, critics make the mistake of attributing to individuals something that is characteristic of a system. It is hard to serve for long at the level of Warden or higher without being involved, directly or indirectly, in a lawsuit, and critics of private prisons have drawn some ammunition from this fact.

The case of "axe-handle Charlie" has already been discussed. Another example is an article in the *Nation*, which cites a Supreme Court ruling that the Arkansas prison system in 1978 was operating under conditions of cruel and unusual punishment.[56] The Director of Corrections in Arkansas from 1971 to 1976 was T. Don Hutto, who later became Vice President of Corrections Corporation of America, then President of CCA International and a member of the Board of Directors of CCA. Since most states in recent years have had jails, prisons, and prison systems under court orders for conditions of confinement, it is very misleading to imply that this particular case is indicative of malfeasance on the part of either CCA or Hutto. To the contrary, Hutto is widely regarded as having had a distinguished career in corrections. While Director in Arkansas, he helped dismantle that state's armed trusty guard system by replacing inmate trusties with qualified staff. He has been elected President of the American Correctional Association and in 1987 received that Association's E. R. Cass Correctional Achievement Award. His prior experience, including his record of reform in a troubled state prison system, is an asset, not a liability, that he brings to his service in the private sector.

Inspections

In January 1983, the Tennessee Corrections Institute inspected Hamilton County's prison and found violations of 62 out of 177 regulations. Earlier reports were similarly poor. In February 1985, four months after the prison was taken over by CCA, the same inspector found 21 violations, most of which were corrected within a few months. Subsequent inspections found even fewer faults.[57] A Hamilton County grand jury inspects the prison four times a year. According to County Auditor Bill McGriff, the grand jury reports since CCA took over "have all been glowing."[58] In contrast, many grand jury reports were critical of the facility under the county.

On January 30, 1987, a grand jury inspected the New Mexico State Penitentiary and the privately run Santa Fe County Detention Facility. After comparing the two institutions, several grand jury members recommended that private management of the state prison be considered. They cited economy, efficiency, and cleanliness as potential benefits.

In Bay County, the State Correctional Internal Inspector found

76 violations of Florida codes or standards at the county jail prior to its takeover by CCA. Four and a half months into the contract, a subsequent inspection found only nine violations, all of which were rectified by the time of a follow-up one month later.[59]

Private Parts Reflect Public Wholes

Whatever effect contracting may have on quality, it cannot outweigh completely the effect of the purchasing agency's own commitment. Quality supplied is determined most strongly by quality demanded. Private prisons will thus largely reflect the public systems of which they are a part. This principle was noted by Kevin Krajick, one of the first observers of the private prison scene, in a brief comparison of two private juvenile facilities: RCA's Weaversville Intensive Treatment Unit, and the Eckerd Foundation's Okeechobee School for Boys.[60]

That comparison is worth elaborating here. It illustrates not so much a difference between RCA and the Eckerd Foundation—both had successful track records running small-scale programs for juveniles—as a difference between the missions assigned to each by the respective states. Pennsylvania asked RCA to quickly create a small, intensive treatment facility for hard-core delinquents. The state was more concerned with speed and quality than with cost. Florida asked the Eckerd Foundation to take over a large, rundown, troublesome, underfunded facility, and to run it for even less money.

The results are described in the two sections that follow.

Pennsylvania, RCA, and Weaversville

Weaversville, as Krajick noted, "is part of a relatively progressive juvenile system; Pennsylvania has made a commitment to running small, well-funded institutions." Krajick quotes the manager of Weaversville as saying, "We're able to do what we do because somebody up there in the state really cares about these kids. They give us whatever we need." The state pays RCA $40,000 per year for each resident, 5 percent of which is RCA's profit.[61]

Though many of the residents are serious offenders, the atmosphere is relaxed. Staff outnumber residents and are well educated and trained; they include teachers, psychologists, and caseworkers. There are daily group therapy sessions. Krajick quotes James Finkenauer, a Rutgers University expert on delinquency programs nationwide, as saying, "Weaversville is better staffed, organized, and equipped than any program of its size that I know."[62]

The employees at Weaversville are enthusiastic about their jobs in spite of pay that is lower than they might get in a comparable state job. Indeed, some of those employees gave up state positions to do the same work in the private sector. They cite as a major compensation the opportunity to do quality work. "There's far more creativity in working for a corporation," says Henry Gursky, project manager at Weaversville. "There is a direction towards excellence and innovation here that seems to be unique to private industry," adds Arthur Eisenbuch, Weaversville's clinical psychologist.[63]

Pennsylvania state officials, who might be seen as competitors as well as sponsors and monitors of the Weaversville facility, also praise the program. Robert H. Sobolevitch, Director of the state welfare department's Bureau of Group Residential Services, says that Weaversville is "the best example of a private operation. This is going to be *the* national model. It's the hottest thing in corrections." While the program is expensive, Sobolevitch reports that costs at Weaversville run slightly under spending at Pennsylvania's comparable state-run juvenile institutions.[64]

At least at Weaversville, the fear of critics that companies "driven by profit" must necessarily sacrifice quality to cut costs has not materialized.

Florida, Eckerd, and Okeechobee

The private takeover of the Okeechobee School for Boys occurred within a totally different context from that which produced the private Weaversville Intensive Treatment Unit. Both Weaversville and Okeechobee were intended to hold hard-core, serious juvenile offenders, but there the similarity ends. Weaversville was produced as a new facility in response to a legal necessity, and it was supported by a jurisdiction already spending relatively high amounts on its own facilities. Okeechobee, in contrast, was perhaps the

most neglected and deteriorated facility within a system of large
state training schools that had been allowed to run down in antic-
ipation of deinstitutionalization. Prior to contracting, Okeechobee
and two other state training schools were facing lawsuits alleging
cruel and abusive conditions of confinement.

Krajick underscored the contrast between Okeechobee and
Weaversville:

> Florida gives Eckerd less than one-half the money per resident at
> Okeechobee that Pennsylvania gives to RCA for Weaversville. Ju-
> venile-justice experts say that Florida imprisons too many delin-
> quents in training schools to begin with, and that all the schools are
> too big for their own good. Okeechobee alone is more than twice
> the size of the Pennsylvania institutional system. . . . [65]

With funding from the National Institute of Corrections, a research team for the American Correctional Association undertook
a study to evaluate the effects of privatization on Florida's Okeechobee School for Boys.[66] Because of late timing, they were unable
to use a before-and-after design for most of their analyses. Instead,
they compared Okeechobee (after the takeover by the Eckerd
Foundation) with the Arthur G. Dozier School for Boys, another
training school of about the same size that the state continued to
run. They gathered and examined data on clients, staff, and management and administration. In addition, because the school
seemed to be suffering from transition problems at the time of
their original study, they had a consultant return eight months
after the study ended for a more subjective follow-up look.

Of the client measures gathered, only one—number of deten-
tions—produced usable data. The ACA analysis of the data, however, was badly flawed. They failed to control for significant
population differences on race and seriousness of offense, while
controlling instead for nonsignificant differences on a widely used
offender classification scale. Since ACA found little to report, the
data concerning clients need not be examined here.

When examining the staff data, the research team found that
staff morale and satisfaction at Okeechobee were lower than at
Dozier. There was a smaller questionnaire return rate at Okeechobee (62 percent vs. 82 percent), and the average length of
employment was much longer at Dozier, so selection factors may

have been operating. However, on about half the survey questions, there were significant differences between Okeechobee and Dozier staff.

Okeechobee staff *more often*:

—saw the environment as threatening to clients and staff;
—saw their work as temporary employment and "just a job";
—were dissatisfied with their jobs and work environment.

They *less often*:

—saw their institution as well organized and well run;
—felt that they were well trained or effective;
—were optimistic about the future of their charges.

In terms of management, the researchers found significant improvements in efficiency of purchasing and greatly increased latitude in personnel procedures. However, Eckerd had serious problems in running Okeechobee that resulted from initial personnel policies that later had to be reversed.

When it first took over the facility, Eckerd reduced the staff from 224.5 to 183 positions. Cottage counselors lived with their charges 24 hours a day, but their work week was redefined from 40 hours (5 × 8) to 80 hours (5 × 16). This (along with other factors) caused great dissatisfaction and enormous turnover among the counselors.

Staff turnover at Okeechobee was very high to begin with, about 87 percent the year before the contract began. During the year of transition, turnover shot up to 167 percent (on an annual basis), then fell back to 118 percent the next year.[67] Meanwhile, turnover at Dozier was very low during all three years (about 10 to 12 percent).

In response to this unrest, Eckerd contributed an extra $236,000 above the contract to bring the staff size back to its precontract level and reduce the work week. The new work week ranged from 40 hours for detention unit counselors to 56 hours for cottage counselors (16 hours a day for 7 out of 14 days). At this point, new Okeechobee cottage counselors, after 90 days, were earning $12,000 per year for a 56-hour week. This was the same hourly rate ($4.12) as new Dozier counselors, who received $8,560 per year for a 40-hour week. In addition, Okeechobee counselors received free room and board, which Dozier counselors did not. Nonetheless, staff morale and turnover remained much worse at Okeechobee than at Dozier. Their total compensation advantage was apparently not worth the onerous work schedule. Later, work schedules for cottage counselors were reduced to 8 1/2 hours a day, 45 hours a week, and all staff were paid overtime beyond 40 hours a week (the initial policy after the takeover provided no overtime pay rate).

Thus, Eckerd's attempt to cut labor costs by reducing staff size and increasing work hours was clearly a failure, which soon had to be reversed. While the year of reduced budget for staff allowed Eckerd to shift funds into making substantial and permanent improvements in the facility's physical plant, those improvements came at a high cost in terms of staff morale. As the ACA study concluded:

> The Eckerd Foundation's assumption that they could "site-adapt" their Wilderness Camp program to fit Okeechobee, was unrealistic. This idea, coupled with the loss of experienced state staff and an immediate reduction in total number of personnel, left the facility both understaffed and for the most part in the hands of inexperienced personnel. The concomitant increase in work-hours led to an even higher rate of personnel turnover and contributed to further lowered staff morale.[68]

There must have been unrest among the residents as well as the staff, judging from Okeechobee's high escape rate. On the other hand, escapes were unusually common at Okeechobee prior to the changeover. The escape rate was 25.6, 27.6, and 25.6 per 100 inmates in the years before, during, and after transfer from government to private hands. This is essentially no change, in spite of the extremely high turnover among the cottage counselors and the other problems of a difficult transition year.[69] At Dozier, the escape rates for those three years were 10.6, 8.0, and 6.3 per 100.

Management of the education program at Okeechobee was made more efficient by the contracting arrangement. Previously, the Florida Department of Education contracted the education programs at Okeechobee and Dozier to local school systems (a community college and the county school board, respectively).

When Eckerd contracted to run Okeechobee, it also applied for, and won, the contract for its education program. This resulted in several efficiencies: educational and institutional policies and disciplinary actions could be coordinated; educational and other staff could overlap and supplement each other's activities; and overhead costs authorized at 20 percent of the education contract could be largely reinvested in the school. At Dozier, the full amount authorized in the contract for overhead costs was used for that purpose by the contracting county school board. At Okeechobee, however, only one-sixth of the funds authorized for overhead was used for that purpose; the remainder was used to pay other expenses at the school. Moreover, after the first year, Eckerd used some of its education contract funds to pay for telephone, utilities, and maintenance accounted for by the education program. At Dozier, the school board paid for none of these costs out of its contract.

The ACA researchers tallied up an inventory of 36 positive results and 22 negative results of the Eckerd contract. The list is too long and detailed to present fully, but a sample from each set is paraphrased here.

Positive results included:

1. Greater flexibility in personnel procedures.
2. Greater flexibility in purchasing and capitalization.
3. Improved training program.
4. New equipment and refurbishment of all occupied cottages.
5. The education program (which must be contracted by the state) was brought under the same administration as the rest of the institution.
6. The Foundation lobbies the legislature for program and capital funds.
7. Improved security and fire safety.
8. Improved food.
9. Improved clothing for clients.
10. Increased supply of maintenance materials.
11. Quicker identification and resolution of problems.
12. Faster renovation and construction.

Negative results included:

1. An initial work schedule for counselors that was too demanding, resulting in lowered morale and greatly increased turnover.
2. A requirement of one to five years employment with the Foundation before transfer of state pension credit to the Foundation retirement plan.
3. Difficulty in changing staff attitudes and philosophy.
4. Insufficient maintenance staff.
5. Duplicative accounting requirements.
6. Department of Health and Rehabilitative Services perceived a loss of information and control.
7. Loss of coordination with the rest of the state juvenile system.

Several positive results that are omitted above concerned employee benefits or perquisites. They are worth a summary mention for two reasons. First, they mitigate somewhat the employee dissatisfaction over hours and working conditions that occurred during the transfer period. Second, they differ from the negative experiences of some other contracts, in which employee benefits constitute a sore point. At Okeechobee, under Eckerd, employees received: a pension plan at least as good as the state offered; $10,000 free life insurance; free dental care; free housing, meals, and clothing; tuition for part-time college study; certain professional and business expenses for key staff; and Foundation-sponsored social events.

It should also be noted that among the negative "results" mentioned in the report were: short client stay; inappropriate referrals to the facility; and no control over population size. Since these are determined by the state, it does not seem accurate to describe them as the "results of contracting."

The ACA study noted in an afterword that a newly changed administration at Okeechobee chalked up a large number of remarkably positive achievements following the first draft of the ACA report.[70] Employee turnover was cut by 75 percent following a return to normal working hours. Staff size was increased and the facility's population declined, resulting in greater client control and a more relaxed atmosphere. The student council met regularly with the superintendent, a grievance procedure was created, and the need for disciplinary segregation declined. Work release and aftercare programs were developed. Sanitation and maintenance improved. Staff training was strengthened. Improvements were noted in the classification system, community relations, and many other areas.

The Silverdale Survey

While a researcher for the American Bar Foundation, Samuel Jan Brakel, a law professor at Northern Illinois University, studied the quality of CCA's program at Silverdale, the Hamilton County Penal Farm, largely from the perspective of the inmates.[71] By means of a questionnaire, Brakel asked a sample of 20 inmates 16 questions covering the conditions of their confinement, programs and services, due process procedures (discipline, grievance, legal access, and release procedures), and relations with the outside world.

At the aggregate level, the total responses ($20 \times 16 = 320$) broke down as follows: 157 positive, 67 ambivalent, and 96 negative.

The areas where CCA was most highly rated by inmates included: physical improvement, upkeep, and cleanliness; staff competence and character; work assignments; chaplain (also counselor) services; requests and grievances; correspondence and telephone; and outside contacts.

Areas with a rough balance of positive and negative ratings were: safety and security; classification; medical care; food; education; discipline; and legal access.

Areas with a preponderance of negative ratings were: recreational facilities and programs; and release procedures. It should be noted that release decisions and allocation of good time credits are the responsibility of the county superintendent of corrections and out of the hands of CCA.

Six of the prisoners were able to compare CCA's management with prior conditions under county administration, at least on some of the questions. These inmates provided 28 explicit before-and-after comparisons: 24 favored CCA and 4 favored the county prior to CCA.

From prisoners' comments and information gathered independently by Brakel, it is evident that much of the before-and-after comparison favoring CCA stems from the fact that conditions under the county had become especially bad. This may be a common problem in evaluating private prisons. Some of these facilities—especially the early ones—may be responses to desperate situations, where a "regression to the mean" effect is possible. On the other hand, while inheriting a "mess" may make it hard to do worse, it does not guarantee that a contractor will do better. Indeed, it makes it harder to do well in absolute terms, because the contractor also inherits the budget, physical plant, staff, and inmates that caused many of the prior problems.

Many inmates at Silverdale were able to make external comparisons of their experience under CCA to conditions at the county jail in downtown Chattanooga or to conditions at the state penitentiary in Nashville. These comparisons totaled 102, with 66 favoring Silverdale, 10 favoring the Chattanooga County Jail, and 26 favoring the state penitentiary. The external comparisons suggest that CCA's improvements are real achievements and not just regression-to-the-mean effects.

Brakel also cites the contract monitor and former warden as having identified "in unequivocal terms" five major areas of improvement: physical plant, classification, staff treatment of inmates, the disciplinary system, and medical services.

A Survey of Contracted Services

It is reasonable to expect that the quality of private sector operation of entire institutions will correlate with the quality of private sector delivery of the separate services and programs that make up the whole. Here there is a longer track record, so we have better information.

In a recent survey, 52 corrections agencies, representing 38 states plus the District of Columbia, reported having at least one service contract with a private vendor.[72] The survey found 32 different services that were contracted privately, covering "literally every aspect of institutional operations."[73] Further details about benefits and liabilities were provided by 50 of the agencies. When asked to identify benefits, 62 percent of the responding agencies mentioned better quality of service.[74] When agencies were asked to state the "single best advantage" of their contracts, half of the advantages listed related to quality of service and 45 percent related to cost.[75] When asked to identify liabilities, using a checklist of 12 possible problems, the 50 agencies produced a total of 161 complaints. About one-third of these (34 percent) concerned service quality or delivery.[76]

It is too soon to do a formal survey of corrections agencies that have contracted for the operation of entire facilities; the number is too small. The closest thing we have to such a review is a report prepared for the National Institute of Justice by the Council of State Governments and the Urban Institute. The researchers obtained documents such as contracts, Requests for Proposals (RFPs), inspection reports, and legislative studies from 22 states. They also visited privately contracted facilities and interviewed corporate and government officials. While emphasizing that information on service quality is very limited, they concluded that these facilities "are perceived by government agency oversight officials as being quite satisfactory. We have seen no indication to date that a government agency has been dissatisfied to any significant extent with the quality of the service provided."[77]

Comparison Yes, Double Standard No

Perhaps the major contribution of private prisons is that they will provide an alternative standard against which to measure public prisons. This is one potential benefit of private prisons that reform groups should examine closely. Privatization may force improvements in government operations by defining higher standards and raising expectations.

However, the existence of an alternative, or comparative, standard should not lead to the creation of a double standard, in which the legal requirements for private prisons are higher than for their public counterparts. It is one thing to anticipate higher quality from private corrections, or to encourage it with incentives in the form of renewed contracts, longer renewal periods, or higher fees. But would be another matter to formally require contracted facilities to meet higher standards than are required of government operations. Charles Ring, in what is probably the best-balanced monograph on private prisons, points out what could happen then: "Plaintiffs' attorneys could argue that state prisons which fail to meet the minimum requirements imposed on private providers are in violation of the state's own standards of what constitutes acceptable conditions and humane care."[78] Just as government and contractor prisons should have the same requirements and procedures of due process (see Chapter 4), so too should they have the same legally required minimum standards of care.

One purpose of contracting is to improve the quality of our prisons, but that purpose will be defeated if demands for excellence are used as a weapon against the process of contracting itself. That is what will happen if private prisons are required to meet uniquely high standards of quality and accountability while at the same time producing substantial cost savings relative to governmental operations that are not being held to the same standards. It is reasonable to ask private prisons to live up to their own claims that they can do better for less, but the comparison must be fair. The insistence that they meet higher standards for less than what it costs government to meet much lower standards ultimately becomes an impossible demand. A major function of competition is to spur all parties on to higher performance. That purpose would be undermined if the private sector were handicapped by the application of double standards.

One promoter of double standards for contracted versus government-run prisons is Professor Ira Robbins. In the Model Contract and Model Statute that he has presented to the American Bar Association, Robbins proposes criteria for private prisons that exceed what is required of public facilities.[79] To give just one example here, Robbins incorporates into his Model Contract 22 standards on staff training developed by the American Correctional Association. The ACA identifies the majority of those standards as nonmandatory for accreditation, but Robbins upgrades them, making all 22 mandatory under the Model Contract.[80]

In my view, a "model" contract or statute would be one that attempted to balance conflicting interests and values, no one of which can be maximized without sacrificing other legitimate concerns. I refer here not just to the conflicting special interests of contractors, contracting agencies, prisoners, and the public, but also to the conflict between more general interests and values:

accountability versus flexibility, security versus due process, quality versus economy, innovation versus regulation or restraint, and so on. Robbins' Model Contract and Model Statute are not well balanced in this sense.[81] The guiding principle running throughout his proposals is the necessity to maximize one value: accountability. Now that is a very important value, but Robbins' approach to it is one-sided. He assumes that accountability is inherently problematic for private prisons, while government agencies are, by their very nature, more accountable and considerate of the interests of inmates and the public. As a result of this perceived difference, Robbins seeks to impose constraints, liabilities, encumbrances, and costs on private prisons far beyond those that exist for government prisons.

To be sure, contractual operations require certain mechanisms of accountability that are different from those used for noncontractual operations. However, this holds for intergovernmental contracting as well, but Robbins is silent on the need for model contracts and statutes to assure accountability when one governmental jurisdiction contracts with another. Robbins requires of private contractors not just *different mechanisms* (because they are contractors) but also *higher standards* (because they are private) for accountability, liability, insurance, standards of operation, monitoring, regulation, and economic efficiency.

When Robbins, in the name of accountability, seeks to impose on private prisons a set of legally mandated requirements that do not exist for government prisons, he creates special liberty interests for privately confined prisoners, and thus new grounds for legal actions against their keepers.[82] This double standard could make private prisons so relatively expensive, so specially encumbered, and so uniquely vulnerable to lawsuits that they cannot survive.[83]

Conclusion

There has been almost no systematic empirical research comparing private and government-run prisons in terms of quality. Until such studies are available, we must rely on the type of anecdotal evidence that has been considered in this chapter. Evidence of this nature should be evaluated with caution. Government-run prisons have been studied extensively for decades. About all that can be said of them as a class is that they vary enormously in just about every area that relates to the concept of quality.

Private prisons, because they are still unusual, are particularly susceptible to the effects of both positive and negative publicity. Much of the literature in the first few years was rather complimentary and optimistic. As the novelty has worn off, critical stories are becoming more common, as is often the case. While neither puff pieces nor hatchet jobs provide a basis for valid conclusions, these types of stories will probably predominate for some time to come. The governmental prison system has survived numerous scandals, along with endless and scathing denouncements, basically because it is the only system we've got. Private prisons have never had the advantage of monopoly, and thus will be much more vulnerable to negative publicity. There is little danger that jurisdictions will commit themselves completely to private prisons on the basis of early positive reports. It is possible, though, that some jurisdictions might completely rule out contractual arrangements on the basis of early scandals. No matter how convincing stories of "success" or "failure" may appear, they should not form the basis of any but the most narrow and tentative of conclusions.

My own conclusion so far is simply that private prisons will fall variously within the same range of quality as do those run by government employees. Some private prisons will be better than some public prisons, and vice versa. As long as there are at least some jurisdictions where prisons and jails might be improved by competition from the private sector, that option ought not to be categorically ruled out. Moreover, even jurisdictions with relatively high quality prisons ought to remain open to competition.

7
Issues of Quantity

Many of the people who are opposed to private prisons take this stance because they are opposed to prisons generally. They fear that cheaper and more efficient prisons will mean more imprisonment. Few of these critics object to the privately administered, profit-making community correctional programs which serve as alternatives to prison.[1] Rather, they are concerned that private prisons will distract attention from these and other alternatives.[2] It is ACLU policy that "new prison or jail capacity should be increased only after existing unconstitutional conditions have been remedied, if ever." [3] Moreover, capacity should not be expanded until all alternatives to imprisonment have been exhausted.[4]

Jerome Miller, of the National Center on Institutions and Alternatives, lobbies hard for alternatives to imprisonment. Miller has voiced strong doubts about for profit jails for adults[5] and his organization's newsletter has attacked and ridiculed the idea of proprietary prisons.[6] However, Miller saw nothing wrong with privately contracting out virtually all of the Massachusetts juvenile corrections system, a revolutionary change for which he was personally responsible. The private exercise of state authority to carry out correctional practices is acceptable to Miller, but only where the aim is to provide treatment rather than increase the prison population.

"Capacity Drives Use"

If, through greater efficiency, more prisons are built, argue the critics, then they will be filled simply because they are there. "As long as you build prisons," a program associate at the Edna McConnell Clark Foundation declared, "you'll fill them. It's a self-fulfilling prophecy." [7]

For this argument to have weight as an objection to privatization, it would have to be shown that capacity which is produced, owned, and operated by private agents on a contingent basis under contract to a government is as likely to be used by the government "because it is there" as is capacity produced, owned, and operated by the government itself. On the contrary, however, the government is more likely to use up "excess" capacity that it already owns than it is to purchase "unneeded" capacity from a contractor. Owners may feel compelled to find uses for their idle properties; renters, however, do not increase their holdings just because new properties are on the market. Thus, the argument that capacity drives use would be a better argument against government ownership of prisons than against privatization.

Nevertheless, those who object to private prisons speak of "the solid evidence which supports the position that the criminal justice system inexorably operates to fill every available cell regardless of the need [or] wisdom of their use." [8] The most widely cited piece of this "evidence" was supplied by Abt Associates[9] in a time-series analysis relating state prison populations to changes in capacity. The researchers concluded that all net increases in prison capacity will be entirely absorbed within two years. When a team of experts at Carnegie-Mellon University headed by Alfred Blumstein, an eminent authority on prison population research,[10] examined the Abt analysis they concluded that it contained a crucially incorrect calculation and was extremely sensitive to the inclusion of two extreme data points. In addition, they criticized the statistical model as overly simplistic because it omitted important variables and ignored simultaneous (two-way) causal effects. Blumstein and his associates concluded that existing evidence does not support the hypothesis that prison capacity directly determines the degree of prison use. While the Blumstein group emphasized that the evidence does not disprove Abt's hypothesis either, they point out that during the 1960s, when there was considerable spare capacity, prison populations declined even though crime was increasing.[11]

Obviously, capacity is not unrelated to the degree of prison use, but expansion of capacity does not automatically produce a rise in imprisonment. Likewise, nonexpansion does not automatically prevent an increase in imprisonment; if it did, there would be no overcrowding. For over two decades, prison reform groups have advocated a moratorium on all new prison construction, hoping that lack of capacity would curtail use. That strategy has backfired, and increasing numbers of prisoners are paying the price in terms of overcrowding and deteriorating physical conditions.

Given current levels of crowding, oversupply of prisons seems like a fanciful concern, but that prospect should be viewed as a hope, not a danger. Overconstruction would allow us to tear down many ancient and run-down monstrosities that have been tolerated up to now only because there are no alternatives. Still, supporters of privatization, who tend also to ascribe to supply-side theories of economics, ought not to dismiss completely the warning that private production of public services can increase the demand for those services.[12] Indeed, both liberals and conservatives sometimes support particular forms of privatization precisely because they want to see more rather than less activity in those specific areas.

Ideally, in the area of criminal justice, demand should drive supply, rather than vice versa. Given the reality of scarce resources, that ideal can never be achieved fully, but any increase in efficiency is a step in the right direction. Greater efficiency creates more room for the system to respond to the requirements of justice and not just to the reality of scarcity. Whether we opt for more imprisonment or for less, our decision ought to be based as much as possible on a sound philosophy of punishment, not merely on the availability or absence of beds. We, the consumers of justice, must see to it that our demand for punishment is relatively inelastic with respect to supply, so that oversupply, if it does occur, will simply drive down the price. To imprison someone merely because there is a bed available clearly would be unjust; equally unjust, however, is the failure to imprison serious felons because space is lacking.

If both oversupply and undersupply can lead to injustice, we should, in principle, err on the side of oversupply, although this is not likely to happen for some time to come. Distortions of supply do not relate symmetrically to distortions of justice. While undersupply leads inevitably to either overcrowding or underimprisonment, oversupply does not necessitate overimprisonment. Nonetheless, oversupply is also undesirable, if only because it is wasteful. What is needed, for both justice and efficiency, is *flexibility* of supply, which the private sector is best equipped to provide.

Vested Interests and Lobbying

Advocates of privatization generally want to see total government spending go down. Contracting, however, even if it reduces unit costs, does not necessarily reduce total spending. This might be the result of effective lobbying on the part of contractors, who have a vested interest in selling as much of their product or service as possible. Critics of private prisons are right to worry about potential distortions in the justice market as a result of political influence by parties with vested interests.

Critics go overboard, however, when they imply that contracting will create special interests where none existed before, and when they exaggerate the power, influence, and supposedly purely self-serving character of private businesses. Some critics portray private prison companies as prepared to hang onto each prisoner for as long as possible, by denying inmates good time credits and undermining their bids for parole, in order to wring out extra per diem payments. Those who fear that this vested interest will pervade the corrections process ask whether prospective jurors who own any stock in a prison company could be disqualified from felony cases.[13]

Opponents of private prisons apparently believe that contractors will be able to manipulate legislatures and public opinion in order to ensure more imprisonment and longer sentences. They speak of the ability of contractors to "buy unlimited television and newspaper time and space, reach the highest political levels and unleash upon America a program to convince the public to lock up more and more people for longer and longer periods, carefully concealing that their motive is profit."[14] Harmon Wray warns that "the most critical flaw in the privatization movement is that it is inherently expansionist." Wray cites the Vera Institute's Michael Smith as noting that "the private sector has an enormous investment in stimulating demand" and he cites Ken Schoen, Director of the Justice Program at the Edna McConnell Clark Foundation, who predicts: "Private operators whose growth depends upon an expanding prison population may push for ever harsher sentences. . . . And the taxpayers will finance the profit-makers while double-locking their doors at night." [15]

Special vs. Public Interests

Lobbying is an intrinsic and (within certain limits) positive aspect of representative government. Whatever government does, and however it does it—whether directly or through contracted agents—the policy-making process will be subject to lobbying by all sorts of groups representing any number of different interests. These groups are not always motivated by economics. Personal, moral, philosophical, ideological, or reputational investments can be at stake, with the same biasing effect as economics and the same potential conflict with the general public interest. Moreover, it should be noted that private, for-profit companies are not the only ones with economic interests; such concerns also affect government agencies and nonprofit organizations.

For example, the National Center on Institutions and Alternatives has a strong philosophical and moral commitment against incarceration and in favor of alternative sanctions. It also tends to identify with offenders. Yet the NCIA is the largest private provider of presentence reports in the country,[16] and in that role it is not completely free to promote its own values exclusively. Surely it would lose business as well as credibility if *all* of its presentence reports argued against imprisonment. Here, then, is a case where an economic interest acts to restrain an ideological interest and to force an agency to focus more on the concerns of the general public. In short, its economic interest keeps NCIA honest and objective, in the sense that it is forced to consider values and definitions of justice other than just its own. This same dynamic can also operate on a profit-making incarcerative organization.

While many Americans denigrate them as "special interest" groups, lobbyists and political action committees often serve shared interests and can be a creative force for change.[17] Corrections experts have long bemoaned the relative lack of organized constituencies for corrections, other than correctional employee unions. One noted expert, John P. Conrad, has concluded glumly: "A strong and durable constituency for corrections cannot be built. . . . The reason is simple. Corrections is unrelated to citizens' personal interests." [18] Adding new parties with incentives to participate in the formulation of social policy, as well as incentives to innovate and experiment in the details of policy implementation, offers at least an opportunity to shake up a generally stagnant enterprise.

Whether industry-sponsored policy changes will be good or bad will depend on whom you ask. Predictably, they will please some and displease others. As noted, critics who expect private prisons to lobby for more imprisonment view that prospect negatively and say that it is not in the public interest. Most of the general public, however, would dispute this claim. Those who said that the courts were not harsh enough rose steadily from 48.9 percent in 1965 to 84.9 percent in 1978.[19] From 1980 to 1986, between 82 and 86 percent of Americans advocated stiffer penalties for lawbreakers.[20] In a recent national poll, 71 percent of the public said that a jail or prison term is the most appropriate sanction for a broad range of crimes, including rape, robbery, assault, burglary, theft, property damage, drunk driving, and drug offenses.[21]

It should not be supposed, however, that private corrections corporations would lobby only for longer sentences. Contractors can be expected to push for higher correctional budgets for rehabilitation, education, job training, work programs, medical services, conjugal visiting facilities, better food, and any number of other improvements in prison environments and programs. The more these are mandated by the state, the more they can be offered by private prisons as well. Contractors may lobby for capital outlays to renovate deteriorating facilities, then bid for the work if it is authorized. As noted above, one major obstacle to significant change of any sort in corrections has been the fact that the interested and active constituency has always been so narrow and weak. Thus, reform-oriented corrections professionals may find in the private sector an ally as well as a competitor, and should welcome this expansion of the constituency.

Private vs. Public Lobbies

The private sector will not bring politics and lobbies to a field where none now exists. Corrections is already a political arena. Wherever governments appropriate and redistribute resources, interest groups of all sorts attempt to influence the allocation of those resources. Among the interest groups now actively involved in correctional issues are: corrections officials and their associations, correctional employee unions and associations, police and their organizations, attorneys and their associations, crime commissions, funding agencies, ex-offender organizations, the American Civil Liberties Union and its state chapters, and a number of other prison reform groups.

Criminal law and criminal justice generally, not just corrections, are political, and strongly influenced in their development by special interest groups. This fact is recognized by analysts all across the political spectrum, from right-wing libertarians to the radical left.[22] Bruce Benson, an economist at Florida State University, has summarized the special interest theory of law in six propositions:

1. Legislators and other public officials supply and enforce laws demanded by politically powerful special interest groups.
2. Effective interest groups tend to be small relative to the population that might be affected by the government activity in question, because of the difficulty of organizing and making decisions when many individuals are involved.
3. Political power may take the form of votes, money, or the ability to disrupt a politically stable situation with such things as strikes, violence, and disorder.
4. Interest group members may be very self-interested but they also may be very well intentioned individuals seeking what they feel is "good" for the society as a whole (although their definition of "good" is typically affected to some extent by their personal circumstances).

5. Bureaucrats (i.e., police, prosecuting [*sic*] judges, prison officials) constitute interest groups that benefit when laws requiring enforcement are passed.
6. Government responds to interest group pressure by favoring the most powerful group (or groups) . . . [however,] conflicting demands tend to lead to compromise, with no group completely satisfied or dissatisfied.[23]

In support of the special interest theory of the development of law and operation of the justice system, Benson[24] cites empirical research by Richard Berk, Harold Brackman, and Selma Lesser[25] on changes in the California Penal Code from 1955 to 1971. The researchers found that just a few criminal justice lobbies dominated, and often practically dictated, criminal justice legislation. Prominent among these lobbies were the California Peace Officers Association, the American Civil Liberties Union, the state Bar Association, and the Friends Committee on Legislation. Benson notes that:

> [An] important finding of the Berk-Brackman-Lesser study was that "public opinion" played no identifiable role in Penal Code revision. The study deemed "inescapable" the conclusion that criminal law was enacted for the benefit of interest groups rather than for the public good.[26]

The result, and often the aim, of this lobbying by bureaucrats and nonprofit organizations has been to expand the size, scope, power, and resources of the criminal justice monolith.

Public employee organizations and unions that promote the campaigns of those who promise them larger budgets, more jobs, and higher salaries are doing exactly what they say private contractors will do. Thus it is ironic to hear the President of the American Federation of Government Employees Council of Prison Locals (which represents Federal Bureau of Prison workers) declare that: "*For the first time*, it is in someone's self-interest to foster and encourage incarceration. It does not take an accountant to figure out that they will act in their self-interest." [27]

Of the one million members of the AFSCME, 50,000 are corrections employees.[28] Organized union labor accounts for some of the strongest lobbies and most lavishly funded political action committees in the country. As Morgan Reynolds notes: "Unions can supply formidable organization, campaign money, workers, and direct influence over some members' votes. Public employees participate in elections at substantially higher rates than the general citizenry does, thereby forming a more potent voting bloc than their share of the work force might suggest." [29]

Correctional workers' unions have used collective bargaining to restrict the ability of administrators to contract for community-based programs.[30] These agreements preserve the jobs of institutional employees and, as a side effect, keep the populations of the institutions higher than administrators may desire. Those who complain that private prison businesses, in pursuit of profits, will discourage the development and use of alternatives to prison, have been silent when organized labor, in pursuit of its own interests, has done the same. Among the policies that correctional unions have opposed, are: deinstitutionalization, contracting out for services, the use of volunteers, establishment or enhancement of due process rights for inmates, increased community and family involvement in institutional programs, prisoner furloughs, work or educational release programs, and a shift of emphasis from custody to treatment.[31] A study of correctional unions in 17 states found that

> Employee organization lobbying, publicity, lawsuits, and job actions
> . . . have often been attempts to counteract progressive correctional
> programs such as community-based facilities and to reestablish an
> emphasis on custody. Another feature of this campaign is that cor-
> rectional unions have advocated longer prison terms and more strin-
> gent parole policies—for example, an increase in the minimum term
> an inmate must serve before he can become eligible for parole.[32]

One final example of a public-sector lobby is particularly relevant to the charge that privatization is inherently expansionistic. As noted in chapter 5, most referenda on bond issues for prison construction yield a mixed message from the general public. People want more prisons but are unwilling to pay higher taxes to finance new long-term debt. Such referenda are often defeated by a well-funded advertising campaign mounted by organized and powerful opponents of new prison construction. Supporters were better organized than usual, however, in a 1981 referendum for a bond issue to build new prisons and expand the system in New York.

There, the biggest spender, shelling out $158,000 to lobby *for* the bond issue, was the New York Department of Correctional Services.[33] The referendum was defeated, but it "had no impact on the construction plans and timetable of the Department of Correctional Services," whose Commissioner exhorted his employees to work instead on the regular appropriations process, and "support the continued expansion of our state prisons with the appropriations in [the next] budget." [34]

Against this background, to argue that privatization will introduce an element of self-interest not otherwise found in the criminal justice system is absurd. This is not to deny that private firms will have concerns that may sometimes conflict with the public interest (or with other conflicting interests competing to be defined as "the public interest"). The point is that these conflicts of interest are not unique to the private or profit-making sector and therefore do not provide legitimate grounds for excluding that sector from participation in the formulation of criminal justice policy.

Private prison companies may very well become important actors in the field of criminal justice policy, just as public actors are today. Indeed, merely opening up the field has taken some political muscle. As Harmon Wray reports, one lobbyist for Corrections Corporation of America managed the campaigns of Tennessee Governor Lamar Alexander and served as his Chief of Staff. Alexander has been strongly supportive of prison privatization. "Others in the CCA-Alexander circle include CCA stockholders who are current and former Alexander cabinet officers, CCA administrators who are former state GOP chairpersons, a CCA lobbyist who was a Democratic state senator, and two prominent public figures [the governor's wife and the state's Speaker of the House] who in 1985 sold their CCA stock to avoid the appearance of conflict of interest."[35]

Competition within the industry can serve to dilute, rather than concentrate, this political power. For example, one of CCA's competitors, Corrections Associates, Inc. (now called Pricor), hired Tennessee's Finance Commissioner Hubert McCullough away from his state office, to become its new chairman and CEO.[36]

With or without the participation of profit-making enterprises, it is important to maintain democratic political controls to prevent any one set of narrowly defined interests from squeezing out all others and from asserting an imprimatur over designation of "the public interest." We cannot prevent "lobbying" (though it may not always be called that) by nonprofit organizations, government agencies, public employee unions, or commercial companies, any of whose agenda may or may not coincide with the public interest. However, allowing these groups to compete, both in the provision of a service and in the public formulation of policy for the provision of that service, is a better method of protecting the public interest than is granting a monopoly to one particular service provider. "Pluralism" is what we call the condition in which the "public interest" must be sorted out from among competing definitions and claims. We regulate the competition to preserve the integrity of the processes by which we determine (1) what services are most in the public interest and (2) who best can supply them. But it is competition, even more than regulation, that prevents concentration of power in either area.

Expansion vs. Flexibility and Diversification

The charge that private corrections companies, to remain profit-able, will require an ever-expanding prison population, is based on a simplistic caricature of capitalism that reflects a misconception of the nature of business under conditions of competition. To be sure, most profit-makers do attempt to drum up business. On the whole, however, businesses succeed not by stimulating spurious demand, but by accurately anticipating both the nature and the level of real demand. This is true whether demand is rising or falling, and particularly if it is shifting. The ability to predict and respond is far more important to a business than any supposed power to artificially stimulate demand.

The supposed need for full occupancy is often referred to by commentators on private prisons as the "Hilton Inn mentality." [37] The phrase is an unfortunate one when used by critics, and not just because of the high quality associated with the Hilton.[38] Many hotels make profits without continuous full occupancy. It is not crucial that demand exactly meet supply. It is far more important that suppliers be able to predict demand and have the flexibility to shift resources and to adjust prices accordingly.

Still, it is clear that private facilities will have an interest in at least stable, if not maximum, occupancy levels. Rather than assuming that contractors will respond insidiously, by violating the rights of inmates or by stampeding the legislature and judiciary into greater use of prisons, critics should recognize that efficient use of contracted facilities is also in the public's interest.

One response based on that recognition would be to write contracts that allow a vendor to temporarily fill a contracting agency's excess space by accepting inmates from another agency or jurisdiction. A higher price could be charged for these "extra" inmates, with the excess shared between the vendor and the primary contracting agency. This arrangement is part of the contract between CCA and Bay County, Florida. Likewise, in Santa Fe, New Mexico, CCA runs the county jail under contract to Santa Fe county but has supplemental contracts to hold prisoners for the city of Santa Fe, the Federal Bureau of Prisons, the U.S. Marshall's Service, and some other counties and cities in New Mexico.[39] In Houston, CCA has a supplemental contract with the Texas Board of Pardons and Paroles to hold preparole inmates in the facility that it runs as a detention center under a primary contract to the INS.[40]

These supplemental contracts benefit all parties by increasing efficiency. Jail space is a scarce resource, but the problem is more one of distribution than of aggregate supply. While some jails are desperately overcrowded, many others, especially small to medium-sized local facilities, have plenty of empty cells. Every year, some jails close for lack of need. The flexibility of private contracts can do much to allocate resources to where they are needed.

Another lesson to be learned from the Hilton Inn mentality is one that is far more applicable to a private enterprise than to a government agency. That lesson is: diversification. Because commercial enterprises survive and prosper by accurately anticipating and responding to shifts in demand, we should not assume that correctional corporations will always be motivated to lobby for expansion of high-security facilities. Such corporations can be expected to diversify both within and outside of corrections. If they anticipate or sense a shift in public demand toward community treatment, electronic monitoring, or other alternatives to incarceration—or, indeed, a decline in total demand for correctional services of any type, through falling crime rates or decriminalization—they will prosper more by shifting resources to other activities than by attempting to buck the trend. Right now, there is a genuine unmet demand for imprisonment. However, if the demand for *alternatives* to prison increases, commercial companies should be able to respond rapidly to such a shift. One INS detention contractor, for example, also provides (and aggressively markets) electronic monitoring services as an alternative to jail.

To sum up briefly, political and economic pressures to expand the use of imprisonment are neither inherent in nor unique to the involvement of private enterprise in corrections. Vested interests in promoting either imprisonment or alternatives to imprisonment can be found in both public- and private-sector organizations. The public interest, whether it lies in greater or lesser use of imprisonment, is therefore no more naturally allied with the special interests of government agencies, government managers, and government employees, than it is with those of outside contractors.

8

Issues of Flexibility

A major promise of proprietary prisons is that they will bring with them the flexibility and innovation typical of entrepreneurial activity and commonly found among small businesses. They will have less of the bureaucracy that tends to preserve the status quo in government and other large organizations. As enterprises subject to competition and market discipline, they will be more free to engage in purchasing and subcontracting without the bureaucratic regulations that are needed to control government spending. They will be able to respond more rapidly to the changing conditions and needs of corrections, and act more quickly to correct mistakes resulting from inaccurate predictions or faulty policies. They will add new expertise and specialized skills, and promote creativity and enthusiasm by bringing in "new blood" and new ideas more often than is possible under civil service.

Joan Mullen, an expert on privatization of corrections at Abt Associates, sees enhanced flexibility as an even greater potential benefit than cost containment:

> The notion that private organizations can provide more for less is undeniably attractive, but probably unrealistic. The greatest promise of the private sector may instead lie in its capacity to satisfy objectives that might be difficult if not impossible to achieve in the public sector—introducing public sector managers to the principles of competitive business; quickly mobilizing facilities and manpower to meet immediate needs; rapidly adapting services to changing market circumstances; experimenting with new practices; or satis-

fying special needs with an economy of scale not possible in a single public sector jurisdiction.[1]

In short, one of the major strengths claimed for private prisons is that their greater management flexibility and more rapid speed of response will promote both minor innovations and major program changes, whether through initiation, expansion, contraction, or termination.

Rigidity vs. Clarity

Critics of contracting argue that it is impossible to write a contract that is as broad and flexible as the mission of a public agency needs to be. Contractors may be unwilling to go beyond the provisions of their contracts. Renegotiating and changing contracts is time-consuming and terminating a contract is often very difficult. Thus, contracts produce their own form of rigidity, and it will be harder for the government, under contracting, to order and control marginal changes. As two sociologists put it: "How can innovation be expected from a contractor who will not offer one iota more than the contract calls for and who does not have even the limited flexibility of the state and national correctional programs?" [2] A political scientist argues:

> Writing and enforcing highly detailed contracts may help to guarantee accountability, but it does so only at the expense of administrative flexibility. . . . As a public corrections official with years of experience in these matters stated, "Either the contractors will be allowed to run wild as they did in the old days, or we'll make the specifications, regulations, and monitoring so rigid that the firms will become as bureaucratized and inefficient as we are. . . ." [3]

This all-or-nothing reasoning, however, is clearly a false dilemma. Private prisons can have latitude in some respects without being given free rein in all respects.

A government prison that is run by unionized public employees may suffer from its own kind of systematized rigidity as a result of a management-labor contract, rather than a government-management contract. For example, one study of correctional unionism reported that: "Correctional administrators interviewed during our research charge that the provisions requiring that assignments and promotions be based on seniority have done more to disrupt the operation of correctional institutions than any other kind of provision." [4]

It is fair to predict that private prison companies will use their contracts to limit what is demanded of them. Within reason, that is one of the intended functions of a contract. But what critics see as rigidity, proponents see as specificity and clarity.

Government agencies can issue grandiose mission statements without fear of penalty if they fail to live up to all their promises. A contract, on the other hand, is meant to cut both ways: to specify as well as to limit what is required. The purpose of a contract is to facilitate, not to restrict, the accomplishment of certain goals. Contracts force the government to confront the question of what are its goals, standards, and criteria of performance. All parties—contractor, government, and taxpayers—benefit from that process. Contracts protect the government by specifying in advance the nature and quality of the service it is to receive. At the same time, contracts also protect the contractor from unanticipated and unreasonable demands.

Contracts will not necessarily protect a vendor from reasonable demands, even if they were previously unspecified. A more flexible contractor will have a competitive edge, when it comes time for contract renewal, over one who uses the contract to behave in a rigid and truly unreasonable fashion. The government's control over contract renewal and rebidding will tend to prevent abusively rigid interpretations of contract provisions by the vendor. To exercise this control, however, the government will have to be prepared to deal with the problem of terminations and transitions.

Contract Terminations and Transitions

In exchange for the flexibility of contracting, government must be prepared to minimize the risk of interruptions in service when contracts change. When a contractor takes over a government operation or when the government resumes control or shifts it to another contractor through competitive rebidding, many details must be anticipated. Capital investments must be protected. Property and equipment must be transferred. Continuity of records must be maintained. The interests of current employees must be considered. In short, terminations and transfers of contracts, even on a nonemergency basis, entail components not found under normal governmental continuity.

The American Federation of State, County, and Municipal Employees maintains a file of instances where it has been necessary to terminate contracts for public services because they proved to be too costly or unsatisfactory.[5] These examples illustrate the problems of transition referred to above, but they also show something else. They indicate that it *is* feasible to terminate a public/private contract. In contrast, how feasible would it be to replace or halt the activities of a government agency staffed by tenured and unionized civil servants whose services were found to be unsatisfactory? It may not always be easy to terminate a contract, but experience has shown that it is nearly impossible to terminate a government agency, even one supposedly made mortal by a sunset law.[6] Thus, a contract situation can be seen as preferable if an agency is poorly managed or staffed. Where contracting, and therefore competition, is possible, bad management (either public or private) is less likely to become entrenched, because a surgical solution is at hand.

The Immigration and Naturalization Service has successfully terminated and replaced several of its contracts for detention facilities. Robert Schmidt, formerly Supervisor of Detention Services for the INS, supervised ten private contracts for six different facilities before he retired. Of those ten contracts, he describes three as "total successes," four as "OK," and three as "total failures." He reports that the INS had little difficulty in terminating the contracts that were failures and replacing them with new contractors.[7] It should be noted, however, that the INS is a national agency with multiple facilities, which helps to ease such transitions.

Contractors with multiple contracts can deal with rough transitions by temporarily reassigning personnel. Corrections Corporation of America uses experienced facility administrators from its central offices to serve as interim administrators when setting up a new contract or changing the administration of an ongoing contract. The Eckerd Foundation used counselors from its other programs to deal with a rough transition period at Okeechobee, during which there were strong fears of violence. According to an American Correctional Association study, the Superintendent and these outside personnel "were able to maintain the safety of the institution through heroic effort and countless hours of overtime." [8]

CCA's contract for New Mexico's women's prison provides for a procedure to ensure the government a smooth transition in case of contract termination. During transfer of operations back to the NMCD or to another contractor, CCA would work under supervision of the New Mexico Corrections Department for a period of 60 days. All records would transfer to the NMCD.

As a final note, since one purpose of contracting is to allow for competition in the provision of correctional services, it would be a mistake to regard potential terminations and management transitions as necessarily negative. Certainly, they can be disruptive, but they may be either good or bad, depending on what went before and what comes after.

Innovation and Risk-Taking

A study of contracting for community correctional services found that flexibility was a major attraction to public agencies.[9] Contracts allow agencies to experiment with new programs without long-term commitment of funds or of tenured civil service staff. Vested interest in these programs does not accumulate inside the agencies. This avoids the tendency toward bureaucratic self-perpetuation that ordinarily makes public programs difficult even to alter, let alone to eliminate.

Of course, flexibility for the public agency translates into insecurity for the private contractor. To survive and succeed, a contractor must solve this problem in a variety of ways: by providing service that is too good to give up; by accurately anticipating and being ready to meet the shifting needs of different clients; by holding down the administrative costs of hustling from one contract to another; by cultivating multiple clients; or by other techniques that must be the stock-in-trade of any competitive contractor.

Flexibility and willingness to take risks are often seen as virtues when associated with small businesses. They can, however, be seen as mixed blessings when it comes to the incarceration business. On the one hand, the structure of incentives seems to favor originality and innovation in the private sector. While failure in corrections can be dramatic and costly for either the government or a private contractor, there are fewer countervailing rewards for success in the public sector. Private actors can be motivated economically to take innovative risks, but public actors' concern with political survival induces caution and reinforces the status quo. Under civil service, the careers of line staff and middle managers are more or less predetermined, while the positions of top officials depend largely on avoiding embarrassing mistakes. Steering clear of bad publicity becomes more important than outshining the competition, especially if there is no competition.

On the other hand, in the coercive environment of prisons, flexibility and innovation are not necessarily desirable. Cumbersome governmental procedures for review and approval of changes in policies and programs are not merely obstructionist. They are necessary to preserve due process constraints on the power of the state. It is important not to lose these constraints when state power is extended through contractual agents.

This is a valid point, though it gets carried too far when it is argued that private firms are *incapable* of responsibility in innovation. According to sociologists Jess Maghan and Edward Sagarin, "Innovation and flexibility, when proposed by the CCA or some other such organization, can be motivated only by profit enhancement, hardly a purpose inspiring to those who are grappling with corrections." [10] We should not feel that we have to choose in an all-or-nothing fashion between due process protections and the ability to innovate. Particular innovations may be either good or bad, but a structure that is conducive to innovation is, on the whole, positive.

Contracting passes some of the risks of innovation from the government to the private sector. This is usually presented as a point in favor of contracting. John Donahue, however, sees it as a drawback. While conceding that "uncertainty about the future is the whole rationale of a market for risk," Donahue questions the wisdom of shifting risk from the government to private parties. His primary argument against doing so is that "governments in general are better at spreading risks than private companies are, simply because they encompass more people." [11] What he means is that governments are better at absorbing costs when risks turn out to be bad risks.

Why should the ability of government to absorb costs be seen as an advantage? If our goal is to avoid costs, the best strategy is to transfer risk to the party most motivated to minimize it, not to the party best prepared to absorb it. In most cases, it is the party least able to bear a risk that is best prepared to act quickly in response to innovations that develop snags or go sour.

Flexibility and the Uncertainty of Social Policy

Flexibility is especially important in the administration of public policy, where the concentration of decision-making magnifies the consequences of ignorance, uncertainty, and error. Policies regarding imprisonment, for example, contain implicit or explicit projections about trends, distributions, and patterns of crime and punishment. Even where broad trends are discernible, however, it is beyond the powers of social science to make highly accurate and reliable forecasts. Because of the scale on which it operates and the ponderous way in which it moves, government is much more dependent than is private enterprise on the long-term accuracy of projections. Of course, the private sector must also be able to predict, if it wishes to make a profit, but it can make better use of short-term (and therefore more accurate) predictions because it can generally respond more quickly to changes in information.

A market in corrections would share in the general advantages of markets over central planning. The advantage most relevant here is that while central planning magnifies the consequences of erroneous predictions, competition isolates and minimizes them. If a state launches a major prison construction plan and hires an army of civil servants, based on a long-term projected trend that does not materialize, or that unexpectedly reverses itself after a few years, the cost will be much greater than if several competing contractors are responding continuously to projected needs. Some contractors will predict better than others, or be able to respond more quickly to altered predictions. These companies will survive and prosper by being able to meet the changing needs of the state more effectively. The less successful companies will have to absorb and thereby contain the costs of their inaccurate forecasts. In contrast, when the state has a monopoly on the prison business, it can simply pass on to taxpayers the full cost of its errors, and thus has less incentive to avoid mistakes in the first place.

Contracting can help respond to changes in prison populations brought about by changes in legislation. In recent years, these changes have generally meant increases, but contracting can help with *decreasing* correctional needs also. In 1984, the Bureau of Prisons signed a three-year contract to house about 60 Youth Corrections Act offenders in a private facility in La Honda, California. Repeal of the Youth Corrections Act that year had made it clear to the Bureau that its YCA population would disappear through attrition over the next few years. The Bureau's director later reported to Congress that: "Contracting to house these offenders gave us the flexibility to handle our population without acquiring additional permanent spaces. This allowed us to respond to the YCA population reduction in the most cost-effective way." [12]

Flexibility Enhances Justice

The flexibility of private prison contracts may also enhance justice, at least according to a "just deserts" model. Public concerns over justice and punishment (usually expressed as "getting tough") have led to changes in many components of the justice system. Abolishing parole, limiting judicial discretion, banning or restricting plea bargaining, and other such reforms are intended to curb abuses and to make punishment more uniform and just. Generally, though not necessarily, this is seen as replacing inconsistent lenience with more consistent firmness and punitivity. One objection to these "get tough" policies has been the fear that they will produce further overcrowding of prisons. Therefore, some criminologists have urged the development of so-called front-door and back-door mechanisms that would seem to defeat the purpose of the antidiscretion reforms. Back-door options include emergency release mechanisms and ongoing early reentry programs. Front-door mechanisms include diversion programs and sentencing guidelines that specifically require judges to take capacity into account. [13]

The search for new mechanisms of diversion and release to prevent or reduce overcrowding rests on a faulty assumption: that prison flow can and should be fine-tuned by the state, while prison capacity remains virtually fixed. A penal system based on the justice model, however, makes just the opposite assumption: prison flow should respond to the crime rate, which is largely beyond the control of the state; therefore, prison capacity must be flexible. Reduction (or increases) in imprisonment under a justice model should occur because such changes are perceived as improving justice, not because of limited (or expanded) prison space.

At least at the margins, then, the prison system must be able to expand and contract in accordance with the shifting demands of justice. Flexibility at the margins will tend to maximize the supply and minimize the cost of imprisonment. Commercial prisons, with efficient management, multiple vendors, and renewable, adjustable contracts, offer an increased prospect of achieving this marginal flexibility.

9

Issues of Security

One of the strongest reservations about private contractors relates to their ability to run high security prisons. The former director of the Federal Bureau of Prisons, for example, has expressed doubts that private firms could ever run maximum security institutions.[1] The Council of State Governments and the Urban Institute recommend that only minimum security facilities be contracted at this time.[2] Their rationale for this appears to be based largely on the expectation that local communities will object to privately run maximum security institutions being located in their neighborhoods.[3]

While private firms have not yet run a maximum security prison, they are running jails that include all levels of security. In February 1987, the Bay County (Florida) jail, which is run by Corrections Corporation of America, had over half a dozen capital murderers along with other offenders in the jail's maximum security wing. Also, some private juvenile institutions are designed for serious, including violent, offenders.

Why should private management be seen as more problematic in a maximum security institution? Probably because, in most people's minds, the higher the level of security, the greater the need for coercion, including the use of potentially deadly force.

Deadly Force

The right to use deadly force is widely regarded as an exclusive prerogative of government, but this is a misconception. Legitimacy in the use of force is determined by conformity to provisions of law, not by the public or private employment status of the person who exercises force. Under certain circumstances, the use of force by private actors is both legal and legitimate.

For example, the power of arrest has been delegated to private railway police, to humane society agents, and to bail bondsmen. The arrest powers of bondsmen were established under common law, while a majority of states empower private railway police by statute. Such police may carry concealed weapons and have all the arrest powers of public police. Though nominally appointed by a public official and sworn into office, they are in fact employed and supervised by the railroads.[4]

Under common law, a private citizen has the right to use deadly force in self-defense, in defense of another, or to prevent the escape of a felon. In 1985, however, the Supreme Court held, in *Tennessee v. Garner*, that deadly force may be used by police against a fleeing felon only where it is "necessary to prevent the escape and the officer has probable cause to believe that the suspect poses a significant threat of death or serious injury to the officer or others."[5] It is not clear what the implications of this decision are for prison guards, but it appears that the powers of police, and probably of corrections officers, are approaching those of ordinary citizens, rather than diverging from them. The *Garner* decision is a recognition of the precept that, whatever the specific rules and regulations, the general principles justifying the use of force by state agents should not be significantly different from those justifying the use of force by civilians. In this connection, an observation from the report of the Council of State Governments and the Urban Institute is significant: "In States that subscribe to the provisions of the Model Penal Code, the proper use of deadly force by private correctional officers would not require further legislation. The definitions in the Model Penal Code appear to sufficiently include private prison guards."[6]

There is no moral distinction between governmental and private actors as individuals that would justify a governmental monopoly on the use of force. Civil servants are not by nature or necessity the most responsible, accountable, or controllable wielders of power. There is, however, a practical rationale for limiting particular uses of force to small and highly visible subsets of the population. The rationale is that, by doing so, it is easier to keep the use of force within the limits specified by law. That is why powers of arrest are generally linked to certification of some sort, such as licensing or deputization. The certification does not confer legitimacy in itself, through incantation or some sort of voodoo jurisprudence. Rather, it aids the enforcement of laws intended to restrict the legitimate uses of force. In keeping with this goal, it is consistent for the state to recognize, allow, or authorize force by nonstate actors under certain circumstances and within the same legal guidelines that determine whether the use of force by a state actor is legitimate.

Also consistent with the practical rationale for limiting and controlling the use of force would be for the state to certify, license, deputize, or swear in all correctional officers, both public and private. This would bind them formally to specific codes that authorize and restrict their permissible uses of force and provide mechanisms for disciplining them if they overstep their authority. The training and other requirements for such certification should be the same for public and private correctional officers.

In the state of Florida, all correctional officers, including those employed by private contractors, must be certified by the state. In New Mexico, legislation authorizing private prisons designates a contractor's employees as peace officers while in the performance of their duties.[7] The California Department of Corrections places one or more of its own officers at each of its privately contracted prisons for parole violators. These state officers have final authority over any security issues that may arise, such as escapes or disturbances, and during any emergency operation may take over command from private security officers.[8] Officers do not carry guns inside most prisons and jails, either public or private, and the use of deadly force against inmates is rare.[9] Some private prisons have guns available outside, with employees who are authorized to carry them.

What happens in the case of a riot, or other emergency? Critics often ask this question, then move on to other issues as if it were unanswerable, or required no answer. The answer, however, is about the same for a private as for a government-run prison. In the event of disturbances at most prisons and jails, force is deployed from outside. Major disturbances often require reinforcement from state police or national guard units. This practice would not be different in a privately run prison.

Routine Security

Experience at most contracted facilities, in terms of routine security, has been positive. At the Bay County Jail, CCA has assigned officers to each floor so that they can observe violations and response time will be quicker. Under the county, there were often no officers on the floor, which was a major factor in a lawsuit filed against the sheriff and the county by an inmate who said the lack of supervision resulted in his being sexually abused by other inmates.

When Buckingham Security took over operation of the Butler County Prison, the first thing they had to do was take back control from the inmates. Even allowing for the partiality of the source, a First Year Report by Buckingham is worth a lengthy quote on this score:

> Prior to Buckingham's arrival, the staff remained out of the areas where inmates lived. They stayed out of the passageways when inmates were moving through them. During the infrequent outdoor periods, a staff member watched from an overlooking window. The myth existed that various areas in the prison belonged to the prisoners whenever they were in them. It was thought to be dangerous to intrude....
>
> Beginning immediately, Buckingham took control of the prison. All staff, including the warden, mingled with the inmates daily.... The entire prison now belongs to the county and the county employees govern all of it at all times. All inmates are now assigned specific bunks in specific cells and the staff knows that each is accounted for.[10]

Among the security reforms instituted by Buckingham were: routine physical security checks (bars, locks, doors, windows, walls and perimeter); a key control system; a professional head-count system; an organized system for inmate files; a tracking system to determine proper release dates; a sally-port system for security doors; and an inmate classification system. The custom of allowing police to wear their guns inside the prison was ended.

At Silverdale, the private prison run by CCA for Hamilton County, Tennessee, security was significantly enhanced following a minor disturbance in August of 1986. In his detailed and objective case study of this prison, Samuel Jan Brakel describes how security measures that were already under way were accelerated after this incident. Guns and other riot gear were placed in a secure area below the control tower (guns are not worn inside the prison); a new fence topped with razor wire was built around the men's unit; a more restrictive checkpoint was set up at the gate; new key control and inmate pass systems were implemented; staff assignments were reviewed to assure 24-hour coverage of all crucial stations; visitation, transportation, and shakedown procedures were tightened; surveillance of cells and dorms was increased; and emergency evacuation drills and procedures were instituted.[11]

Escapes

There have been escapes from private prisons, but their record in this regard is no worse than their public counterparts, and often better. Certainly no private facility has been as lax in its security as the District of Columbia's Oak Hill Youth Center, a "high security" detention facility for juveniles in Laurel, Maryland, where a recent check of the official log showed that 30 percent of the 197 detainees were missing and listed as escapees,[12] or the new Prince George's County (Maryland) Jail—much celebrated for its "new generation" design—which 11 times during its first year released wrong prisoners under mistaken identities.[13]

During the first 7 months of operation at the Marion Adjustment Center, there were 4 walk-aways, 3 of whom were recaptured within 24 hours. In a comparison state facility, walk-aways averaged 1.5 per week.[14] Differential selectivity of admission at these two facilities, however, makes this comparison questionable. A before-and-after comparison is more instructive. At the Okeechobee School for Boys, the escape rate was 25.6, 27.6, and 25.6 per 100 inmates in the years before, during, and after transfer from government to private hands. The failure of the escape rate to rise is significant in light of the extremely high employee turnover that occurred during the transition year[15] (see chapter 6).

Over the first few years of private management at Silverdale, the number of escapes went down slightly. This was in spite of the fact that the population was increasing and moving sharply toward a higher mix of felony cases. During most of 1984 (until October 15), the prison was under county management. There were 42 escapes during 1984, all but 9 of which occurred while the prisoners were on outside work crews under the control of the sheriff. In 1985, there were 39 escapes—9 from within the compound. In 1986, of 35 total escapes, 7 were from within. During this three-year period, the population rose to 358 from a base of 250–300, and the number who were state felons rose from 10 percent to 34 percent. Thus, where more escapes might have been expected, given the changing nature of the population, there were about the same or slightly fewer under private management.[16]

Strikes

The National Labor Relations Act (NLRA) makes it unlawful for an employer to interfere with the right of workers to strike. Public employees are specifically excluded from NLRA coverage and in most jurisdictions there are laws making it illegal for at least some categories of civil servants to strike. In a review of legal issues relating to private prisons, Mary Woolley concludes that private prison employees do possess the legal right to strike.[17] Woolley asserts that these workers are covered by the NLRA unless Congress clarifies or amends the Act or the National Labor Relations Board reverts to an interpretation that was abandoned in 1979. (A 1975 ruling held that a private fire department was exempt from the NLRA and had no legally protected right to strike, because it provided an essential municipal service; this interpretation was rejected in a 1979 case involving private busing of public school students.)[18]

Public Employee Strikes

Those who fear strikes by correctional workers would be better advised to oppose public employee unionization than to oppose prison privatization. Although strikes are generally more common in the private sector, they are rapidly increasing among public employees. From 1960 to 1984 there was a tenfold increase in the number of public sector work stoppages and a thirty fold increase in number of days idle.[19] A state-by-state study of public employee unionization showed that, in each state, the number of strikes increased dramatically in the years immediately after enactment of collective bargaining legislation. In some states, the effect was astounding. Michigan had only one strike in the seven years prior to its legislation, compared to 290 strikes in the six years thereafter. New York jumped from an average of 4.1 strikes a year before, to 27.75 strikes a year after.[20]

Strikes and other job actions are illegal for correctional officers (guards) in all states except Hawaii, and generally they are illegal for most other correctional employees as well.[21] The absence of a right to strike, however, has not prevented public prison guards from engaging in many strikes, sickouts, and other job actions.

Under the leadership of the American Federation of State, County, and Municipal Employees, strikes by correctional workers have been not merely local, but sometimes regional and even national affairs. In 1974, under coordination by the AFSCME, prison guards in Rhode Island and at six penal institutions in Ohio walked off their jobs.[22] In 1979, almost all the guards at New York's 33 correctional facilities went out on a strike that lasted 17 days. During that time, the strikers were responsible for several incidents of violence and property damage directed at National Guardsmen called in by the Governor.[23] A study of correctional employee unionism in 17 states found that correctional officers had engaged, illegally, in strikes or similar job actions in about half of the research states.[24]

Contrary to popular impression, prison strikes do not generally create situations that are difficult to control. Lockdowns are frequent, but inmates tend to stay on good behavior during strikes even when supervisors attempt to run things on a near normal basis without a full lockdown.[25] Thus, the risk of strikes in private prisons is neither as new nor as serious as most people suppose. Still, it is a risk to be avoided or minimized as much as possible. Whether the risk will be higher or lower in a private prison remains an open question.

Strike Risks under Contracting

Privatization provides an opportunity to deal with the problem of strikes in a fashion more realistic than simply outlawing them. Mary Woolley recommends that work stoppages be addressed in both enabling legislation and contract. For example, in the event of a strike, state police could be required to perform as guards, as they do already during emergencies at correctional institutions. The cost of contingency staffing could be covered by insurance or performance bonds.[26] Another possibility, not mentioned by Woolley, would be to couple legislation requiring that all correctional officers—public and private—be certified, with legislation providing for automatic decertification of officers who participate in a strike.

The Council of State Governments and the Urban Institute recommend that private prison contracts should "require sufficient advance notice of the end of an employment contract period, the onset of labor difficulties or major grievances that could result in a work stoppage or slowdown." [27] The contract between CCA and Hamilton County specifies that "A default shall immediately occur if any threat to the security of property or persons . . . is caused by strike (whether by employees or inmates) . . . "[28] The contract—like other prison contracts—also specifies procedures for the county to resume immediate control of the prison in the event of default or serious disruption, such as a strike, a riot, or bankruptcy.

State police and the National Guard would be the ultimate recourse in a strike by private correctional officers, as is the case now when public employees walk off the job. However, the cost of such intervention could be negotiated and specified in the contract, so that it might or might not distribute differently from how it currently does. Also, a performance bond can be used to defray the government's cost if it has to take control of a contracted facility.

a lov of opportunities
↑ for guards

Since a strike or other disruption would allow the government to terminate a contract, unemployment as the result of a strike will be a credible threat to private officers. In contrast, such threats do not often deter strikes in the public sector. Although numerous strikes took place in Ohio prisons from 1970 to 1975, it was not until May 1975 that any striking officers were fired. Likewise, when Walpole State Prison officers were fired for striking in 1973, the Governor of Massachussetts was pressured into rehiring them, by an AFSCME threat to declare a strike by all state employees.[29] Amnesty for strikers is a universal demand in public employee strikes and generally (assuming that there has been no violence or other illegal acts incidental to the strike) they get it.

In government-run prisons, strikes typically last only a few days; a three-week strike is considered extreme.[30] There are several reasons to believe that labor unrest would be resolved even more quickly in a proprietary prison. Private management has a greater and more personal stake in rapidly ending a strike and resolving the underlying issues. They also have more direct control over many matters at issue, and where they do not, that fact is clearer than in a public situation, where a strike is often not merely against management but against the executive and legislative agencies as well. Private correctional officers, unlike their public counterparts, do not have a claim on the support of noncorrectional public employees, especially given the opposition of public employee unions to privatization. Even inmates in a private prison might be in a better position to prevent or resolve a strike. Inmates suffer most from any strike, but ordinarily they have no power to influence the outcome.[31] As third-party beneficiaries to a contract, however, they will have a new legal standing from which to petition for a court injunction against a strike or threaten to sue the company.

Finally, the experience of the federal government is reassuring on the question of strikes against contractors. In a review of almost 30 years of contracting experience under Circular No. A–76, "Performance of Commercial Activities," the Office of Management and Budget lists the fear of strikes as one of the common misconceptions about contracting:

> Available evidence has not borne out the fear that contracted services would be more susceptible to employee strikes than if they

were retained in-house. There have been two cases of strikes by contract employees and in both cases contingency plans proved effective. The Circular requires that contractors be held accountable in the case of strikes and that contingency plans be included in contracts.[32]

In sum, there is nothing special about the government's ability to provide security in prisons. Force can be exercised legitimately, legally, responsibly, and effectively by private actors subject to the same rules of law as public employees. Experience with security in private facilities, including jails with maximum security wings, has been fairly positive so far. And the threat to security posed by a labor strike is at least as great if not greater under governmental as compared to private management.

10

Issues of Liability

Critics of privatization warn that governments will not escape liability by contracting the administration of their prisons, as some advocates supposedly claim. In contrast, some opponents of private prisons seem to imply that government *can* escape liability (through sovereign immunity) if only it stays away from contracting. Lawyer and privatization critic J. Michael Keating summarizes the liability picture as follows:

> What seems reasonably clear is the likelihood that private jail and prison operators will be subject to all of those statutes fashioned to render state agencies liable for their misconduct, such as the Civil Rights Act, while remaining ineligible for the benefits derived from those statutes and common law doctrines formulated to preclude or limit the liability of public bodies, such as state tort liability statutes and the doctrine of sovereign immunity.[1]

From context, it is clear that Keating regards this legal vulnerability of private prisons as an argument against them, but it is not at all clear why this should be so.

Since critics of private prisons are particularly concerned about prisoners' rights and the accountability of those who exercise power, they should regard the increased liability of private prisons as an argument in favor of contracting. Prisoners in private facilities gain by the addition of an extra layer of liability, accountability, and responsibility for their rights and welfare. They are certainly not worse off in this regard than they would be under total government management. It is therefore ironic for prisoners' rights

181

groups to raise liability concerns in opposition to contracting. One would think that these litigious groups would be reassured, not alarmed, by the legal vulnerability of private prisons.

So far, there has been at least one case in which an inexperienced private detention vendor was sued, made a monetary settlement, and went out of the detention business.[2] The government was also sued in this case, but only for declaratory relief, not monetary damages. When the government is sued for damages, it passes the cost on to taxpayers; no government agency yet has been litigated into bankruptcy. This may be a plus in terms of stability, but it is a minus in terms of accountability.

Civil Rights and Wrongs

On at least one liability issue, there seems to be universal agreement: with or without privatization, government remains ultimately responsible for the constitutional rights of citizens, including prisoners. Government may not shirk its constitutional duties, nor can it avoid liability. Careful legal scholars holding opposite views on the general wisdom and propriety of private prisons are nonetheless in agreement that both government and contractors definitely can be held responsible under the Civil Rights Act (42 U.S.C. Section 1983) for violations of constitutional rights by private prison contractors.[3] Private prisons will qualify as Section 1983 defendants because they will be acting "under color of law" and thus "state action" will be present. Therefore, both private prisons and their contracting units of government can be sued under the provisions of this Section.[4]

The most pertinent case so far has been *Medina v. O'Neill*,[5] the facts of which were as follows:

In 1981, a vessel arrived in the Port of Houston carrying 26 stowaways, and the Immigration and Naturalization Service was alerted. Ordinarily, the INS orders that stowaways be detained on board the same vessel for immediate return transportation. In this case, however, the ship lacked facilities for detention, so 20 aliens were placed in a local jail, while 6 were placed with a private security firm, in a 12 foot by 20 foot cell designed to hold no more than a half-dozen people. The next day, 10 of the aliens in the local jail were transferred to the custody of the private firm and placed in the cell that was already filled to capacity. A day later, the aliens attempted to escape and a private guard accidentally killed one of them with a shotgun.

The federal district court ruled that the plaintiffs were entitled to sue the INS for violation of constitutional and statutory rights. The ruling had three significant parts. First, the actions of the private party were held to constitute "state action." Second, the conditions of confinement were held to violate constitutional standards of due process. Third, the INS was held to be responsible for ensuring that the detention met constitutional standards.

In 1988, the Fifth Circuit Court of Appeals vacated and reversed two of the three parts of the district court ruling. The Appeals Court held that "(1) INS officials had no statutory duty to provide appropriate detention facilities for excludable aliens, and (2) [the] aliens' due process rights were not violated." [6] Significantly, however, the Appeals Court did not negate the district court's ruling that the contractor's conduct constituted "state action." That ruling was allowed to stand despite the fact that excludable aliens have practically no rights under the U.S. Constitution, and even though the connection between the INS and the private firm in the *Medina* case was very weak. All costs for the detention and transportation of stowaways must be borne by the carrier on which they arrive.[7] Though it may designate someone other than the carrier to provide detention, the INS itself does not have to financially contract for that service in the case of excludable aliens. Compared to this, any correctional facility privately managed under a direct, formal contract to the government is operating even more clearly "under the color of law." In sum, there seems to be little doubt that violations of constitutional rights by private prison staff constitutes "state action" under Section 1983,[8] thus allowing plaintiffs to sue either the government or the private provider.

Professor Ira Robbins both prefaced and concluded a lengthy discussion of the liability issue with statements that one argument in favor of prison privatization has been the claim that it will reduce or eliminate government liability.[9] It is this claim, he says, that makes the issue of liability so significant in the debate over private prisons. Robbins' documentation on this point, however, is a statement by an *opponent* of contracting, not a supporter.[10] In point

of fact, it is virtually impossible to find any supporters of privatization who claim that contracting can actually immunize government against legal responsibility (as opposed to lowering risks by
providing better services and insuring or indemnifying government
against those risks that remain). Charles Thomas calls the argument about liability a "straw man" and reports that "no representative of any private corporation has even one time in any
document I have ever found—and I've reviewed hundreds of
them—ever made that allegation." [11] My own review of the literature is consistent with that report. [12]

The existence of government liability is a nonissue, because all
parties agree that it is there. What remains to be seen is whether
that liability results in higher or lower legal costs to the government
under private as compared to public operation of prisons. In any
case, the liability argument can be turned in either direction. Which
is stronger as an argument *for* contracting: the claim that the government can thereby escape from liability, or the claim that it
cannot do so? To argue that private prisons will not reduce the
liability of either government or contractors seems to me to be a
very strong argument *for* privatization, because it emphasizes that
accountability and protection of prisoners' rights will not be compromised. Indeed, the legal recourse of prisoners may well be
increased.

In testimony to the President's Commission on Privatization,
Professor Robbins has noted that prison contracts will create two
categories of third-party beneficiaries to the contract: prisoners
and the public. This expands prisoners' rights by giving them the
potential benefit of a contract cause of action, which they would
not have had before. In addition, this new cause of action will
generally have a longer statute of limitations than a suit under
Section 1983 or an ordinary tort action. [13]

To nail down this unique form of liability, [14] Robbins has recommended that clauses be inserted in both statutes and contracts
explicitly declaring that prisoners and the public are intended to
be third-party beneficiaries to written agreements between the government and private contractors. [15] That would give standing to
enforce the contract not only to the government agency but to
prisoners and to any member of the general public. The ACLU,
or any other group that now sues prisons on behalf of inmates,

would no longer need inmate plaintiffs; as part of the public, it could sue private prisons on behalf of itself.

To broaden the scope of claims that could be brought by third parties, Robbins places in his Model Contract a clause in which the private provider agrees "to provide inmates with proper care, treatment, *rehabilitation, and reformation.*" [16] As goals of imprisonment, rehabilitation and reformation are not only controversial, but almost certainly impossible to achieve fully. When offenders released from private prisons are convicted of new crimes, will members of the public (and the newly convicted offenders themselves!) be able to sue the contractor for damages because of this "breach of contract"?

Sovereign Immunity

Another liability question is whether private jailers should be allowed to protect themselves against monetary damages by asserting the defense of sovereign immunity.

In principle, there is a basic distinction between "policy-making, planning, or discretionary decision-making activities, which remain fully protected by the sovereign immunity defense, and operational or ministerial activities, which are not immune." [17] In practice, however, the distinction between making and implementing policy is often fuzzy. To minimize or avoid legal challenges on delegation grounds, this distinction should be clarified as carefully as possible.

In some states, legislation authorizing prison privatization includes a statutory prohibition against the defense of sovereign immunity. In Florida, legislation permitting correctional privatization at the state and local levels specifies that private companies are liable for damages in tort with respect to the care and custody of prisoners under their supervision; the Tennessee Private Prison Contracting Act denies the defense of sovereign immunity to private contractors or their insurers. [18]

Most states have waived sovereign immunity either generally or substantially. [19] In those states, liability for the tortuous acts of correctional employees will exist whether those acts are committed by government or by contract employees. On the other hand, many states waive immunity only if the government purchases liability insurance, and then only up to the amount of coverage.[20] Thus, even where sovereign immunity is waived, the waiver is generally limited, and liability is capped. Given the large insurance coverage required of private prisons, and the historically modest size of damages awarded in correctional lawsuits (both discussed below), a legislated cap on the liability of private prisons may not be necessary at this time.[21]

Serious questions can be raised about the advisability of imposing a legal double standard, in which state actors are protected by sovereign immunity while private actors performing the same function are not. The major argument for sovereign immunity is that public officials need that protection in order to perform their jobs effectively. The major argument for denying sovereign immunity to contractors is that they need to be held responsible.

The implicit theories behind such a double standard are that: (1) government actors can be trusted while private actors cannot; (2) government actors respond best to carrots while private actors respond best to sticks; and (3) immunity allows people to act according to their true characters, which for public actors means altruistically but for private actors means selfishly. But it simply won't do to assume that public and private actors have different human natures or respond to incentives in radically different ways. Indeed, many people change from a public-sector job to a private-sector job without any simultaneous change in character.

The doctrine of sovereign immunity was originally based on the notion that because the King ruled by Divine Right, he could do no wrong. This notion has now been replaced by one that is only slightly less questionable: that "public servants" are also touched by grace, because they are disinterested and benevolent and act only for the public good; hence, they should be granted immunity so that they can act boldly on their presumed commitment to maximize social welfare.

Qualified (or "good faith") immunity for government actors also rests on the proposition that it would be unfair to prosecute persons who are legally required to exercise discretionary power in their jobs. However, government officials and bureaucrats apply for those jobs and assume the concomitant obligations voluntarily.

Some are attracted to such positions precisely because they want to exercise discretionary power. Others accept the power as part of a job that they want largely for personal gain (satisfaction, salary, job security). Few are driven by self-sacrifice. Except perhaps for military draftees, government employees are not legally required to hold their jobs in the first place, or to remain in them. Therefore, a civil servant who by virtue of his job is required to exercise discretionary power is in no different position from a contractor, who by virtue of his contract may be required to exercise discretionary power.

It may be that some jobs—like police officer and prison warden—are so fraught with discretionary power and potential litigation that the public interest requires a grant of immunity as one of the incentives needed to fill these posts. Where this is true, I see no reason why it would be less true for contractual police or wardens than for those who are direct government employees. Qualified immunity is a device to make a risky job more attractive (i.e., more profitable) to a government employee. The alternative would be to pay civil servants enough to enable them to buy liability insurance. Exactly the same logic applies to contractors: they too need an incentive, in the form of either qualified immunity or fees high enough to pay for extra insurance.

Actual Risk vs. Legal Exposure

As discussed above, prisoners in private facilities have at least as many avenues of civil redress as do their fellows in government-run prisons. Total liability, in other words, is not decreased. Spreading the liability neither immunizes the government nor relieves it of its ultimate responsibility for the rights and welfare of prisoners.

However, it is still possible that government, by contracting, could reduce the *actual risks* (and therefore costs) for which it remains liable, as opposed to reducing its *legal exposure*. That is, the financial damages likely to be suffered by government as a result of its legal liabilities can be cut back. Lowering liability risks not only avoids financial damages, it reduces litigation and insurance costs as well.

Liability risks can be reduced by:

1. Running prisons better, and thus avoiding lawsuits.
2. Achieving certification, which greatly enhances the defense against lawsuits.
3. Carrying adequate and cost-effective insurance.
4. Agreements in which the contractor defends the government in court and indemnifies it against legal damages.
5. Developing extensive legal expertise and resources, both for preventing and for fighting lawsuits.
6. Settling quickly out of court, which is easier for private firms than for public entities.

Private prison contractors today are reducing risks by all of these methods.

Corrections Corporation of America believes that litigation, and thus liability exposure, can be reduced by taking a proactive, rather than a reactive approach. For example, they invite the ACLU to inspect their facilities. As they put it, "That's good free advice; and they're the ones most likely to sue us." [22] When they won the Texas contracts, CCA took a positive step toward assuring that they would be able to comply with the massive and comprehensive court orders governing corrections in that state. They retained as counsel a former Texas Department of Corrections attorney intimately familiar with the *Ruiz* decision.

At several of their facilities, including Laredo, Bay County, and Silverdale, CCA is required to supply legal assistance to inmates beyond the mere provision of a law library. To represent inmates in lawsuits against them, CCA retains private counsel under contracts that enable the lawyers to act like public defenders, immune to any control by CCA. One benefit to CCA is that they hear about a potential problem before a suit is filed and therefore can resolve it more easily. To represent CCA when it is sued, the company hires other outside counsel; the job of their own legal staff is mainly to keep them from being sued in the first place.[23]

Prior to its contract with CCA, Bay County, Florida, was under court order to reduce overcrowding in its jail and faced a lawsuit for the death of a prisoner. The uninsured county commissioners were named personally as defendants.[24] Nine months after CCA's takeover, three prior lawsuits against the county over jail conditions "were dropped in the wake of substantial improvements in conditions." [25]

Changes in procedures instituted by Buckingham Security when it took over operation of the county jail and prison at Butler County, Pennsylvania, were designed to take back control of the facility from the inmates. Those changes should also make less likely any serious injuries or harmful incidents and reduce legal liability that might result from a lack of proper procedures in the event of a significant incident. One measure of the effect of these changes (which were detailed in Chapter 9) is that prior to Buckingham's takeover, emergency trips to the hospital had been averaging four or five a week, but after the takeover they were rare.[26]

The liability experience of private prisons has not been all positive, however. Corrections Corporation of America recently resolved a $100 million lawsuit filed against the company and 11 other defendants in Hamilton County, Tennessee. The suit, which alleged that a female inmate died as a result of inadequate medical treatment, was settled out of court for $100,000.[27] As will be noted below, this amount is not unusual for a medical malpractice case.

The Modest Size of Correctional Damages

It is too soon to tell whether private prisons will be sued less often, less successfully, or for lower amounts than government prisons. In the final analysis, the effect of privatization on liability costs will depend more on operational differences than on legal differences. It is worth noting, however, that while the volume and total cost of litigation by inmates is enormous,[28] and the costs of outside insurance and self-insurance are high, a recent national survey by Contact Center, Inc., indicates that monetary damages and settlements in corrections tend to be rather modest.[29]

In the Contact Center study, the Federal Bureau of Prisons and 33 states returned surveys reporting their costs for inmate lawsuits in 1983 and 1984. In compensatory damages, punitive damages, settlements, and court-awarded attorney fees, these 34 jurisdictions paid a total of $5,920,922 over the two-year period.[30] Using adult inmate population figures for these systems on June 30, 1984, combined payouts come to a per capita, per diem value of just four cents.[31]

Though a big award could have a serious effect on a small county, it is evident that for large systems, liability costs resulting from privatization would have to be several times what they are now before they would substantially affect costs on a per unit basis. And for successful suits to multiply, the total volume of litigation would have to explode, since only a minuscule proportion of inmate lawsuits result in damages or settlements.[32]

Insurance and Indemnification

Although liability risks in corrections are generally low, the cost of insuring against them can be high. In 1986, CCA spent about $940,000 on premiums for $5 million in general liability insurance, which did not cover officers of the corporation. No claims were filed against CCA or its officers during that year. By 1987, CCA had established a self-insurance plan covering both the corporation and its officers. For this plan, $5 million from their initial public stock offering was placed in an interest-bearing trust fund. An outside firm was paid about $150,000 a year to service or administer claims. CCA projected savings of about $800,000 on insurance premiums for 1987.[33]

At one time, CCA was required by its contract with Hamilton County, Tennessee, to carry $25 million of insurance, and by its contract with Bay County, Florida, to carry $15 million. At first, the company did obtain $25 million coverage, but later they found it impossible to find an insurer that would underwrite a policy that large. The company felt that its assets ($30 million in lines of credit and $12 million in net worth) were adequate to cover risks beyond a $5 million insurance plan.[34]

Other corrections companies also carry large amounts of insurance. Behavioral Systems Southwest carries $5 million.[35] Pricor, which manages four correctional facilities, carries $2 million in general liability insurance.[36] Wackenhut Corrections Corporation typically provides $5 million in coverage and can provide more on large contracts. In addition, WCC has behind it the enormous financial strength of its parent, the Wackenhut Corporation, with assets of $300 million and revenues of over $400 million in 1988.[37]

In addition to carrying high levels of insurance, private prison companies typically offer contracts in which they indemnify the government against the total cost of any harm resulting from the operation of their facilities. In Bay County, as elsewhere, CCA promises to defend the county in court against any legal actions arising out of the operation of the jail. The contract contains the following indemnification provision:

> CCA shall save and hold harmless and indemnify the COUNTY, the members of the Board of County Commissioners, county employees, and agents, including attorneys, and their respective legal representatives, heirs and beneficiaries, whether acting in their official or individual capacity, and shall pay all judgments rendered against any or all of them for any and all loss or damage of whatever kind against any and all liability, claims, and cost, of whatsoever kind and nature for physical or personal injury and any other kind of injury, including specifically deprivation of civil rights, and for loss or damage to any property occurring in connection with or in any way incident to or arising out of the occupancy, use, service, operation or performance by CCA, its agents, employees or representatives of any of the provisions or agreements contained in this Contract, including any Appendices, for which the COUNTY, the members of Board of County Commissioners, county employees and agents, attorneys, or other persons, as noted hereinabove, whether acting in their official or individual capacity, who may become legally liable resulting in whole or in part from the acts, errors, or omissions of CCA, or any officer, agent, representative, or employee thereof, and for which CCA shall pay all judgments which may be rendered against the COUNTY, members of Board of County Commissioners, county employees and agents, including attorneys, and other persons as noted hereinabove, whether in their individual or official capacity.[38]

As formidable as this sounds, CCA is financially able to shoulder the risk, and may even be overinsured against it. In its own survey of monetary damages in correctional negligence cases, the largest award CCA could find was a medical malpractice judgment for $750,000, which went to the family of an inmate who died in a prison hospital.[39] This study dovetails with the Contact Center finding that nearly all the large (six-figure) awards went to victims of medical malpractice.[40] Health care is the most frequently contracted component of corrections, representing about 23 percent of all correctional service contracts.[41] Apart from this troublesome area, which correctional officials are often glad to contract out, liability risks in corrections are no greater than those that occur in many other enterprises, both public and private.

Ira Robbins has proposed that every private prison contractor should be required to carry insurance in the amount of $25 million per occurrence.[42] Such a requirement would slap a big "Sue Me" sign on the back of every privately employed warden, an open invitation to lawyers in search of deep pockets. Many states place dollar limits on their own liability. In Virginia, for example, this limit is $25,000.[43] The law does allow higher awards where they are covered by insurance, but it is hard to see what incentive a state agency would have to voluntarily carry insurance greater than $25,000. Thus, in Virginia, under Robbins' proposal that private prisons must carry $25 million in liability insurance, the incentive to sue a private prison would be 1,000 times as strong as the incentive to sue an uninsured state prison.

One has to wonder if Robbins, a foe of private prisons, really just wants to see them sued out of existence. On the other hand, Robbins is a sincere champion of prisoners' rights, and the private companies would be insured, so perhaps he just wants to see that prisoners' interests are well protected. But if that is the case, why not insist at the same time that states also be required to set their own liability limits at $25 million per occurrence? Actually, overinsurance is not a good idea for either type of prison. In addition to inviting opportunistic lawsuits, overinsurance may create a "moral hazard" by weakening the insured's incentive to guard against risk.

Overinsuring only the private prisons will create other problems also. Since contractors will pass their insurance costs on to the state in the form of higher fees, a massive insurance requirement could price them out of the market. In theory, governments could be required to calculate what it would cost them to carry that much insurance themselves, when comparing their own costs against contractors' bids. In practice, however, that is unlikely to happen if the government is not actually required to have that much insurance itself. This would become another hidden cost that presents an inaccurate picture of the differences between public and private corrections.

Briefly, privatization does not offer government any easy escape from its responsibility and liability for imprisonment of offenders. What it does offer is the prospect of sharing that liability, buffering the government through indemnification, and possibly reducing the number of lawsuits through improved management.

11

Issues of Accountability and Monitoring

Critics claim that contracting reduces accountability because private actors are insulated from the public and not subject to the same political controls as are government actors. Also, the critics charge, contracting diffuses responsibility; government and private actors can each blame the other when something goes wrong. Further, contracting may encourage the government to neglect or avoid its ultimate responsibility for prisons; supervision may slacken.

This chapter will focus on the issues of accountability and monitoring as they apply to both public and private prisons. The first step is to recognize that accountability can take many different forms.

Administrative Accountability

Accountability does not come easily under any sort of system. Blame avoidance is endemic to both public and private bureaucracies. While a major purpose of any contract is to identify areas of responsibility, critics of contracting are right to point out that this does not guarantee accountability. Contracting could even confuse and diffuse responsibility and accountability. The state may attempt to avoid responsibility by pointing its finger at the contractor; the contractor in turn, may hide behind the contract by insisting that its responsibilities are limited to those that are explicitly spelled out on paper.

On the other hand, the process of contracting encourages the government to define the purposes of imprisonment, the responsibilities of prison managers, and measures of performance by which those managers will be judged. These definitions and measures can then be applied to governmental as well as to private prisons.

To limit a vendor's ability to hide behind a contract, contracts can contain provisions incorporating detailed and comprehensive specifications or standards that are spelled out in state statutes, corrections department policies, consent decrees, American Correctional Association standards, and other authoritative sources. Even without such provisos, those contractors who are willing to live up to the spirit of a contract will have an edge over competitors who use their contracts as shields to protect themselves against all unanticipated demands, including those that are reasonable.

Legal Accountability

Governments are held accountable not only through the political process but, more importantly, through the rule of law. This is especially the case in the area of corrections. It is primarily the legal system that protects due process and other rights of prisoners. Legal accountability on the part of proprietary prisons can be no less than that of government prisons and will probably be greater, since the private sector enjoys no rights of sovereign immunity.

The importance of the rule of law was discussed at length in Chapter 4. The issue of liability was examined in Chapter 10. Here, it may be instructive to compare the accountability of contractors to that of judges who have been appointed for life. Judges and wardens, of course, perform very different functions, but both exercise considerable power over other citizens. Compared to judges, the problem of imposing legal and political accountability on wardens, either public or private, is much more simple.

Life-tenured judges are appointed by an elected representative of the people. Contractors are selected through a politically and legally regulated process either by elected representatives or by officials who in turn are accountable to elected representatives. Once appointed, tenured judges are accountable in three ways, each with a parallel for contractors.

First, even life-tenured judges are subject to the rule of law. They are not free simply to rule as they see fit, without legal constraint. Contractors are even more subject to legal restrictions since, unlike judges, who often have certain absolute immunities, contractors do not enjoy even limited immunities. They are fully vulnerable to prosecution in criminal courts, and to lawsuits in civil courts.

Second, the decisions of all but nine judges—those on the U.S. Supreme Court—are subject to appellate review. Likewise, correctional contracts can be written so that all contractor decisions affecting the rights or liberty of prisoners are subject to review by governmental and judicial agents. Even if there is no such contractual provision, it is becoming increasingly clear that correctional contractors act "under color of law" such that their conduct constitutes "state action" under 42 U.S. Code Section 1983. This means that prisoners, or others acting on their behalf, can sue not only the contractors but the contracting government agency, and officials thereof, for any actions that violate constitutional rights (see "Civil Rights and Wrongs" in Chapter 10).

Third, even tenured judges are ultimately accountable through articles of impeachment. In a similar vein, the ultimate mechanism of accountability for contractors is termination or nonrenewal of the contract. The difference is that judicial impeachment is a rare event, while breaking or failing to renew a contract is commonplace. Unlike impeachment, termination and nonrenewal are not reserved for only the most extreme cases of misbehavior or nonperformance.

In short, there are effective legal remedies for malpractice or abuse of power by private prison contractors. Private wardens are merely a special, and not a difficult, case within the broader problem of how to apply the rule of law to the men and women who operate the legal system.

Economic Accountability

Economic competition is a powerful mechanism of accountability and discipline. Vendors who are subject to competition are not only accountable to the government, through their contracts; they are accountable also to other parties who have interests that sometimes conflict with, but mostly parallel or derive from, those of the government. Chief among these other parties are competitors, insurers, and the capital market, i.e., investors.

Competitors hold each other accountable on standards of cost and quality set by the purchaser of their services. Less effective or more costly contractors will lose business to rival firms. Competition, comparison, information, accountability: each follows naturally from the one before. In competing for contracts, vendors provide comparative information about themselves and each other (including information about government-run prisons). Such knowledge is essential to accountability.

Insurers provide independent evaluations of quality in the form of risk assessments. Their premiums impose discipline by punishing or rewarding high or low risk. A company with a high-risk profile may be unable to obtain any insurance at all.

The independence and discrimination of investors and knowledgeable investment advisors adds a powerful form of "supervision" in the private sector to supplement the direct supervision and regulation required by the state. Contractors who are successful because they run well-managed and profitable businesses will be able to attract investors. Newly invested capital, in turn, can be used by such a business to improve its services even further.

But wouldn't potential investors just concentrate on a company's bottom line (profits) and neglect or even discourage attention to quality of service? This is not likely. Investors have a stake in the reputation and the future of their company, not just in immediate or short-term profits. Stock prices anticipate the future. A private prison corporation that is headed for scandal, lawsuits, prosecution, or uninsurability as a result of mismanagement, will see its stock begin to fall even before it actually begins to lose contracts. Moreover, if employees are also stockholders, this distributes the supervision motive to where it will do the most good. In severe cases of mismanagement, investors can force reform from within or from without, through takeovers if necessary.

Citizens who invest in a private prison company are risking their money; they have an incentive to consider whether the company's prisons are needed and will be well built, well managed, and in good favor with government and taxpayers for a long time to come. In contrast, those who buy general government bonds don't have to be so careful. They know that the government guarantees them a fixed return, regardless of the success or failure of the project they are capitalizing.

Critics sometimes claim that private prison companies, by their very nature, and particularly because they are accountable to stockholders, will have to put private goals and interests first and the concerns of the public second. If this is the case with private prisons, it will make them unique among commercial enterprises. It is true that a profit-making company must sooner or later make profits if it wishes to stay in business. It is also true that businesses are answerable to the interests of their owners and investors. Neither of these facts, however, places private interests above all others. Would we say of other commercial enterprises that they must place their stockholders ahead of their customers? Or that a company is accountable to its Board of Directors before it is accountable to the law?

Economic controls do not displace political controls, but they can operate more quickly and allow finer adjustments. As Joseph Kalt points out, the "political 'marketplace' . . . meets relatively rarely; when it does voters are presented with a bundle of numerous and durable choices that cannot be marginally altered. Moreover, political competition is plagued by high transaction costs; the costs of organizing and promoting changes in the bundle of policies offered by the government are substantial." [1] In contrast, renegotiating and changing a contract is quicker and more discriminating than reelecting a new administration. If wholesale change is called for, however, that too can occur through contract termination, without the long interval required between elections.

For proprietary prisons, market mechanisms of supervision, discipline, and accountability add to those of the political and legal systems. Economic accountability supplements, more than it conflicts with, political and legal accountability.

Political Accountability

Since prisons carry out public policies, they of course must somehow be held accountable to the public. Where policies are codified into law, mechanisms of legal accountability will serve. Where policy is administratively created or interpreted, however, it is desirable that there be mechanisms for public input, public scrutiny, and public control. These mechanisms may be characterized broadly as "political" and can take many forms.

Direct popular election is the most obvious form, and it is clear that an elected jailer is politically accountable, at least in principle.[2] In practice, however, direct election is not necessary for effective political accountability. If it were, only those jails that happen to be administered by an elected sheriff would be politically accountable. Other jails, and all prisons, are run by administrators who are appointed or hired, not elected.

The political accountability of a contractor is like that of an appointed, rather than an elected, official. Appointees and contractors are only indirectly accountable to the electorate, but this does not make them less responsible. One study compared the fiscal accountability of cities having a mayor/council structure to that of cities with a council/manager structure. It found that in mayor/council cities the actual cost of refuse collection was 41 percent higher than what was shown in their official budgets, compared to 22 percent higher for the council/manager cities.[3] Since the first step toward accountability is the provision of accurate information, it is significant that informational accountability was greater under the system with a hired professional manager—which resembles a contractual arrangement.

Of the many millions of public functionaries and workers responsible for the execution of public policy, only a tiny proportion are directly accountable to the electorate. All the rest can be said to be accountable only in the sense that somewhere up a line of command, or up a network of crisscrossing chains of supervision, there lies an elected official. But the workers and supervisors involved in running a prison under contract, by virtue of the fact that they are all simultaneously liable to the threat of termination, can make a good case that they are more accountable politically than are most government employees. Only the highest government officials and administrators are politically accountable by virtue of election or appointment.[4] Working down the ranks from middle management to lower management to line staff, public employees become progressively less politically accountable. Most government employees enjoy civil service protections that make them virtually immune to being fired. They may be reassigned, but they are not likely to find themselves involuntarily unemployed. In one year, for instance, "only 300 of the 2.8 million federal employees reportedly were dismissed or terminated for incompetence."[5] Public employees at state and local levels of government are also very difficult to discipline. In an extreme example of political and legal nonaccountability, when government correctional employees go on strike—illegal to begin with—they often continue their job actions even in defiance of court orders.[6]

At the federal level, the judicial branch of government is insulated from direct electoral accountability and the legislative branch seems to be getting more so. Members of the House of Representatives are rarely ousted from their posts. In the 1986 elections, 98.4 percent of House incumbents seeking reelection were returned to office.[7] The executive branch, to be sure, is more susceptible to electoral influence, at least at the top. However, to the extent that most federal employees who work in executive agencies are entrenched in civil service jobs and insulated from the political process, the accountability of the executive branch at the highest level may not translate into accountability at the operational level.

If accountability does, indeed, become progressively weaker as one moves down a chain of command to the level of those who actually deliver public services, contracting can help shorten that chain and strengthen the linkage by making everyone involved more directly vulnerable, and therefore more accountable, to officials and administrators at the highest levels. In the case of prisons, contracting can also be used to hold government, as well as vendors, accountable. Where poor management has become entrenched and resistant to reform, contracting provides a surgical solution. In Bay County, Florida, part of the motivation for contracting the jail was a belief on the part of some county officials that the sheriff was too powerful and too difficult to control.[8] One official said he believed that sheriffs, most of whom are reelected continuously, should not be elected officers at all, but professional employees hired by the county commission. The commission itself is elected, is responsible for the budget, and is given statutory authority to incarcerate offenders in a jail or prison. The official argued that sheriffs derive much of their political power, in effect, from the points of their guns. Citizens are intimidated by sheriffs in a way that they are not by county commissioners. Sheriffs control large budgets and extensive job patronage in addition to the power inherent in their discretionary arrest authority. "People are absolutely scared to death to disagree with the sheriff, no matter who he is," said this county official, who cited acts of intimidation against himself and other functionaries.

Bay County knows too well that simply leaving the jail in the hands of an elected sheriff is no easy solution to the problem of accountability. A jury awarded $10,000 damages against the sheriff in a lawsuit brought by an inmate complaining of inadequate medical care when the jail was under the sheriff's administration.[9] The sheriff was also charged with sexual harassment in another lawsuit brought by several female employees. In addition, the sheriff's department was the subject of internal and external investigations regarding money that was missing from the department's evidence locker: $12,600 in 1983 and $2,270 in 1987. The money was never accounted for.[10]

Community Accountability

The only time that a prison or jail is directly accountable to an identifiable segment of the public is at birth. Before a new lockup can be constructed, it must be located in a community willing to accept it. Public fears about safety and effects on property values must be overcome, but despite often strong and widespread resistance, it is not impossible to convince at least some communities to accept prisons in their backyards. This is because prisons bring jobs to the unemployed and unskilled in a depressed area. They buy food, fuel, and other items, often locally.

Because they must rely on persuasion and offers of benefits rather than governmental power to overcome community resistance and fears, private prison companies may be forced to be more accountable to the public than is the state. Private firms do not have the power of eminent domain. When Arbor, Inc., wanted to open a work release facility in Chicago, it created a community board of advisors and hired locals to help renovate an abandoned building. In contrast, when the state proposed a similar facility in the same area without consulting the community, local protests aborted the plan.[11]

Site planning also played a role in the final decision by the Kentucky Corrections Cabinet to award a contract to the U.S. Corrections Corporation for the Marion Adjustment Center. The state's first choice of contractor was unable to find a community willing to accept its proposed facility, while USCC won approval for its location from Marion County's Fiscal Court.[12] Some Marion County residents, however, remained opposed and instituted lawsuits, which were not successful in removing the prison. A study for the Commonwealth of Virginia describes the results of USCC's public relations efforts:

> The "NO PRISON" signs which grace the residents' front yards are gradually disappearing and only a small group of 3–4 hard-core foes remain. U.S.C.C., actively working on better public relations in the community, held an open house the last week of July and invited all the townspeople (over 90% attended). Tours of the facility were given and questions answered. The residents complimented the owners and director on their quality staff and were amazed when told that the tour guides were not staff but rather (college-educated) inmates. Two mothers made a specific point of thanking U.S.C.C. for the employment opportunities presented to their newly employed sons. This is noteworthy since unemployment is a persistent problem in the small farm community.[13]

Visibility of Prisons

Prisons are more open to public inspection than most people think. Nonetheless, except during periods of crisis, they tend to have low visibility to the broader public. Private facilities are currently subject to a great deal of publicity. Most of this is due to their novelty, but even after the novelty wears off they are likely to remain controversial and to draw at least some attention indefinitely. In addition, having a mix of governmental and contractual operations invites comparisons which make each type more visible than it would be alone.

Even people with strong objections to private prisons credit them with drawing attention to problems and issues that are common to all prisons and worthy of public examination. A vocal critic of private prisons, Michael Keating, Special Master of Rhode Island's state facilities, nonetheless notes that the use of private providers "opens up the process to outsiders," and exposes facility operations to public view.[14] The contract for the Okeechobee School for Boys specifies that failure of the Eckerd Foundation to allow public access to records shall be grounds for termination of the contract.[15]

Experience in other parts of the criminal justice system supports the idea that contracting increases visibility and critical evaluation. For example, privately prepared presentence investigation reports (PSIs) are subject to much closer scrutiny by more parties than are PSIs prepared by government investigators. The most important part of a PSI is the section where a disposition is recommended. As Herbert Hoelter, director of the National Center on Institutions and Alternatives, points out:

> In many state and federal jurisdictions, the *recommendation* section of the PSI, the section which demands the most accountability, is not disclosed. The opposite is the case with the private report, where the recommendations and relevant rationale for them are subject to full disclosure. Any responsible private report must demand a higher standard as a result of its disclosure and exposure.[16]

Prison Constituencies

Most citizens have little incentive to monitor the management of prisons. As individual voters they can have little effect on prison policies, and still less on prison personnel. Most citizens will never serve time. Apart from dramatic events, like riots or escapes, they have no interest in routine information about local jails. Hence, there is no general public constituency for prisons.[17]

Prisoners, of course, are interested in prisons, and in recent years they have gained considerable legal power to promote their interests. However, they have almost no political power. Prison reform groups, like the American Civil Liberties Union, through its National Prison Project, have some political influence, but most of their efforts are legal, rather than political.

The most politically effective constituency for corrections is correctional officials themselves, who influence their executive and legislative overseers not through the ballot box, but through control over information. It is well known that bureaucracies attempt to control the flow of information so as to advance or protect their own interests. Various measures, such as the Freedom of Information Act, limit the ability of public bureaucracies to control information completely. However, when the agency that generates the bulk of routine information about itself also stores that information and controls its dissemination, accountability is compromised. Under contracting, there is at least some independence of interest between the agencies that generate information and those that then receive and control it. In addition, with on-site monitoring, there will also be an independent primary source of information.

Monitoring

All parties, including vendors, agree that monitoring is important for private prisons. Private prisons need to be monitored partly because they are contracted and partly because they are prisons. As contractual operations, they need to be monitored for compliance with contractual provisions. As prisons, they need to be monitored for performance. Clearly, compliance and performance are over-lapping concerns, but it is worth noting them separately to emphasize their mutual importance. Moreover, as will be argued below, monitoring for performance—as distinct from monitoring for contract compliance—should not be viewed as a need that is special to contracted prisons only.

In a report for the National Institute of Justice, the Council of State Governments and the Urban Institute reviewed prison management contracts from the early 1980s and the Requests for Proposals (RFPs) issued by government agencies that shaped those contracts. They found that both the RFPs and the subsequent contracts were, overall, quite general.[18] As a guide for future contracts, the report recommended a monitoring process with the following components:

1. Statistical summaries of reported unusual incidents, such as escapes, deaths, major injuries or illnesses, assaults, disturbances, staff use of force, and major disciplinary actions (i.e., loss of good time, lockdowns, or solitary confinement).
2. Surveys of inmates regarding programs and conditions.
3. On-site inspections using standardized evaluation forms that focus on actual conditions and behavior, not just written procedures. These should be conducted by outsiders at least annually and by on-site or local monitors on a continuous basis.
4. Timely feedback to contractors, so they can adjust their practices, and to government officials, so they can make informed decisions on contract renewal.

The report also recommended that, for comparison, the same monitoring procedures be applied to publicly operated facilities.

Though government may be more inclined to monitor contractors than to monitor itself, it should not be assumed that any monitoring will occur automatically. The government needs to provide a specific mechanism for monitoring. Since contracting does relieve bureaucrats of many daily headaches, they may be tempted to treat it as a quick fix and neglect their duty to oversee.

Something like this apparently happened for a while in Florida, with the Okeechobee School for Boys. The Department of Health and Rehabilitative Services, which was responsible for monitoring the contract at Okeechobee, requested but did not receive authorization for a full-time monitor, so the task was assigned to a staff member with other responsibilities in West Palm Beach. However, after the lack of monitoring was criticized in the first draft of an evaluation study by an American Correctional Association research team, the Department of Health and Rehabilitative Services initiated a regular, formal auditing process.[20] In its final draft, the ACA study noted that,

in addition to the HRS response, the private administration at
Okeechobee responded to the initial ACA report by moving "in
a very positive direction." [21] The ACA's own monitoring found
the contractor to be in compliance on 91 percent of the items in
its contract.[22] The lesson here seems to be that both government and contractors benefit from outside scrutiny as well as
from a system of monitoring.

Monitoring has, in fact, been a regular feature of most recent
prison and jail contracts. At the Marion Adjustment Center (a
preparole facility), an on-site state employee (a parole officer)
monitors the contract, approves inmate furloughs, and gives final approval or disapproval to all good-time determinations
made by private employees.[23] The situation is much the same at
the Bay County Jail and Annex, except that the monitor is a
county employee who also has an office and duties downtown.
At Silverdale, the county prison and women's jail at Hamilton
County, Tennessee, monitoring is provided by the county's Superintendent of Corrections, who was the warden at Silverdale
before the Corrections Corporation of America assumed management. The superintendent handles all release and good time
decisions and makes all work assignments for prisoners doing
county work outside the walls. He also serves as liaison between the prison and the county commission, the courts, the parole board, the probation board, and the state department of
correction.[24] Hidden Valley Ranch was monitored daily by a
federal official when it was under contract to the Bureau of
Prisons. At the Butler County Jail, run by Buckingham Security
Limited, the contract is monitored by a county employee and
disciplinary protocol is outlined in the contract.[25]

Reports[26] that the Immigration and Naturalization Service had
to hire 12 employees to provide 24-hour monitoring at their contracted Houston detention facility are not accurate. Essentially,
the contractor rents space to an INS staff of about a dozen at that
site. Most of those people spend most of their time on work for
the INS that is independent of the contract. Only one is designated
officially as the contract monitor and even he spends only about
30 to 40 percent of his time on monitoring duties. An evening
monitor spends 20 to 30 percent of his time on activities related
to monitoring.[27]

Informal Monitoring

In addition to formally designated monitors, prison contracts can be monitored in many other ways. External observers and watch-dogs, like the media and the ACLU, are at least as interested in private as in governmental prisons, if not more so. Internal "monitoring" will be provided by prison inmates, who are veteran whistle-blowers and will take legal actions against private wardens as energetically as they do against the government. Significant input from prisoners could be very useful in contract renewal de-cisions. While it would not be wise to give inmates any formal power over the choice of their keepers, some kind of mechanism for inmate evaluation of their treatment would help to reinforce accountability.[28] Critics who fear neglect or abuse of inmates as a result of a cost-cutting ethic in private prison management might be reassured by this provision for evaluation by "insiders." [29]

Insurance companies provide a form of monitoring for private prisons that is often lacking for the government. Insurers have a vested interest in gathering valid and objective data about areas of performance that relate to legal liability costs. The premiums they set for different vendors or types of vendor will give an in-dependent assessment of risk and, thereby, of quality. This is anal-ogous to the use of household fire insurance premiums to evaluate fire departments, or the use of hospital liability premiums to eval-uate hospitals.[30]

Sauce for the Gander

It should be emphasized that monitoring is as much a benefit as it is a burden to the corrections system. Monitoring adds another level of supervision to an activity that needs as much of that as it can get. More importantly, it brings a new element of *independence* to the system of checks and balances controlling an awesome ex-ercise of domestic power: the deprivation of human freedom. As noted in Chapter 4, independent review is vital to due process. Here, the point is that independent monitoring promotes objec-tivity and rigor in the overall supervision of a prison. It is easier to be consistent when imposing standards on outsiders than when enforcing them on ourselves or our colleagues.[31]

T. Don Hutto, a former commissioner of corrections in two states, and now the President of CCA International, a division of Corrections Corporation of America, observes that: "As a director of corrections, I did a better job of monitoring and evaluating private sector contracts than I did of monitoring and evaluating my own operations. I also did a better job of monitoring and evaluating the jails, which I did not have responsibility for operating. Through the contracting process, government can be more objective about the goals it wants to reach." [32]

In any case, whether it is seen as a burden or a benefit, both sides of the private prison debate agree that monitoring is very important. Indeed, monitoring and other mechanisms of insuring accountability are so important in the prison context that they should not be seen as special to contractual operations. It is necessary and desirable to monitor the operation of correctional facilities no matter who is running them.

Government-run facilities are routinely inspected, audited, regulated, supervised and monitored not just by correctional agencies but by other agencies, and sometimes other branches and other levels, of government. Beyond these routine forms of monitoring, there are others. One third of jails surveyed in 1986 were under a court order. [33] At least 60 jails are supervised by a court-appointed jail master. [34] In 1984, 31 states and the District of Columbia had at least one major prison operating under a court order or a consent decree. For six of the states and the District of Columbia, the entire prison system was under a court order or a consent decree. [35] In 1986, 14 states had court-appointed overseers, such as masters or compliance monitors, for their prisons. [36] Court orders and consent decrees are analogous to contracts, and jail or prison masters are like contract monitors. [37]

Judicial monitoring of government-run prisons can be extremely expensive. Monitoring and enforcing a court order may require a special master with a staff of attorneys and investigators and an annual budget running up to three-quarters of a million dollars. [38] Moreover, such masters commonly serve long and indefinite terms on any single case. [39] Even when a consent decree is supervised directly by a judge, without a special master, that also entails a cost.

As a digression, it would be interesting to apply to special masters, who administer or oversee court-ordered prison reforms, some of the concerns raised by critics of private prisons about issues of delegation and accountability. Who monitors the monitors?

When judges issue broad and detailed orders specifying exactly how prisons and prison systems must be run, they can be accused of eroding the principle of separation of powers. The broader the judges' concerns, the more they encroach on the policy preroga- tives of the legislature. The more detailed the judicial orders, the more they encroach on the administrative realm of the executive branch.

When judges appoint special masters to supervise the enactment of their orders, they thereby delegate power and authority to pri- vate individuals. By virtue of this delegation, prison masters may be considered officers of the court, but the structure of their re- lation to the court is functionally equivalent to a contract, and many of the arguments raised against delegation to prison con- tractors can be raised with equal validity (or invalidity) against special masters.

There is no legislative mandate for the delegation. The guide- lines for the masters' interpretations may be vague. The account- ability of special masters is low.[40] With large budgets and substantial fees, special masters could be accused of having a vested interest in producing continuous findings of violations, an accu- sation parallel to the charges of conflict of interest leveled against profit-motivated contractors.

In reply to this last charge, it may be claimed that the profes- sional ethics of special masters will inhibit them from finding vi- olations just to feather their own nests. I tend to agree, but I think the defense applies just as well to the ethics of professional prison contractors. More significantly, however, I think that both con- tractors and special masters are kept honest not just by their ethics, but by the fact that they have a material interest in their reputations for honesty and integrity.

To make my point clear, I am not arguing that the practice of appointing prison masters is either unwise or unconstitutional. I am saying that objections to delegations of authority over matters of prison administration, based either on some nondelegation doc- trine or on concerns about accountability, have no more categorical validity when applied to prison contractors than they have when applied to special masters.

To return to my primary theme, monitoring should not be seen as a new burden created by contracting. Rather, private prisons serve to focus attention on an important question we should ask of all prisons: How best can we monitor, regulate, and evaluate them?

The Council of State Governments and the Urban Institute, as noted above, have suggested what monitoring and evaluation ought to encompass. More important than the specific ingredients of monitoring, however, is a recognition of the importance of the process, and of the fact that it is just as important for public as for private prisons.

The requirements and procedures for monitoring prisons ought to be similar for both government and contracted prisons. At least two states—Massachusetts and Pennsylvania—have implicitly recognized this principle. They have developed standardized monitoring systems, to be applied to both state-run and contracted facilities for juveniles. In both states, procedures call for examination of institutional records, site visits by an outside team, and interviews with staff. In addition, the Massachusetts procedures include interviews with inmates.[41]

While monitoring is necessary for all prisons, it is not sufficient. Monitoring has not, by itself, saved governmental prisons and jails from poor management or physical deterioration. What is required, beyond supervision, is motivation. Court monitoring has included threats of heavy fines, or total shutdowns, to spur reform of governmental prison systems. This has produced some good results, but it is clearly a meat-ax approach, suitable only for extreme cases. In contrast, one of the major advantages of private contracting is the opportunity to systematically structure incentives so that performance will respond to feedback on a regular and routine basis.[42]

12

Issues of Corruption

Wherever large sums of money and great discretionary power come together, especially if accountability and control are weak, there will be a risk of corruption. Corruption has been a problem in prison contracting historically and it is a problem in other types of government contracting today. It is therefore quite reasonable to be concerned about the possibility of corruption in correctional privatization.

Writing for the American Federation of State, County, and Municipal Employees, John Hanrahan asserts:

> In recent years, there have been scores of publicized cases of payoffs and kickbacks in connection with state and local governmental contracting; of price-fixing and bid-rigging; of major contracts being given to cronies and campaign contributors of public officials; of contractors' conflicts of interests, and of contracts going to companies with links to organized crime.[1]

Certainly, these are real problems, with potential for subverting the contracting process. Prison contracts, just like other types of government contracts, carry with them temptations and opportunities for corruption.

To use the possibility of corruption as an argument against contracting per se, however, is illogical. It is fallacious to imply that corruption-related problems are uniquely inherent in private contracting, or would necessarily diminish if contracting were not allowed. Political corruption is a corollary of government, not just of government contracting.

Corruption as a Corollary of Government

People who spend other people's money are always tempted to find ways to keep some of the money or to spend it on themselves. This trait is not limited to contractors and their governmental collaborators. Public administrators who do not use contractors have other ways of cheating. They may wastefully expand their budgets and activities, thereby increasing their salaries, their perquisites, their status, and their power. They can cheat by building and protecting sinecures for themselves, thereby lowering the ratio of work to reward. They may pad their payrolls, their offices, and their staffs. In addition to their own cheating, they may countenance the cheating of other administrators because it doesn't cost them anything directly, and it serves as camouflage.

Payroll padding, nepotism, cronyism, patronage, bribery, payoffs, featherbedding, dishonest budget inflation, conflicts of interest, misuse of public funds, links to organized crime, and many other kinds of corruption are known to occur within public employee unions and within governmental units that provide services directly, rather than through contracts. Thus, the potential occurrence of any of these (for example, the involvement of organized crime) is no more legitimate as an argument against contracting public services per se than it would be as an argument against the existence of government, or of unions.[2]

Bernard McCarthy has studied the many ways in which correctional officials and employees sometimes abuse their discretionary power for personal gain in the form of money, drugs, sex, or other goods and services.[3] He identifies three categories of correctional corruption. *Misfeasance* includes granting special privileges or preferential treatment, selective use of authorized rewards and punishments, the sale of paroles or other releases, and misuse or misappropriation of state resources for personal purposes. *Malfeasance* includes theft, embezzlement, traffic in contraband, extortion or exploitation of inmates or their families, protection rackets, assisting escapes, or engaging in criminal conspiracies. *Nonfeasance* includes overlooking inmate violations of rules or criminal activity, and failure to report or to stop corrupt acts by fellow workers.

All forms of corruption, whether misfeasance, malfeasance, or nonfeasance, involve the abuse of public power to pursue private ends. Corruption is not caused by private ownership of agencies that provide public services. Nor would corruption be prevented if a law were passed requiring that all state-mandated services be produced directly by government employees. In the Soviet Union, for example, the state controls the production and distribution of virtually all goods and services. Not coincidentally, corruption is pervasive.

It is ironic that some critics of private prisons are fond of quoting Dostoevsky—that the degree of a nation's civilization can be seen in the way it treats it prisoners—and wondering aloud what Dostoevsky would think of private prisons.[4] The clear implication is that based on this country's use of private prisons, Dostoevsky would draw some negative conclusions about our civilization, but in comparison to what? Let's consider one striking comparison that the great Russian novelist would surely make if he had not died in 1881.

If Dostoevsky had been alive in the Soviet Union during the last 70 years he would have been witness to one of the most brutal and lawless prison systems in history. He'd have seen political prisoners jammed shoulder to shoulder into airless cells and box-cars and shipped to punitive slave camps where they were worked, starved, and frozen to death. If he visited contemporary American prisons, including private prisons, Dostoevsky would probably be impressed by the civil and human rights protections, the food and medical care, the standards of decency, even the space, he would generally find there, at least in comparison to the Soviet Gulag.[5] It would indeed say something about our civilization, but nothing that would discourage private sector involvement in the running of prisons.

What this comparison would tell the author of *Crime and Punishment*, himself the victim of repression and harsh punishment, is that it is not state and governmental control that guarantees good prisons. It is the rule of law, an institution that is strongest in capitalist and mixed economies with their free markets, property rights, and libertarian traditions, and weakest in socialist systems where the management of nearly everything is defined as the exclusive prerogative of the state.

In short, private sector involvement in the exercise of power is not the cause of corruption nor is government monopoly the cure.

The "Lessons" of History

Michael Keating is representative of other private prison opponents in the picture he paints of the early history of correctional contracting:

> For much of the Nineteenth Century while correctional facilities, especially in England, were nominally in the hands of government, they were actually under the control of keepers or petty tradesmen, who were in effect private contractors rather than salaried employees. Although they were required to submit accounts to supervising courts, only mass escapes or gross corruption threatened their tenure. Having once obtained their appointments or "contracts" through judicial patronage, these early correctional entrepreneurs were able to settle down to a lifetime of profitable extortion. Everything in the facility was for sale; even release required the payment of a fee to your friendly keeper.[6]

Although contracting for prison labor is quite different from contracting for institutional management, it is portrayed by critics as indicating something basic about the character of private enterprise involvement with prisons. Historically, contracting for prison labor—while found in all parts of the country—was most common in the South and is often associated with the culture of slavery and the economics of Reconstruction. Some profess to see a continuation of this tradition in the fact that private prisons today are concentrated in the South. A more likely explanation of this phenomenon is the fact that organized union opposition is weaker there. Harmon Wray, however, sees a deeper historical pattern running from slavery, convict leasing systems, and chain gangs, to contemporary private prison management and the employment of prisoners by modern private industry. He observes darkly: "Constitutionally, slavery is legal as punishment for crime, and our Southern prison populations are, of course, overwhelmingly poor and disproportionately black and Hispanic." [7]

Other critics imply that privatization is both racist and a tool of class oppression:

Corporate America is upper-class white. Only a few of its hirelings are minority people. Privatization places in the hands of the haves a tool to exploit and further enrich themselves at the expense of the have-nots.[8]

John DiIulio describes a bleak history of for-profit corrections from the pre-Civil War years to the post-World War II years. His summary judgment is measured but critical:

It is highly unlikely that the ugliest features of this history will repeat themselves. Increased external monitoring aside, the corrections profession has grown well beyond the days when such situations were tolerated or encouraged. But the record does teach that prisons and profits can be a most unhealthy mix.[9]

In his review, however, DiIulio himself does some unhealthy mixing by lumping together three different types of profit-related activity: private management of institutions, leasing of convict labor, and profit-seeking behavior by public prison officials. Much of the corruption and abuse found in the last two areas originated within government, rather than the private sector. Many state-run prisons attempted either to turn a profit through their own activities or to profit by leasing involuntary convict labor to outside employers. These things were not done just by private prison managers. Thus it is not accurate to attribute them specifically to privatization, as though they were not also common in the absence of privatization.

DiIulio has supported his historical observations, in part, by citing two of the earliest and best-known observers of American penitentiaries, Alexis de Tocqueville and Gustave de Beaumont.[10] While their writings do contain information useful to critics of private prisons, it should be noted that Tocqueville and Beaumont provide a two-edged comparison of private and governmental prison management. They were critical of the exploitation of prisoners' labor both by contractors and by governmental prison administrators. They noted that this exploitation was minimized when there was a balance between governmental and private management:

It appeared to us, that the evil which we have thus pointed out, has been generally avoided in the new penitentiaries in the United States. In these establishments, neither the system of entire domestic [governmental] management, nor that by contract, have been exclusively adopted.[11]

These scholars concluded that corruption and exploitation were equally possible under either private contracting or internal public management. The cause in both cases was some form of monopoly and the cure was some form of competition to avoid consolidation of power. For example, contracts were rotated among contractors. Also, different activities and industries were contracted to different parties so that no one proprietor had too much power.

The history of private prison management, like the history of convict leasing, contains many grim examples of corruption, profiteering, and abuse of prisoners. It must be remembered, however, that most of this took place at a time when corruption was also much more prevalent in government-run prisons and in the criminal justice system generally. Some states ran their prisons as profit-making enterprises with as much ruthlessness and exploitation without the aid of private contractors as others did with them. Wardens and sheriffs had considerable discretion and autonomy, and ran their institutions like feudal fiefdoms, as illustrated by this example from the 1920s:

> In one county the cost of feeding a prisoner was eight cents a day while the sheriff received forty-five. In many counties, the sheriff is permitted either directly or through concessionaires, to sell special articles of food, tobacco, or other so-called luxuries, to prisoners. He is thus permitted to starve them to the point where they or their friends purchase food to supplement the daily ration. He thus enjoys the extraordinary privilege of reaping a profit not only from starvation but from the relief of starvation.[12]

Malcolm Braly, author of *On the Yard*, recalls in his memoirs a variation on this theme that he observed during a stint in the Nevada State Prison:

> [E]verything in the kitchen was for sale and everyone who worked there sold food. The convict politicians [powerful inmates] bought control over most of the meat, butter, eggs, milk—the good stuff—and the mainline [most convicts] got whatever was left over.[13]

At the New Mexico State Penitentiary, prior to this country's bloodiest prison riot in 1980, there prevailed an extensive pattern of theft, extortion, graft, embezzlement, and other forms of corruption among employees and officials of the corrections department. Officials helped themselves to "fill-it-up" privileges at the state gasoline pumps, free automobile repair, free dry cleaning, free haircuts at the prison barber, and free dental and medical services for the whole family, including discount medication and injections, at the pen infirmary. Officials also helped themselves to food from the pen kitchen, purchasing eggs and meat at fifty cents to the dollar. Whole truckloads of meat being shipped to the penitentiary from the prison farm at Las Lunas would disappear on a regular basis.[14]

In some counties today, the sheriffs are allowed to keep for themselves any money not spent on food for prisoners. When the Wisconsin legislature tried to end this practice in that state recently, the bill was vetoed by the governor. The legislature is now trying again, amidst reports that some sheriffs have squeezed out meal profits equal to their salaries. One sheriff in 1988 was discovered to have fed prisoners baked goods that had been donated to the county as food for goats.[15]

Nearly all the abuses found by historians in private prisons can be found also in the history of governmental prisons—including abuses related directly to the profit motive.[16] *Corrections Today* recently reprinted an article first published in 1945 by E. R. Cass, a leading figure in correctional history, in which Cass decried the exploitation and corruption of jails run for profit on the fee system.[17] What was most objectionable about these jails, according to Cass, was not that they made a profit, but that the profit was based on abuse of power. Those who set the fees, imposed the fees, and enforced their collection, kept the money for themselves. Under the fee system, the sheriff was "a public official whose chief interest is to increase the population of the jail, and thus add to his fees."[18] Some of these sheriffs would release offenders early but continue to collect fees until the nominal expiration of the sentence. Significantly, the jails disparaged by Cass were run entirely by the government. The private sector played no part in them.

Almost all the arguments from history presented by critics of private prisons suffer from a common fallacy: they fail to make contemporaneous comparisons. Instead, they compare the worst aspects of private prisons from the past with the features of modern prisons (or worse, with idealized, not actual, versions of modern prisons). Of the possible comparisons between historical, modern, public, and private prisons, critics focus almost exclusively on the one analogy that puts private prisons in the worst light. Never do they compare modern private prisons with public prisons of earlier eras. That would be equally valid (or invalid) but unfortunately (from their perspective) it would make private prisons look far superior. It would also make more obvious the fallacy of noncontemporaneous comparison.

At a minimum, a valid historical analysis would have to compare private prisons to public prisons within the same political and legal jurisdictions at the same point in time.[19] However, even if such proper comparisons show private prisons to be worse than their public counterparts during some earlier era, it is questionable whether such differences would still apply in the socially, politically, and (most important) *legally* different world that exists today.

The Revolution in Prisoners' Rights

At a time when the prison environment was more generally corrupt, contracting often represented an extension and application of that corruption, but it was not the cause of it. In today's political and legal environment, especially with the firmly established revolution in prisoners' rights, such extreme and flagrant abuse of power is very unlikely. William C. Collins, formerly a Senior Assistant Attorney General for the State of Washington and a specialist in correctional law, cautions against comparisons that ignore the enormous changes of the last two decades:

> While the private operation of jails has some historic precedent, legal and management issues in jail operation have changed so dramatically in the last 10 to 20 years, especially with the growth of inmate rights and court involvement, that contracting issues or problems from the 19th century have little relevance in the waning decades of the 20th century.[20]

Important as the prisoners' rights revolution and heightened judicial oversight of prison management have been, however, they do not mean that corruption is no longer a problem in corrections. And it is likely to remain a problem as long as officials and workers at all levels of prison administration have extensive discretionary power and relatively low visibility.

Controlling Corruption through Law and the Market

Just as the private sector is not the source of all corruption, neither is state monopoly of correctional operations a solution to corruption. Abuses of inmates under the nineteenth-century practice of leasing out their labor were as much abuses by the state as by private firms. It was not so much the state as the law that finally ended those abuses, and it is the law, not the state, that protects against abuses and violations of prisoners' rights in contemporary prisons. The way to further guarantee the rights of prisoners is not to insist that prisons remain in the hands of government employees, but to maintain the rule of law.

The independence of the judiciary allows it to oversee and regulate the government's prisons. Prisoners' rights are thus protected, and the power of their keepers constrained, by the checks and balances inherent in the distribution and separation of powers. Contracting, when it operates properly, extends the concept of separation, and constructive tension, between agents of administration and agents of oversight. When there is corruption and collusion between contractors and government officials, the regulatory function of contracting breaks down, but it is the collusion, not the contracting, that is the problem.

Co-optation is a subtle form of collusion. In private prisons, it is possible that an on-site governmental monitor could become co-opted by the contractor, even if only through friendships. The Council of State Governments and the Urban Institute suggest that this possibility "can be alleviated by periodically changing monitors, by proper training, and by continued interaction between State home-office personnel and the monitor." [21]

The "revolving door" syndrome, in which government purchasers move directly into jobs with private vendors, can produce another subtle form of collusion, which could be called "anticipatory collusion." As Joan Mullen points out, however, there are established methods of dealing with this problem, including "conflict-of-interest provisions attached to public employment, openly competitive procurement procedures, and broadly composed contractor selection committees." [22]

Problems of corruption in public-private contracting are rooted in departures from conditions of genuine competition. Government monopolization, by outlawing contracting, would not solve these problems. With honest government, by definition, there would be no corruption in the delivery of public services. But governments are not automatically honest; they must be kept that way. Open competition among contractual agents of government is one effective method of keeping them honest. "The answer," in the words of Robert W. Poole, Jr., "is to have rational, open bidding procedures and objective selection standards—and to make sure that they are adhered to. This can be done by requiring that all such rules, procedures and criteria be matters of public record and by holding bid openings and other important decision-making sessions in public." [23]

13

Issues of Dependence

Critics worry that some vendors will obtain contracts by "low-balling," that is, they will make unrealistically low bids. After the contract goes into effect, the government will gradually lose much of its capacity to resume the operation itself, and high capitalization costs will prevent new competitors from entering the field. Once the government becomes dependent on a contractor, that contractor will be free to jack up prices. Worse, the contractor may go bankrupt, leaving the government without any correctional capacity. Worst of all, contracting may devolve into exclusive franchises that simply replace public monopolies with private monopolies.

All of these are realistic possibilities against which we should seek safeguards. None of them, however, is so unavoidable as to justify a moratorium on private prisons.

Lowballing

A common objection to contracting of all sorts is the danger of "lowballing." In lowballing, an unrealistically low bid is used to win an initial contract. Losses are then recovered through cost overruns or inflated subsequent contracts. If competitors cannot quickly enter the market and if the government would incur high costs in resuming the operation itself, the existing contractor can raise its price gradually but continually.

A contractor's greatest leverage over the government may be as much psychological as financial. When a prison or jail is contracted out, it relieves public officials of many worries and headaches. To take back a facility, or even to recontract it to a new firm, would be a hassle. The emotional cost of that hassle would be borne by the bureaucrats assigned to handle the necessary transactions and paperwork, whereas the financial cost of renegotiating the same contract at a higher price can be passed along to taxpayers.

The strategy for a contractor seeking to hook the government, then, would be to raise prices through a series of modest increases, each one being too small to be worth the bother of a new bidding process. Obviously, there must be some limit, but it could well be higher than what the price would have been under either fair competition (no lowballing) or continued government monopoly.

Is there a solution to this problem?

First, it should be noted that taxpayers can be "lowballed" by public agencies as well as by private contractors. A public agency can start a program with a low budget or as a "pilot project" and then increase the budget after the program is entrenched and a constituency strongly interested in its continuation has been established. Public agencies also produce "cost overruns" when they exceed their budgets or inflate the costs of construction and financing by dragging out the time to completion.

The caveat that private companies may raise their rates in the future implies that public agencies, in contrast, will not. The fact is, however, that since World War II the price of goods and services has increased much more rapidly in the public sector than in the private sector,[1] partially because contractors are often required to index their fee increases to the Consumer Price Index.

Experience in contracting for other public services has shown that while some lowballing probably does occur, it can be controlled. Moreover, it is not so extensive as to have made contracting more costly, on average, than direct public delivery. A nationwide study of garbage collection sponsored by the National Science Foundation demonstrated significant savings through contracting. Costs of municipal collection were shown to be 29 to 37 percent greater than contractor prices.[2] This comprehensive study presumably included some firms that had been lowballers and now were overchargers, if that practice really is endemic to private contracting. However, these inflated fees, if any, were not enough to outweigh the strong savings provided by contracting overall.

Recent experience with prison contracting does not support the fears of lowballing. Joan Mullen reports that the INS, which has the most extensive experience in contracting for custodial confinement, has encountered increasing, not decreasing, competition for its business. INS contracts are renegotiated annually and must go to the lowest bidder. "This requirement, plus an INS history of early contracting with low-cost nonprofits, appears to provide little opportunity for the provider to include substantial cost increases in the contract." [3]

Financial reports by Corrections Corporation of America for its early years do show annual losses to the corporation overall, but these are not the result of lowballing. Each of CCA's facilities is profitable, and the company's total return from operations is positive.[4] Costs of developing a new market, however, have produced high central office costs, which can be expected to diminish, as a percentage of total costs, as the field matures. Now that Wackenhut, another corporation that is national in scope, has joined CCA in market development, those costs should spread more widely and have less effect on particular contracts.

"Cost Overruns"

One alleged example of lowballing is an oft-cited *New York Times* story that referred to what it headlined as a $200,000 "cost overrun" at Silverdale, the privately operated prison in Hamilton County, Tennessee.[5] Prior to the contract, the county ran the facility at a cost of $24 per inmate for an average population of 243. After the contract began, vigorous enforcement of laws against drunken driving raised the average population to more than 300. The contractor did not charge any more than the $21 per inmate agreed to in the contract, but the county was sending far more prisoners than anticipated to the facility. While it is true that the county thus spent more money on Silverdale than it had planned, it is very misleading to label the excess expense a "cost overrun." [6]

A more accurate term, suggested by Charles Ring, is "population overrun."

Some Hamilton County officials were upset because they had
accepted a bid that turned out to have been higher than necessary.
But this is not a valid criticism of private contracting generally, or
even of this particular contract. After all, if the average population
had declined, the county would have garnered unexpected benefits
from the contract. Would the county then have volunteered to pay
a fee higher than contracted, to compensate the company for its
lower than projected revenues?

Contracts based on specific prison population predictions are
inherently risky. This risk can be distributed by negotiating contracts that specify lower or higher fees depending on whether projected volume rises or falls. However, neither party to a contract
can avoid all such risks without paying some sort of premium to
the other party. To judge a contract only after the fact, without
taking into account how events might easily have been different,
is like pronouncing your insurance policy a waste of money because
you did not have an accident. No one can predict the future perfectly, but competitive bidding and contractually set prices provide
a motive for all parties to predict as well as they can. Bidding by
private contractors generally tends to keep prices both as low and
as accurate as possible even though unanticipated events may later
show the winning bid to have been, in retrospect, either too high
or too low.

—Those who cite the $200,000 cost "overrun" story generally miss
the most significant part of the tale. When it was clear that the
large number of drunk driving offenders was likely to be a permanent factor, the contractor and the county worked out a new
price agreement that provided for a much lower per diem payment
for those particular offenders.[7] The cost of the contract is renegotiated annually in any case, but the county's Superintendent of
Corrections was able to arrange an informal adjustment even before the contract was reworked.[8]

Defenses against Lowballing

As illustrated by the adjustment just discussed, contractors have
a vested interest in accommodating, not exploiting, their govern-

mental customers. Hard bargaining may be part of the contracting game, but so is flexibility. The best contracts are those that are mutually beneficial. While one party may sometimes gain temporarily at the expense of the other, a lopsided contract is unstable and not in either party's long-term interest.

A contract with a sliding scale can protect the government against a population overrun, or even work in its favor. At the Bay County jail complex in 1988, the contract with Corrections Corporation of America was set at $31.01 per day for the first 300 inmates, about $10 lower for the next 20, and only $7.88 for every inmate over 320. When the population reached 400 (a bit over the designed capacity), both CCA and the county were surprised, but the county was delighted to be paying such a low fee for one-fifth of its detainees.[9]

Public agencies can guard against lowballing by evaluating proposed budgets for their realism and reliability, rather than following a rigid rule specifying that contracts must go only to the lowest bidder. The lowest bid is not necessarily the most realistic bid. Also, regular renegotiation or renewal of contracts, with at least the potential for competition through open bidding, can make lowballing a costly strategy. No private company can raise its fees very high above a reasonable profit margin without inviting exposure and competition. Competing contractors have the information, motivation, and organizational resources to control each others' prices to a much greater degree than taxpayers are able to control government costs.

Consolidation and Market Entry

Ironically, one concern about privatization of corrections is that it will not be competitive enough. Capital costs are said to be so high as to restrict market entry, thus allowing early entrants to use their capital advantage to squeeze out would-be competitors with predatory pricing. Further, big corporations may use political power as well as economic power to control the market. Critics fear that the private sector in corrections will become "a privileged group of large, monolithic service providers concerned more about profit than performance, creativity and compassion."[10] They worry about "the small, independent social service agencies. Hundreds of them, particularly those supported by federal grants, have disappeared while the private sector's bigger corporations—Eclectic, Magdala, the Volunteers of America and others—survive and prosper." [11]

Some critics even foresee the possibility of dependence at a national level, with unsettling effects on prisoners: "An American gulag archipelago, in which the prisons are under the jurisdiction of private corporations working together, or a single corporation that has established a dominant if not monopolistic position, could easily result in the transfer of prisoners from one area of the country to another . . ." [12]

Market dominance and consolidation are not bad in themselves; it depends on whether they result from economic or political processes. Critics are right to be wary of political distortions of the contracting process. Even lobbying, a legal form of political influence, can be objectionable, but only if it departs from the model of open competition based on relevant criteria established by agencies accountable to the public. What must be avoided is unfair competition, not successful competition. It may be true that small, independent, nonprofit agencies supported by federal grants will not be able to survive in a competitive market. If so, it will not be because profit-making and competition are somehow incompatible with "performance, creativity and compassion." Instead, such shakeouts are likely to make the industry more stable, more reliable, and higher in quality.

Critics often cite the experience of defense contracting and predict that the Pentagon's $500 hammer will be matched by the Corrections Department's $500 million slammer. The analogy is not a very good one. Research, product development, and capitalization costs are not anywhere near as high for corrections as for the defense industry. Nonetheless, the comparison to defense contracting might still be useful because the lessons that have been learned there in recent years may have application to contracting for prisons. The 1984 Competition in Contracting Act was partly a result of scandals in defense contracting and was designed to reduce expensive sole-source and cost-plus contracting. Success in achieving this goal has been reported as "substantial." [13] Some of the techniques used to keep defense contractors competitive would presumably work for prison contractors as well.

By the same token, lessons from defense contracting about the limits of competition may also apply to the prison industry. These would include lessons about not pushing competition purely for the sake of competition; about limiting the number of contracts in order to maintain economies of scale and to avoid overcapacity; and about the shortsightedness of buying only from the lowest bidder.

There may be an analogy between developing and producing a small number of expensive weapons, such as Stealth bombers or MX missiles, and a U.S. state that decides—as an experiment—to authorize the construction and operation of one, and only one, maximum security prison. With such a poor ratio of high investment risk to low potential return, it is unlikely that this state will attract much competition or realize low prices.

However, capital costs for prison contractors, unlike those for many defense contractors, are not necessarily so high as to restrict market entry; they will vary a great deal by size and type of facility and will depend on whether the contract calls for new construction, renovation or conversion of other property, or takeover of existing governmental facilities. Start-up costs for single, especially low-security, facilities are well within reach of small businesses or groups of investors. As a new corporation, CCA was able to site, finance, build, and open a 350-bed prison within 7 months, for $5 million. The U.S. Corrections Corporation, founded by two men with an initial investment of $1.9 million, opened its first facility at a seminary purchased for $695,000. If this is all it takes to enter the market, it is well within the resources of numerous potential competitors.

Market entry is likely to get easier, not harder. When corrections is no longer an exclusively government-operated monopoly; when enabling legislation has been passed and other legal uncertainties resolved; when jurisdictions have in place mechanisms for contracting and monitoring; when conventions and standards for prison contracts begin to develop; when investors gain confidence in the industry—as all these things occur, it will become progressively easier for new companies, including small ones, to enter the market and compete.

Facility Ownership and Government Dependency on Contractors

If a jurisdiction's prisons are not only managed, but also *owned* by a private corporation, will this make the government so dependent that it loses effective control over the company and the prison?

James Gentry suggests that the physical plant of prisons should be owned by the government, because that would allow for shorter contracts and for easier transfer to subsequent bidders.[14] While he recognizes that private ownership facilitates speed, savings, and innovation in prison construction, Gentry thinks these could be achieved under state ownership by design competition and lease-purchase agreements separate from management contracts.

Separating management and ownership does have some advantages, but it also has disadvantages. One problem is that design and operation are intimately related. Efficiency may be lost if a management company is neither allowed nor given any incentive to invest in the design and construction of the facilities it will operate.

The argument against private ownership of prisons assumes that the physical assets of a prison are so expensive, specialized, and nonredeployable that the market will be resistant to new entrants and firms will require long contracts to recover their investments.[15] These long contracts will lock governments in to single suppliers. An alternative to a long contract would be a periodically renewable contract with provisions specifying the terms for immediate government purchase of the facility if and when the contract is terminated. It might be objected that this would give the vendor something to hold over the government, to deter it from terminating the contract. However, if the government wishes to take over the facility itself, it will be no worse off than if it had built and financed the prison in the first place, and if it switches to a new contractor it can have the new contractor take over the same financing role as the previous contractor.

On the matter of dependency, it may well be asked: who has whom over the barrel? Even where a state or county contracts

away most of its own correctional capacity to a single private vendor, does that put the government at the mercy of the vendor?
Clearly, the dependence works both ways. There is only one cus-
tomer, in a given jurisdiction, for correctional services. The vendor
may own the buildings, but either they will be difficult to convert
to other uses (which puts the government in a good bargaining
position) or they will not (which means that the government could
also acquire and convert other buildings). Either way, private ownership of the prison does not leave the government in an untenable
position.

Further, the company does not "own" its human capital. By
canceling a contract, the government instantly creates a pool of
surplus labor having just the characteristics now needed by the
government, or another contractor, as the new employer.

The Threat of Bankruptcy or Default

It is not inevitable that the government will become dependent on
contractors, but it can happen. To the degree that dependency
does occur, the government will have to worry about that contractor going bankrupt. Even if the company never does go bankrupt, it can use the mere threat of bankruptcy to gain concessions
from the government, at least to the extent that the government
is in fact dependent on the contractor.

Thomas Coughlin, Commissioner of the New York Department
of Correctional Services, supports his concern over this issue by
citing a case in a related area. In 1978, the New York Department
of Mental Retardation contracted with a private, nonprofit agency,
the United Cerebral Palsy Association of New York, to run a
substantial part of a large facility in New York City. Three years
later, the company was $17 million in debt and filed for bank-
ruptcy.[16] The state resumed operation of the facility.

The most worrisome aspect of bankruptcy or default is the prospect that a jurisdiction might find itself suddenly without the capacity to hold and care for its prisoners. Until there are a number
of regionally or nationally viable correctional contractors prepared
to enter the market in a particular jurisdiction, it would be wise
for the government to retain some capacity of its own. This is

possible even in a jurisdiction so small that it has only one jail or prison. Such a jurisdiction would need to retain supervisory capacity for monitoring purposes, in any case.

What disappears when a contractor goes broke is the financial structure and highest level of management, both of which the government will still have. A bankrupt prison company leaves its line staff and most of its middle management behind, ready for a new employer. The plant and equipment can be purchased by the government from the failed company (or its creditors) at liquidation prices with money from insurance carried by the former vendor as part of the contract. Or another company could step in and take over a failing competitor—or purchase its assets—and the government could switch the contract to the new company.

I do not mean to play down the fact that bankruptcy would cause serious problems. However, it need not leave the government empty-handed, or force it to empty its prisons or jails.

Since bankruptcy is a worst-case scenario for private prisons, for the sake of perspective it ought to be compared to worst-case scenarios for government prisons. While a government is unlikely to go bankrupt, some prison systems have experienced interruptions of services comparable to what might occur in a bankruptcy. Courts have ordered the immediate closure of public prisons and threatened to close down whole systems. Fiscally strapped and debt-ridden state and local governments have been forced to release prisoners for purely budgetary reasons. Frustrated sheriffs, transporting prisoners from overflowing jails, have left them shackled to the gates of overflowing prisons unwilling to accept them.[17] Convicts have been housed in warehouses, quonset huts, tents, gymnasiums, trailers, schools, boats, and other makeshift accommodations.

Clearly, many public prison systems are already in a state of crisis and disruption, for which private prison contracts offer some relief. In such systems, bankruptcy or other failures by a contractor would mean little more than a return to the status quo ante.

Some Recommendations

To protect against defaults or bankruptcies, the Council of State Governments and the Urban Institute make several recommendations to contracting jurisdictions. During bidding, and periodically throughout the contract, companies should be judged on financial soundness and stability. Contracts should specify who is to pay the costs created by termination (this could vary by whether termination is for cause or otherwise). Performance bonds (equal, for example, to the cost of one year's contract) should be considered. There should be a contingency plan to cover staffing, placement of inmates, and control of the facility during emergency transitions.[18] State officials in Kentucky required in their Requests for Proposals that prison contractors be prepared to post a performance bond equal to 70 percent of the annual value of the contract.[19] In its Santa Fe contract, CCA posted a performance bond, with a $325,000 certificate of deposit as collateral.[20]

Contracts and the Expansion of Government

While the general concept of *privatization* is often attractive to conservatives and libertarians, because it implies a shrinking of government, the specific mechanism of *contracting* has received support from some liberals for just the opposite reason. These supporters hope that contracts, by operating more efficiently, will be able to provide more government services in spite of limited tax revenues. Whether this is seen as a danger or an advantage, it must be recognized that contracting can be used to extend, as well as to reduce, the scope of government.

A major cause of government growth is the existence of special interest groups that encourage government spending in those areas that most directly benefit the group and its clients. Paul Starr argues convincingly that "the most common privatization proposals, such as contracting out and vouchers, would hardly diminish the domain of 'special' interests." [21] He warns against the creation of "an enlarged class of private contractors and other providers dependent on public money." [22] Starr correctly notes that those who produce public services—whether as public employees or as private contractors—have a vested interest in increasing government expenditures on those services.

Liberals have been blamed by conservatives for promoting the growth of a parasitic "New Class"—defined by its relationship to the means of public production—that thrives on the growth of government. Unlike labor and capital—the two sides of the old class structure—the New Class does not produce wealth but participates in (and benefits from) its governmental transfer. The New Class consists of the interest groups and lobbyists who call for government services and programs, the politicians who order them, the functionaries and professionals who administer the programs and deliver the services, and the originally targeted individuals and organizations who receive what is left at the end of this long pipeline (or trough, as the cynics refer to it). Now conservatives themselves may be vulnerable to charges that they have simply added private contractors to the ranks of the New Class.

Contracting, by itself, is not going to limit the scope of government, but it can restrain the cost. It is not a way of restricting the demand for government service, but a method of controlling the price. To do so, however, contracting must be competitive. It does no good to substitute private monopolies for public ones. This is one danger of privatization to which even its advocates should be especially sensitive. While designed to inject characteristics of the private sector into operations of the public sector, contracting could have the reverse effect. Characteristics of government could be extended through the use of private enterprise. We might end up with the worst, rather than the best, of both worlds.

Something akin to noncompetitive contracting occurs when government agencies create "off-budget enterprises" (OBEs).[23] OBEs, according to Hans Sennholz, are governmentally created and managed enterprises, whose spending and borrowing are not recorded on any budget. Familiar examples would be airport, housing, parking, sewer, water, and other authorities, but there are many other types as well. OBEs make it harder to control the growth and cost of government. Indeed, OBEs have arisen in response to attempts to statutorily or constitutionally restrict government spending and debt, which is why most of them are found at the state and local, rather than federal, level.[24] OBEs allow governments

> to spend and borrow without constraint, to dispense patronage without civil service restrictions, and to bestow favors and benefits on special groups. An OBE is an anomaly of organization: a government entity unfettered by many of the statutory constraints applicable to government, a corporation without stockholders but with

a board of directors consisting of politicians or their appointees, a non-profit business that competes with business or is protected from competition as an unregulated monopoly.[25]

There are important differences, however, between municipal authorities or other OBEs and private contractors supplying public services. Contracting reveals more expenses than it hides, and the fees paid to contractors are on-budget. Contractors are not independent authorities; they are accountable to their government monitors who are, in turn, accountable to the public. In contrast to contractors, "OBEs pay no taxes or license fees, post no performance bonds, face little paperwork and regulatory tape that strangle individual enterprise." [26]

Exclusive Franchises

While correctional contracting may not create off-budget enterprises, it may in other ways contribute to what Sennholz is warning against: expansion of the power of government. In particular, a contract that took the form of an *exclusive franchise* would corrupt the process of competition into just another form of governmental monopoly. The State of Tennessee flirted briefly with this when it took seriously a bold proposal by the Corrections Corporation of America to lease the entire operation of the Tennessee Department of Correction.

The distinction between an exclusive franchise and market dominance is important. With an exclusive franchise, there is formal protection against competition; in market dominance, there is not. If one company runs all the prisons or jails for a single jurisdiction, that does not by itself create either a monopoly or a dependency situation. As long as there is no exclusive franchise, then the potential for competition will still exist.

Competition occurs through time as well as across space. Even with a long-term contract, a competitive environment can be maintained through provisions for periodic renewal, review, and possible termination. Nonetheless, wherever possible, government should strive to preserve actual, as well as potential, competition. It could do this by continuing to run some facilities itself, thereby retaining its own capacity to compete. Or it could divide its facilities

among different contractors and hold open the possibility of re-
distribution of facilities at a later point. A classic example of competition between contractors and the government, over time,
comes from a field other than corrections. In Phoenix, the city
public works department, by outbidding private competitors, successfully regained one sector of the city's garbage collection that
it had lost to a private contractor a few years earlier.

In correctional contracting, Texas, California, and the Immigration and Naturalization Service, as large systems, have had no
trouble maintaining contracts for secure confinement across multiple providers. Competition that is preserved in large systems like
these, or across jurisdictions nationwide, is competition that is
available for smaller systems as well. Corrections Corporation of
America and Wackenhut Corrections Corporation currently operate facilities in only a handful of states. However, they are already large enough that they could provide competition in any
state. The absence of private prisons and jails in most states is due
to such factors as strong union opposition, absence of enabling
legislation, and caution or lack of interest on the part of correctional and other governmental authorities. It is not because the
nature of corrections makes it impossible for competition to develop rapidly in response to real demand.

Dependence vs. Competition

Objections that government may become dependent on particular
contractors, that capital costs will restrict market entry, that markets will be consolidated or distorted by a few powerful corporations, that corruption may undermine open competition, or that
exclusive franchises may occur, raise a number of legitimate concerns. However, to present these objections, not as warnings of
dangers to avoid, but as arguments against the very concept of
privatization, is self-contradictory. The objections rest on an underlying recognition that competition is desirable. They thus implicitly reaffirm that which they seem to deny. With the market
model accepted as a standard of judgment, an imperfect, distorted,
or manipulated market is obviously undesirable, something to
avoid. But preserving a nonmarket, government monopoly of ser-

vices would not avoid or solve the problem of imperfect competition.

The AFSCME warns governments against becoming addicted to contractors, but what they offer in its place is mandated dependence on organized public employees. If dependence is a real problem, will that problem be solved if there are no private vendors? Is it not also a form of dependence when a service can be supplied only by government employees, especially when they are organized into unions that control the labor market? Private prison companies can help free some governments from dependence on public employees and their unions.

In sum, as an objection to private prisons, the forecast of government dependence on contractors has a self-defeating character. To object that the private supply of a public service may not be sufficiently competitive is not a very good argument for public monopoly. The more essential a service, the greater the need for a diversity of contingent sources of supply.

14

Private Prisons and the Privatization of Punishment

The Future of Private Prisons

The future of privatization in one form or another in corrections seems fairly secure. Contracting of services and of nonsecure facilities is already a permanent feature of corrections. At this point, contracting for the management of secure facilities is still unfamiliar and controversial, but it gives every indication of gaining widespread acceptance. The forces behind its emergence are still in place and growing stronger. Crowding in existing prisons is increasing, along with judicial pressure to do something about it. The judicial solution—closing institutions or capping them, and fining jurisdictions that do not respond to court orders—only serves to increase population pressures at other institutions and financial pressures on government. While crime rates have declined slightly in recent years, public demand for imprisonment has not. Polls show that the public believes in longer sentences than are now being served and is upset over early release as a response to crowding. At the same time, the public often rejects the issuance of bonds to build new prisons on governmentally borrowed money. Proprietary prisons offer a way out of this dilemma, at an affordable price. As a result, they are likely to be viewed as a viable option by increasing numbers of federal, state, and local governments.

That privatization is a viable option has been argued and documented at length in this volume. I have examined here every known criticism of private prisons and jails, and I do not dismiss any of them lightly. However, I have been unable to find any criticisms of private facilities that cannot be matched by equally serious and analogous criticisms of noncontracted facilities. Virtually all potential problems facing private prisons have close counterparts among the problems troubling prisons run directly by the government. All prisons, both public and private, face challenges in the areas of authority, legitimacy, procedural justice, accountability, liability, cost, security, safety, corruptibility, and so on. They face these challenges primarily because of the nature of their mission, not because of their incorporation as public or private entities.

Some students of bureaucracy argue that all organizations are public; that they vary only in their mix of economic and political authority and in the degrees to which they exercise, and are constrained by, each type of authority.[1] Public choice theorists make a parallel argument in the opposite direction: that public actors and organizations respond to the same basic incentives of self-interest as do those in the private sector.[2] From either of these perspectives, "public" and "private" prisons are more alike than they are different.

Still, they are different, and these differences should be explored, experimented with, and exploited. The goal of running prisons that are safe, secure, humane, efficient, and just, is too important to reserve to the government. If that goal can be served better by private companies, they should be allowed a chance to prove it. If it is best served by the government, then the government, too, should be required to demonstrate that fact empirically, not merely announce it by edict.

The Privatization of Punishment

At the beginning of this book, I suggested that private operation of prisons and jails can be seen as an extreme test of the limits of privatization, because the administration of criminal justice, and especially of punishment, is widely regarded as a core function of government and the exclusive prerogative of the state. If the penal function can be privately performed, what function cannot be?

However, while I have entered into what might be regarded as an extreme area of privatization, I have also explored, so far, only the most limited form of privatization: namely, contracting.

To say that contracting is a limited form of privatization is not to minimize its significance. Indeed, the significance of contracting can be seen in the number and variety of arguments that have been raised against it.[3] By examining these arguments in the case of incarceration, and finding them lacking, I have challenged their validity in other areas as well. Nonetheless, as a method of privatization, contracting poses little threat to the sovereignty or scope of the state. Contracting does not deny government's responsibility to provide or arrange for a particular public service; it only rejects a government monopoly over the immediate production of that service.

A purist might argue that the term "privatization" ought to be reserved for the total transfer of a function from the government to the private sector. In relative terms, privatization could be said to occur only to the degree that the government formally divests itself of responsibility for and authority over an activity. Privatization of imprisonment in this purist sense of the term is not an issue for practical policy consideration at this time, or for the foreseeable future. It might be worthwhile, however, to address the issue here as a theoretical question. Perhaps we can put the current policy debate over "private prisons" in perspective if we try to imagine what autonomous private prisons—as opposed to contractually managed prisons—might be like and how they might be justified. I cannot do justice in one chapter to the concept of a completely private criminal justice system.[4] Moreover, I shall ignore two-thirds of that system (police and courts) and look only at one type of post-conviction sanction: imprisonment. The full privatization of all justice functions would require a more thoroughly libertarian society than the one we have now, but we can try to envision what private prisons might be like in such a society. To do so, we need to start with some basic principles of libertarian philosophy.

Libertarian Views of the State

While a rationale for privatization can be found within a variety of nonsocialist ideologies, the philosophy of governance most favorable to it is libertarianism. I use the term "libertarian" here in a very broad sense, to encompass all political philosophies that give priority to the liberty and rights of individuals over the welfare and rights of society or the state. I include the ideas of classical liberals,[5] minimal-state libertarians,[6] and some individualist anarchists.[7]

For all their many differences, there are a few common axioms among the ideas I lump together here as libertarian. These are:

1. Individual rights are natural, inalienable, and supreme.
2. The most fundamental of these are the rights to life, liberty, and property.
3. No individual or group may rightfully initiate the use or threat of coercive force against anyone else.
4. Within certain limits, individuals have the right to respond with force to the initiation or threat of force by others.
5. The state has no rights or legitimate powers not originally held by individuals, and therefore no unique claim to the legitimate use of force.
6. The proper function of government (if any) is to enforce and protect individual rights under the rule of law.

The challenge raised by anarchist libertarians is: given the axioms listed above, how can government in the form of a state exist at all without violating individuals' natural rights? The true anarchist's answer is: it can't.

Robert Nozick, in *Anarchy, State and Utopia*, answers the anarchists with an "invisible hand" theory of the state, which he offers as conceptually possible, rather than as historically accurate. Nozick reasons that in a hypothetical, Lockean state of nature, private protection agencies would arise spontaneously, charging a fee to protect individuals against the violation of their rights by others. These private agencies would play the roles now played by governmental police, courts, jails, and prisons. By the nature of its business, however, one of these protection agencies would, over time, become dominant in any given geographic area, and thereby take on the characteristics of a state. It would have a de facto monopoly over the use of force, even if it did not claim this as an exclusive right de jure.[8]

Individualist anarchists like Murray Rothbard,[9] "anarchocapi-

talists" like David Friedman,[10] and some other libertarian legal
analysts[11] believe, contra Nozick, that it is possible for multiple
and competing protection agencies to coexist within the same area.
Market mechanisms, they claim, would keep the competition from
being violent; thus, the existence of even a minimal state is neither
necessary nor desirable.

While most arguments about the feasibility of a stateless society
are theoretical, some libertarians use historical arguments. Viewed
historically, the notion that punishing criminals is the exclusive
prerogative of the state appears to be an invention of the state.
That is, its origins are not ancient, but coincident with the development of modern nation-states. Prior to that development, responses to offensive behavior or injury primarily took the form,
not of vengeance or unrestricted violence, but of restitution and
compensation. As described by Randy Barnett:

> The image of state criminal punishment arising from a bloody
> Hobbesian jungle is pure myth. Monetary payments had replaced
> violence as the means of dispute settlement and functioned well for
> over 600 years. It was only through the violent conquest of England,
> Ireland, and other parts of Europe that state criminal punishment
> was reluctantly accepted.[12]

As a historical example of a "stateless" society, Rothbard cites
1,000 years of ancient Celtic Ireland.[13]

Unfortunately, there is no modern example of a stateless, completely libertarian society, and it seems unlikely that libertarian
ideals can ever be fully realized, any more than other ideals. Nonetheless, discussions of ideal types (like the "free market" or the
"state of nature") have long been used to clarify philosophical
principles that may then be applied to the real world. It is not
necessary to resolve here the question of whether a more fully
libertarian society should take the form of a "minimal state" or
whether it ever could or should be completely "stateless." Either
way, attempts to limit the scope of government could include provisions for the existence of relatively autonomous private prisons.[14]

Libertarian Principles of Crime and Punishment

To define criminal punishment as the exclusive prerogative of the
state is to accept a collectivistic (whether statist or communitarian)

concept of crime and punishment. In the collectivist view, all crimes, whatever individual victims they may have, are also crimes against some collectivity (the community, society, the state). Thus, crimes are prosecuted, and punishment imposed, primarily on behalf of the collectivity. Individual victims may even be excluded from the process entirely, unless their testimony is crucial, in which case victims may be compelled to testify, along with other witnesses.

Because it is designed to serve the collectivity, the criminal justice system must be driven and directed primarily by representatives of the collectivity. However, to the extent that such issues as delegation, representation, and accountability are resolved (as I have argued in preceding chapters they can be), a public/private contract for the operation of a prison or jail is not incompatible with the collectivistic view of crime and punishment. In contrast, the idea of autonomous private prisons requires an individualistic concept of crime and punishment.

From an individualistic and libertarian perspective, crime is seen as a violation of a particular individual's rights. These rights are natural, not to be created or removed at will by society. If a system is created to protect these rights, it is still individuals who must move that system. Whether this means that only victims have a right to punish criminals is a matter of debate.

Some libertarians believe that punishment is the exclusive right of victims. For example, Rothbard asserts:

> In the libertarian society, there are only two parties to a dispute or action at law: the victim, or plaintiff, and the alleged criminal, or defendant. It is the plaintiff that presses charges in the courts against the wrongdoer. In a libertarian world, there would be no crimes against an ill-defined "society," and therefore no such person as a "district attorney" who decides on a charge and then presses those charges against an alleged criminal.[15]

Murder poses a special problem for libertarians which they attempt to resolve by referring to the victim "or his heirs." But this just creates more problems. If a murder victim dies intestate, who—if anyone—would have the right to punish the murderer?[16]

The phrase "or his heirs" implies that the right to punish is transferable. If so, why should it be transferable only to heirs? Rothbard allows that a criminal might be permitted to buy his way out of punishment.[17] Presumably, then, a victim could sell his right to punish to the highest bidder. Criminals would be protected from wealthy zealots (or sadists) by the principle of proportionality, which "imposes the maximum limit on punishment that may be inflicted before the punisher himself becomes a criminal aggressor."[18] Within this limit, punishment will be imposed only when there is some specific individual or group, beginning with the victim, that wants to see a criminal punished more than the offender is willing—or able—to escape punishment.[19]

Defining punishment as a transferable right raises many questions. The biggest problem with such a view is that it ignores the moral dimension of punishment. Even if we accept the idea that all rights (including the right to our own bodies and lives) are ultimately property rights, this does not mean that every violation of rights should be reduced to economic terms. A crime is not just a harm, which arguably can be translated into an economic cost. It is also a wrong, which cannot be so reduced.

One central thrust of libertarianism is its emphasis on individual rights. Libertarian concepts of justice are normative and rights-based, not utilitarian. It is contrary to libertarian principles to treat individuals coercively as the involuntary means to some end. A libertarian justification of punishment must therefore be a nonutilitarian one.

The Justification of Punishment in Libertarian Society

Since the publication of John Rawls's *A Theory of Justice* (1971) and Robert Nozick's *Anarchy, State and Utopia* (1974), there has been a greatly increased emphasis on individual rights among philosophers and political theorists, with a corresponding decline in the influence of utilitarianism.[20] Utilitarian theories of criminal justice are collectivistic, viewing society as the victim of all criminal acts and justifying coercive treatment of offenders as the means to a societal end. The end is crime control and the means include rehabilitation, deterrence, and incapacitation. Rights-based theories of criminal justice, in contrast, place the rights of individuals above the interests of social groups and emphasize restitution or retribution rather than crime control as the purpose of criminal sanctions.[21]

Andrew von Hirsch's *Doing Justice*, which appeared soon after the books by Rawls and Nozick, reflected a shift among criminologists and penologists away from utilitarian conceptions of criminal justice.[22] *Doing Justice* sets forth what has come to be called the "justice model." Following Kant, this model calls for penal sanctions on moral grounds, as the "just deserts" for criminally blameworthy conduct.[23]

Deterrence, incapacitation, and rehabilitation as purposes of imprisonment are contrary to libertarian precepts. First, they are utilitarian strategies that place a premium on collective welfare, rather than individual rights.[24] Second, they are not merely reactive to past behavior, but aim primarily at molding future conduct. The offender is coerced not because of what he has done but because of what he (or others!) might do. This has the effect, if not the intent, of a rationalization for the initiation of force.

Punishment cannot be justified by a libertarian on the grounds that it is *also* deserved; only on the grounds that it *is* deserved. Otherwise, the justification is either superfluous or it involves a degree of coercion beyond that which is called for by considerations of justice alone. In the latter case, it is an attempt to justify the initiation of force, which violates a fundamental axiom of libertarianism.

Rights, Duties, and Punishment

How does a nonutilitarian, retributive view of punishment fit in with libertarian principles of individual rights?

To believe in rights is to believe in duties. Those are alternative statements of the same concept. To believe in duties is to accept, implicitly but of logical necessity, the corollary of punishment. When we say that people have a duty to refrain from violating the rights of others, we are saying that there must be some negative sanction if they fail to meet that duty. Duties are given meaning by the consequences that attach to their nonfulfillment. The meaning of a duty, like that of any other norm, must be socially constructed through the attachment of sanctions to behavior. A norm (a rule, a law, a duty, a right) that had no sanction attached to its violation would be empty and without meaning.

Recognizing that rights and duties are socially constructed norms, libertarians understand the importance of sanctions in the creation and maintenance of such norms.[25] Thus, the maintenance of the basic libertarian proscription against force and fraud requires that acts of force and fraud be punished. The recognition that rights must be socially defined through punishments, however, does not mean that these sanctions may only be imposed by collectivities, or in the name of the collectivity.

The belief that a particular social rule is based on a natural right—or should be treated in this fashion—implies that every individual has a right to participate in the social definition and maintenance of that rule. This means that every individual can help enforce the rule and punish those who violate it, since punishment is essential to the definition and preservation of the rule. Thus, the natural right of individuals to be free from force and fraud gives citizens license to punish acts of force and fraud.

Another way of expressing this idea is to say that sanctions serve to uphold values. Failure to reward ethical behavior and to punish misdeeds undermines the values of right and wrong. Persistent failure to punish theft, for example, would erode and eventually destroy the value we place on property rights.[26] Thus, legal sanctions are *integral* to legal norms and values. It is in this sense that we may say that punishment is necessary to preserve the "integrity" of the law.[27] This refers not just to integrity in the sense of probity, but also to integrity in the sense of completeness or unity.

The Sanction of Imprisonment in a Libertarian Society

Some libertarians argue for restitution as the only valid function of the criminal sanction. Randy Barnett and John Hagel believe that all the rights relevant to criminal justice can be divided without residue into two categories: victim's rights and offender's rights.[28] No third parties, including abstract third parties like society or the state, have rights in their scheme. Only the victim has a right to restitution and may use force against the offender for this, and only this, purpose. The offender, in turn, has a right to proportionality in the amount of force used against him for purposes of restitution. "In short, the criminal's rights pick up at the exact point that the victim's rights leave off." [29]

Other libertarians, however, reject a purely restitutionary view of criminal justice. Libertarian philosopher John Hospers, for example, objects that restitution, by itself, is morally deficient because it does not take desert into account.[30] Restitution rests on theories of strict liability, while retribution requires an understanding of the intent, and therefore of the culpability, of the offender. Richard Epstein, a law professor, cautions against combining criminal trials and civil actions into a criminal proceeding—of rolling up restitution and punishment into one ball. To do so, Epstein asserts, blurs important distinctions, confounds issues, and creates more problems than it solves.[31] Defining criminal justice in purely restitutionary terms ignores the important moral distinction between a crime and a tort. Restitution concentrates on repairing a harm (the essential element of a tort), not on punishing a wrong (the essential element of a crime). The wrong done by a crime extends beyond the harm done to the immediate victim. Without reifying "society" or "the state," it can be said that crimes threaten the conditions, and undermine the values, necessary for free and civil association among all individuals. A violation of the rights of one individual is thus in some measure a threat to the rights of all individuals. Failure to punish the violation will weaken and undermine the rights of all, and will erode the values that define those rights.

This is what gives others, besides the immediate victim, the right to punish criminals. It also explains why restitution, though it may be essential to some other types of justice, is not central to criminal justice. It is independent, just as the filing of a tort is independent of the prosecution of a crime. Let torts be used to compensate victims for harms. Punishment of crimes is still needed to uphold the values served by criminal justice.

Given a retributive theory of punishment, another question remains. Is there any special reason, consistent with libertarian principles, why it should take the form of imprisonment? In a libertarian society, the purpose of law is to enhance individual liberty and to secure the natural rights of individuals, provided they do not interfere with the rights of others. The function of government, under law, is to maintain the minimal conditions necessary for free and voluntary interaction among human beings. In broad terms, the law prohibits initiation of force or fraud; beyond that, it leaves people alone.

As libertarian philosopher J. Roger Lee points out, only one form of legitimate punishment follows directly from this emphasis on maintaining the conditions for free and voluntary association.[32] That punishment is imprisonment: the removal of the civil liberty of free association. While individual liberty is a natural right, the civil liberty of free association with others is not. Rather, it is a conditional privilege that must be earned by refraining from the introduction of force or fraud in our interactions with others. Imprisonment, in Lee's view, is justified as a withdrawal of this liberty from those who violate that minimal condition of civil association. It is permissible to remove this liberty from those who, by the use of force or fraud, limit the liberty of others. Lee notes that, while society may also require criminals to make restitution and to work off or pay for the cost of their confinement, those are not punishments. They are civil remedies, not criminal sanctions, even though they may be combined with the sanction of imprisonment.

A libertarian, or rights-based, jurisprudence, leading to a justification of imprisonment, can be summarized as follows:

1. Law is an expression, and a definition, of natural rights.
2. A crime is a willful and intentional violation of an individual's natural rights.
3. In response to crime, penal (punitive) sanctions are called for, to uphold the right that has been violated.
4. Imprisonment, the removal of the right to civil association, is an appropriate punishment for crime because it defines, expresses, and upholds the norms of civil association, which crime violates and undermines.

Having developed an argument that imprisonment would be justified as a sanction for crimes in a libertarian society, the question remains: what would a libertarian prison look like?

The Libertarian Prison

J. Roger Lee and Laurin Wollan, Jr., in an article that is both visionary and realistic, have described the rationale and general design for a libertarian prison. My discussion throughout this section relies heavily on their excellent article.[33] Lee and Wollan define a libertarian prison as "one which is itself based, in its workings, on such principles as freedom from coercion, maximization of autonomy, and individual enterprise." It may or may not be run by a business corporation. It is, however, conceived and organized along the lines of a "free market enterprise." [34]

The only official (governmental, societal) purpose of a libertarian prison is to suspend the civil privilege of free association in society at large.

> And that is the extent of the permissibility. Nothing more is sanctioned. It is not, for example, permissible to kill criminals, to torture them, to deny them avenues for sex or for other pleasures, to make them contemplate their evil ways, to retrain them, to mold them, etc. No sanction for any such behavior comes out of the fact that the criminal has breached the trust which is ordinarily placed in people. [35]

Because it is only the civil liberty of the *offender* that is suspended, others (for example, his family) would be free to visit, do business, or even to live with him inside the prison. With the crucial exception of those special restrictions required to maintain the sheer fact of imprisonment, prisoners would be subject to no regulations other than those that apply also to citizens on the outside.

Work is a fundamental human (and humanizing) activity. In a libertarian prison, inmates would have the right to work, and to earn as much as they can. This would not be "make work," but productive work filling real needs as identified by a free market. Inmates could be entrepreneurs, creating their own jobs and owning their own businesses, or they could work for others. This would neither reward crime nor take jobs away from noncriminals. Inmates would not simply be "given" jobs. They would compete for them or create them. Inmate income would derive from wealth created by their work, not from tax money.

Inmates would not be able to keep all the money they earned. Like all the rest of us, they would have bills to pay: for food, shelter, clothing, and so forth. These bills would not necessarily come from the government. Many costs would be privatized, by transferring activities from the public to the private sector.

One bill, however, would be special: for restitution. Restitution is consistent with libertarian principles, and a desirable goal, even though it is independent of the purpose of imprisonment. It can occur before, during, or after imprisonment, and it should occur; but it is not directly a penal matter.

Labor may be required in a libertarian prison both to make restitution and to pay for the cost of imprisonment. By their crimes, offenders obligate society to punish them. In declaring an act to be criminal, society makes a threat, or promise, to punish anyone who commits that act. Punishing criminals, then, is more a mater of society fulfilling an obligation than of offenders paying their debts.[36] It is not by committing a crime that offenders incur a debt to society, but by forcing society to punish them. Thus, they cannot pay their debts simply by being punished, because their punishment is itself an expense for which they are responsible. As the willful and blameworthy cause of an expense, an offender should be held responsible for the cost of that expense.

Notwithstanding the universal obligation to pay one's bills, convicts in a libertarian prison would not be forced to work through physical coercion (violence or threat thereof). They would not be enslaved, indentured, nor leased like chattel. Offenders with (legally acquired) wealth or independent means could support themselves and make restitution without working, if they chose to. Those who either refused or were unable to support themselves, and had no wealth to be garnisheed for this purpose, would meet the same fate as those in a similar position on the outside.[37]

Crimes committed inside prison would be punished by new prosecution, thereby adding to the sentence, as is already the case. In most current prisons, however, the longer the sentence the weaker any possible disincentive to crime inside prison. The limiting case (in a state without capital punishment) is the "lifer," whose punishment cannot be increased. In a prison with an internal economy, on the other hand, the longer an inmate's sentence, the greater his stake in the stability of his local socioeconomic system. While sentence time cannot compound indefinitely, fines and restitution payments can.

The economy of a libertarian prison should flourish, like any free economy. Participation by inmates in such an economy gives them a vested interest in social order. The pursuit of voluntary cooperative exchanges in prison may or may not have long-term rehabilitative effects on inmates, but just as important would be the institutional effect. In a laissez-faire prison the source of inmate power would shift toward an economic basis and away from brute force and intimidation. This new informal mechanism of control would be less in conflict with the formal mechanisms, thus easing the task of governance.

Entitlements of Condition in Libertarian Prisons

Libertarian prisons would help clarify many of the moral dilemmas of imprisonment. One of these is the problem of special entitlement of prisoners to benefits that are not legally guaranteed to citizens on the outside. A government that believes in rehabilitation and in humane treatment may require that prisoners be provided with free counseling, job training, recreation facilities and programs, good food, comfortable climate control, clean clothes and linen, health care including medical, dental, and psychiatric treatment, prescription drugs and eyeglasses, and a safe, clean, and sanitary environment. These and other benefits may be required by law, administrative policy, or court order. A court order in New Mexico even mandates that prisoners be given free tobacco. Most citizens outside of prison are not legally entitled to receive benefits like these without charge. Not even the basic necessities of life such as food, clothing, shelter, and emergency medical care are universal entitlements in our society. Why should they routinely be provided for prisoners?

The answer, which is quite cogent in a nonlibertarian prison, is that prisoners are not free to fend for themselves. If we deprive prisoners of this freedom, we are thereupon obligated to provide for them—and we must debate endlessly the question of what, and how much, we must provide. In a libertarian prison, prisoners would not be deprived of either the opportunity or the obligation to earn things for themselves. Of course, the opportunities might not be as great as they are on the outside, so perhaps the obligation ought to be relaxed somewhat also.

When we assume coercive custody of convicted offenders, we must also accept some responsibility for their welfare. However, this responsibility does not have to extend to more than the basic necessities for survival: food, clothing, shelter, and emergency medical care. Beyond that, neither the courts nor other branches of government should impose either a floor or a ceiling on the living conditions that prisoners are able to create for themselves. Considerable inequality of conditions would no doubt result, but equality of condition is not a goal of libertarian society. Convicts in a libertarian prison would have to obey rules, and those rules should be applied and enforced equally, but within those parameters prisoners should be as free as possible to achieve the varying, and therefore unequal, lifestyles they would be able to pursue on the outside.

Contemporary Precursors to Libertarian Prisons

The libertarian prison envisioned by Lee and Wollan may seem like a remote prospect, at least in pure form. It is not entirely fanciful, however. Apparently unknown to Lee and Wollan, in 1973 John Price, an anthropology professor, published an article titled "Political Enterprise in a Prison: The Free Market Economy of La Mesa Penitenciaria." [38] That prison, in Mexico, matched Lee and Wollan's ideal type description of a libertarian prison in a remarkable number of particulars. The following is from Price's abstract:

> Conjugal visits by the prisoner's spouse, as well as long and very open family visits, are regularly permitted. In these contacts quantities of food, clothing, and money are allowed to be given to the prisoners. A market system then develops out of the barter of these goods, the purchase of bedding and special sleeping quarters, and the operation of stores, restaurants, and small manufacturing firms. The resulting prison society is thus similar to the social realities outside the prison, and it draws the inmates into daily economic decisions. . . . While La Mesa Penitenciaria has very serious problems, such as its heroin trade, for most of its inmates it is a humane prison. [39]

For a faint approximation of a libertarian prison in this country, consider a short period in the recent history of the Maine State Prison (MSP). [40] For about 40 years, this maximum security prison at Thomaston has allowed inmates to produce wooden craft items and novelties that are sold at a store run by the prison on nearby U.S. Route 1, a major tourist thoroughfare. For many years, the

crafts trade was limited and subsidiary to a state-run industry program that produced goods for state use.[41]

In 1976, a new warden was hired who instituted changes that
allowed the inmates greater economic liberty. As a result, Maine's
novelty sales program blossomed rapidly into what was undoubt-
edly the most economically successful inmate crafts program in the
country. What the new warden did was to appoint a supervisory
novelty committee, composed predominantly of inmates, and to
significantly raise the upper limits on value, variety, and volume
of output allowed per inmate. The revenue cap, for example, went
from $5,000 a year in 1976 to $15,000 in 1978.[42] To circumvent
even these limits, more enterprising businessmen took on partners,
buying their quotas in exchange for a share of the profits.[43]

In contrast to most prison industry programs, which employ only
a small fraction of the population,[44] the crafts industry at MSP, at
its peak, involved from half to three-quarters of the inmates. In
1979, the prison store had gross sales of over half a million dollars.[45]
To keep the store open longer hours in the summer, inmates themselves paid the overtime salaries of the state-employed store
managers. Some inmates were said to earn over $38,000 a year,
with claims as high as $100,000 for the most successful "novelty
kings." [46]

An unusual aspect of the MSP program was that it allowed
inmates to form businesses and employ other inmates. This pro-
moted labor specialization, managerial skills, and productivity.
The inmate economy was also allowed to have a legal and transferable currency, in the form of canteen coupons.[47] This currency
allowed the development of a secondary economy within the
prison, offering such services as a barbershop, laundry, and television rentals.

The novelty committee levied a tax on sales at the prison store.
The revenue was used to buy lounge furniture, athletic equipment,
movie rentals, and other amenities that the state could not or would
not provide.[48] The committee also issued patents for new product
patterns designed by inmates. Although inmates were restricted
in the number of patents that they could own personally, these
were effectively transferable property rights. When patent holders
left prison, they would sell their patterns to others.[49] One inmate
controlled 50 patterns, only 10 of which could be in his own name.[50]

In short, what developed at the Maine State Prison was not just an inmate work program, but an environment that allowed prisoners to become entrepreneurs.

Unfortunately, the laissez-faire atmosphere at the prison may have extended beyond purely economic matters. In 1980, four years into this experiment in inmate capitalism, a team of outside experts called in by the Bureau of Corrections concluded that the staff had lost control of the prison to the convicts, and recommended a complete lockdown. The warden resigned rather than follow this directive, but the Director of Corrections stepped in and confined all prisoners to their cells for two and a half months. Following a thorough search of the prison, 50 dump-truck loads of materials and possessions were confiscated and hauled away. Knives and tools useable as weapons were found, but no guns or ammunition.[51]

Following the lockdown, the prison was reorganized and many new restrictions were placed on the crafts industry. The cap on gross income was cut from $15,000 to $8,000, canteen coupons were declared nontransferable, and procedural restrictions were placed on inter-inmate employment.[52] Some commentators view the lockdown and its aftermath as an overreaction. For example, Jeffrey Shedd asserts that:

> In the final analysis, Maine State Prison was locked down because it didn't fit into the correctional experts' picture of prison life. [This is a picture in which] there is no place for ambitious and talented individuals finding a way around bureaucratic restrictions on their activities, for prison workers' wages being determined other than by administrative fiat, for some inmates benefitting from others' desires for haircuts, laundry services, loans, or anything else. In short, the MSP lockdown occurred, not because authorities did not have control over the prison, but because they did not have control over the *economic lives* of the inmates.[53]

This statement may be too strong. Even if MSP did not have a record of violence as bad as many other maximum security prisons, there was ample and independent substantiation of the investigators' charge that inmates had gained, and staff had lost, too much power. Whether loss of control by management can be blamed on having a strong and relatively unrestricted inmate economy, however, is another matter.

Inmate economies of one sort or another are inescapable.[54] If legitimate occupations and legal currency are not available, hustling and illegal trafficking in goods and services (drugs, alcohol, cigarettes, food, protection, sex, gambling, and so on) will abound. Some of the most out-of-control prisons, with severe problems of mismanagement, staff corruption, and domination of some inmates by others, have been prisons with little or no inmate industry.[55]

In 1980, the crafts program at the State Prison of Southern Michigan at Jackson, with 685 inmates participating, sold only $5,887 worth of goods at its prison store, about one-tenth the level of sales the previous year at Maine State Prison (where the total population was only about 360).[56] The crafts program at Southern Michigan is tightly controlled. No inmate can produce more than one type of item at a time, or order more than a fixed amount of raw materials a month, or have more than $200 worth of goods for sale in the prison store at one time. The limit on ordering materials means that no inmate may profit by acting as a wholesaler to other inmates. And no inmate may employ any other inmate.

But controlling the economy at the State Prison of Southern Michigan has not controlled violence. In 1981, there was a major riot there. A comparison of the Michigan prison system with that of Texas, which has long had a self-sustaining (agricultural) prison industry, found much lower rates of disorder in the latter.[57] Recently, the Michigan prison system was the subject of a federal investigation of drug-related corruption among guards, with charges that officials may have protected inmate crime rings. Inmates were reported to be smuggling drugs and guns into prisons, where a black market in drugs was thriving. A deputy warden at Jackson State Prison was arrested on charges of accepting a $10,000 bribe from a leader of the drug ring. One inmate testified that 85 to 90 percent of inmates at the prison sold marijuana. Another said he made $5,000 a month dealing dope and another boasted of earning $15,000 a week from the trade.[58]

In any prison, some inmates will exercise power over other inmates. When a major source of this power comes from legitimate economic activities, it is easier for authorities to supervise and to influence its exercise. Moreover, those whose power comes from legal activities and is economic rather than violence-based will have a greater stake in maintaining stability and a peaceful order. Thus, there is no reason why the positive features of a self-sustaining inmate economy need to be sacrificed in the name of control. Inmate self-employment, employment by other inmates, legal currency, and high degrees of economic freedom and opportunity are not incompatible with good prison management. While restrictions on the ownership or location of certain kinds of tools, raw materials, or products does make sense in terms of safety and security, income and production limits do not.

The experiment in inmate capitalism at the Maine State Prison was a far cry from the ideal of a libertarian prison. Further, any attempt to create a libertarian environment inside prisons today would probably encounter problems at least a great as those that occurred at MSP. The experience at Maine, however, does at least suggest the possibility of constructing a relatively free economy even in an otherwise very unfree environment.

Contracting Revisited: A (Comparatively) Modest Proposal

I do not know if a completely libertarian society, with autonomous, self-supporting, and completely private prisons will ever be possible, though I do think the idea is philosophically defensible. What I have sketched here, admittedly superficially, is more of a vision than a currently feasible proposal. Next to that vision, however, the *contracting* of prisons and jails (as opposed to their complete privatization) seems downright traditional and nowhere near as radical a departure from current practices as critics seem to believe. Contracting is a reform, not a revolution, and as such, it deserves at least to be given a try.

Contractual operation of correctional facilities offers many potential benefits. I will recount only a few of the more salient ones here.

1.   Perhaps the greatest advantage of contracting in any context is that it makes the true costs of a service highly visible, allowing them to be analyzed, compared, and minimized. This consequence of contracting can benefit even jurisdictions that do not themselves contract. They may observe the process elsewhere, or carefully consider contracting some of their own operations but decide

against it. Either way, contracting provides competitive price and product information that government can use to compare and evaluate its own operations, and see if they could be made more efficient. By revealing otherwise hidden costs, contracting enables legislators and taxpayers to see where money is going and to decide more rationally whether a program ought to be continued, expanded, revamped, or discarded.

2. Where a jurisdiction does choose to privatize some of its facilities, contracting may enable new prisons to be financed, sited, and constructed more quickly and cheaply than is possible under customary procedures for governmental construction. While this process typically takes government two to five years, it has generally required just six months to a year for private prisons. Further, private firms are more apt to design for efficient operation, carrying these savings forward into future years.

3. In part because of its greater speed, but also because of greater freedom in matters ranging from personnel to purchasing, contracting allows greater flexibility, which promotes innovation, experimentation, and other changes in programs, including expansion, contraction, and termination. Government can take programmatic risks through a contractor that it might avoid itself, for fear that the changes could not easily be undone.

4. Contracting adds new expertise and specialized skills. This may be particularly true for smaller counties and cities. Businesses commonly hire outside consultants to help them reorganize and develop new programs. In a similar fashion, larger correctional contractors can use their most experienced staff from the central office to establish a new facility under contract, then turn it over to a more permanent local staff.[59] The experience and resources of the central office, which may exceed those of a smaller city or county by far, remain available throughout the life of the contract.

5. Contracting reduces the tendency toward bureaucratic self-perpetuation and helps limit the size of government. While it is true that contractors have a vested interest in encouraging greater government spending on that which they provide, this impetus toward growth may be easier to control than is the government's own seemingly insatiable craving for internal expansion.

6. Contracting increases accountability because market mechanisms of control are added to those of the political process. In

the electoral competitions that underlie political accountability, decisions are made by a large number of voters, each of whom has only limited information and, with only a minuscule margin of influence, little incentive to gather more. In contracting, competitive bidders are motivated to supply relevant information to a small number of politically accountable decision-makers. If it is reasonable at all to suppose that a diffuse public can hold political actors accountable for their own actions and decisions, then it is even more reasonable to suppose that those actors in turn, as a small and well-informed decision-making body, can hold contractors accountable for theirs.

7.   Private prisons will tend to be highly visible, in contrast to state prisons which, at least historically, have been ignored by the public and given (until recently) "hands-off" treatment by the courts. Though the attitude may be ill-informed, there does seem to be greater public suspicion toward those who would wield power "for profit" than toward those who would wield it for other reasons, or for its own sake. Vigilance over those who run prisons is always a gain, though the standards of supervision, and of performance, ought to be the same for both public and private actors.

8.   Contracting promotes the development and use of objective performance measures. When the government spends taxpayers' money to provide services, it has little natural incentive to measure objectively the quality of its own performance. In contrast, it is in the nature of a contract to specify service requirements, and to some extent broader goals as well. All correctional contracts include provisions for monitoring and have language that at least implies the need for some measurement of performance. Unfortunately, we do not have validated, reliable, and standard measures of performance for the operation of prisons, but there has been a lot more discussion of the need for them in connection with private prisons than there was when the government's monopoly was unquestioned. Accreditation by the American Correctional Association may not be fully satisfactory as a measure of performance, but the fact that it is often required for contracted prisons and jails, while remaining rare among those run by the government,[60] suggests that contracting does encourage the measurement of performance.

9.   By creating an alternative, contracting encourages compar-

ative evaluations; this raises standards for the government as well as for private contractors. In spite of the lack of objective measures, discussed above, there has always been plenty of criticism of government performance in running prisons and jails. There has not, however, been very effective public pressure for reform. Most criticism of government corrections has been based on absolute rather than relative standards. "Good enough for government work" is an attitude that is tolerated by those who ultimately pay for government work, but only when they can see no realistic alternative. If the people standing in line at the Department of Motor Vehicles had a clear vision of a commercial alternative, public pressures for reform might be as strong in this area as they are, say, for the postal system. By offering the public a visible choice, privatization may be a force for correctional reform.

10. Where reform is greatly needed, but public management has become entrenched and resistant to change, contracting can provide a surgical solution. It is certainly easier to replace a bad contractor with a better one than to replace an entire government agency or operation with another governmental one. The replacement of a government operation with a private one may fall somewhere in between. Where it becomes necessary or desirable to thoroughly reform a particular prison, or even a small system, contracting can produce wholesale and sudden change.

Beyond the advantages that I recap above, I have presented in this book many other arguments that can be made in favor of the private operation of prisons, jails, and other correctional or confinement facilities, and I have attempted to answer all the objections and criticisms of which I am aware. In the end, however, the best case for private prisons does not rest on a priori claims that they will be inevitably or necessarily superior. The strongest case rests simply on a plea for open-minded comparison, and for evaluation against real alternatives rather than against absolute and ideal standards. The private players ask only for a chance to prove themselves in competition on a level field. We should ask no less of the government's team.

Notes

INTRODUCTION

1. E. S. Savas, *Privatizing the Public Sector: How to Shrink Government* (Chatham, NJ: Chatham House Publishers, 1982), p. 1.

2. Seymour Martin Lipset and William Schneider, *The Confidence Gap: Business, Labor, and Government in the Public Mind* (New York: Free Press, 1983).

3. Ronald A. Cass, "Privatization: Politics, Law and Theory," *Marquette Law Review* 71(1988): 449–523, at 499.

CHAPTER 1

1. This section draws heavily on Charles H. Logan and Sharla P. Rausch, "Punish and Profit: The Emergence of Private Enterprise Prisons," *Justice Quarterly* 2 (1985): 303–305. Adapted with permission of the Academy of Criminal Justice Sciences.

2. U.S. Department of Justice, *Prisoners in 1987. Bulletin* (Washington, DC: Bureau of Justice Statistics, April 1988).

3. U.S. Department of Justice, *Prisoners in 1983. Bulletin* (Washington, DC: Bureau of Justice Statistics, 1984).

4. Roy H. Reynolds [Note], "The Role of Special Masters in Federal Judicial Supervision of State Prisons: The Need for Limitations," *American Criminal Law Review* 26 (Fall 1988): 491–511, at 491 (citing information from the ACLU's National Prison Project).

5. If construction is paid for by a 20-year bond at 10 percent interest, the real cost will triple the original figure. To these interest costs must be

added an allowance for overruns. In a survey of 15 states, cost overruns on prison construction averaged 39 percent above the initial budget. Overruns would include the effects of inflation during the time from bidding to completion; hidden costs would include such things as architect and agency fees, construction supervision, equipment, and insurance. After calculating these costs, a proposed Connecticut prison reported to cost $50,000 per bed would actually have cost $62,000 per bed, almost 25 percent more. See Bruce Cory and Stephern Gettinger, *Time to Build? The Realities of Prison Construction* (New York: Edna McConnell Clark Foundation, 1984), p. 16.

6. Gail Funke, "Who's Buried in Grant's Tomb? Economics and Corrections for the Eighties and Beyond" (Alexandria, VA: Institute for Economic and Policy Studies, 1983), p. 3.

7. Edwin W. Zedlewski, "The Economics of Disincarceration," *National Institute of Justice Research in Brief* (Washington, DC: Department of Justice, March 1984).

8. U.S. Department of Justice, *Report to the Nation on Crime and Justice: The Data* (Washington, DC: Bureau of Justice Statistics, 1983), p. 93.

9. Cory and Gettinger, *Time to Build?*, p. 17.

10. Rex Reed and David W. Holm, "The Monopoly Economics of Juvenile Custody: Could Private Competition Keep Costs Down?" *Independence Issue Paper* No. 1588 (July 29, 1988):1.

11. U.S. Department of Justice, *BJS Data Report, 1988.* (Washington, DC: Bureau of Justice Statistics, April 1989).

12. *Tennessee Journal* 14, No.47 (November 21, 1988):2–3.

13. Robert Poole makes several points in rebuttal to the broad characterization of contracting out as "destroying jobs." First, it is in the interest of labor, as well as taxpayers and consumers, that workers be employed as efficiently as possible. Second, a contract can be made to specify that displaced government workers be given first preference for contracted jobs. This is the federal government's official policy on contracting out. Third, both government and nongovernment workers are given a stake in higher productivity by the existence of competing firms; they may even want to form their own firms through employee stock ownership plans. This is the case with at least one of the private prison contractors, Behavioral Systems Southwest. Finally, it should be remembered that the purpose of both government agencies and private contractors is not to provide jobs but to provide services. See Robert W. Poole, Jr., "Objections to Privatization," *Policy Review* 24 (1983): 105–119.

14. Ralph de Toledano, *Let Our Cities Burn* (New Rochelle, NY: Arlington House, 1975), p. 49.

15. Warren I. Cikins, "Privatization of the American Prison System: An Idea Whose Time Has Come?" *Notre Dame Journal of Law, Ethics and Public Policy* 2 (1986): 455.

16. Todd R. Clear and George F. Cole, *American Corrections* (Monterey, CA: Brooks/Cole, 1986), p. 306.

17. Kevin Krajick, "Prisons for Profit: The Private Alternative," *State Legislatures* 10 (1984): 14.

18. American Civil Liberties Union, *Policy Guide*, Policy #243, Board Minutes, April 12–13, 1986.

19. Ira P. Robbins, "Privatization of Corrections: Defining the Issues," *Judicature* 69 (1986): 326. The primary constitutional issue referred to in the ABA resolution is the question of private delegation of state authority. Ironically, the ABA, which as a private organization accredits law schools and thereby determines who can sit for bar exams, has survived repeated attempts to challenge this private delegation of the state's licensing authority to the ABA.

20. Martin Tolchin, "Bar Group Urges Halt in Use of Privately Run Jails," *New York Times*, February 12, 1986.

21. Testimony of Thomas Beasley, Chairman, Corrections Corporation of America, to President's Commission on Privatization, Washington, DC, December 22, 1987.

CHAPTER 2

1. Though the term "corrections" became standard during the heyday of rehabilitation, it is still used even by those who regard punishment as the primary purpose of criminal sanctions. "Penal" facility is likewise generic although more closely associated with a punitive orientation. Some would object to calling pretrial detention or juvenile court placements "penal" and therefore "prisons" because officially they are not punitive. However, in this book, such distinctions will not often be important and the term "prison" will frequently include jails and secure juvenile facilities.

2. Any combination of the elements—private ownership, private operation, private management—is possible. There has even been one private company that managed a jail owned by the county and staffed by county employees, thus combining governmental operation and ownership with private management.

3. U.S. Department of Justice, *Children in Custody. 1982/83 Census*

of Juvenile Detention and Correctional Facilities (Washington, DC: Bureau of Justice Statistic, September 1986), p. 3.

4. Michael A. Kroll, "Prisons for Profit," *Progressive*, September 1984, p. 22.

5. The community-based contractors are all nonprofit agencies, by state regulation. So far, the secure facility contractors have also been nonprofit, but "DYS officials assert . . . that there would be little opposition to allowing for-profit contractors." Joan Mullen, Kent John Chabotar, and Deborah M. Carrow, *The Privatization of Corrections* (Washington, DC: National Institute of Justice, February 1985), p. 62.

6. U.S. Department of Justice, *Children in Custody 1982/83 Census*.

7. Unpublished figures supplied by the Bureau of Justice Statistics for 1985 indicate 34,080 juveniles being held in 1,996 private institutions.

8. U.S. Department of Justice, *Children in Custody 1982/83 Census*.

9. U.S. Department of Justice, *Children in Custody: Advance Report on the 1982 Census of Private Juvenile Facilities, including Comparisons with Public Facilities* (Washington, DC: Bureau of Justice Statistics, March 1984).

10. Data from handwritten and unpublished tables at BJS.

11. Mullen et al, *Privatization*, pp. 56–58.

12. Kevin Krajick, "Prisons for Profit: The Private Alternative," *State Legislatures* 10 (1984): 10.

13. Matthew J. Bronick, "The Federal Bureau of Prisons' Experience with Privatization" (Washington, DC: Federal Bureau of Prisons, June 1989), Tables 3 and 4.

14. U.S. Department of Justice, *Children in Custody 1982/83 Census*.

15. All data for this paragraph are from handwritten and unpublished tables at BJS.

16. Kevin Krajick, "Punishment for Profit," *Across the Board* (1984): 23.

17. James O. Finckenauer, *Juvenile Delinquency and Corrections: The Gap Between Theory and Practice* (Orlando, FL: Academic Press, 1984), p. 182.

18. Ibid., p. 178.

19. Krajick, "Punishment for Profit," p. 25.

20. Mullen et al., *Privatization*, p. 65.

21. Ibid., pp. 62–63.

22. Krajick, "Punishment for Profit."

23. Mullen et al, *Privatization*, p. 65.

24. Phone conversation with William R. Key, Juvenile Court, Memphis, July 6, 1987.

25. *Los Angeles Times* May 29, 1986.

26. Ibid.

27. *San Jose Mercury News*, March 15, 1985.

28. Behavioral Systems Southwest, "Prospectus" (Pomona, CA: Behavioral Systems Southwest,1985).

29. *Money*, May 1986, p. 32.

30. Mullen et al., *Privatization*, p. 67.

31. Behavioral Systems Southwest, "Prospectus."

32. Mullen et al., *Privatization*, p. 67.

33. Ibid.

34. Peter Young, *The Prison Cell* (London: Adam Smith Institute, p. 8.

35. *Philadelphia Inquirer*, April 4, 1984.

36. *Money*, May 1986: 32.

37. Corrections Corporation of America press release, August 29, 1989.

38. Krajick, "Prisons for Profit," p. 11.

39. Corrections Corporation of America, "Second Quarter and Six Month Earnings Announced," July 25, 1989.

40. Corrections Corporation of America, *Annual Report 1986* (Nashville, TN: Corrections Corporation of America, 1986), p. 24.

41. *Hartford Courant*, January 3, 1984.

42. T. Don Hutto and G. E. Vick, "Designing the Private Correctional Facility," *Corrections Today*, April 1984, p. 85.

43. Mullen et al., *Privatization*, p. 68.

44. Ibid., pp. 67–68.

45. National Criminal Justice Reference Service, "Privatization Program Search" (Rockville, MD: National Criminal Justice Reference Service, 1985, computer printout).

46. Conversation with Robert Schmidt, Immigration and Naturalization Service, May 21, 1987.

47. American Correctional Association, *Director of Juvenile and Adult Correctional Departments, Institutions, Agencies, and Paroling Authorities* (College Park, MD: American Correctional Association, 1987), p. 509.

48. Mullen et al., *Privatization*, pp. 68–69.

49. Commonwealth of Virginia, "Study of Correctional Privatization" (Richmond, VA: Secretary of Transportation and Public Safety, 1986), pp. 66, 71; *Chicago Tribune*, May 19, 1985.

50. News release from Wackenhut, June 12, 1989.

51. Robert Schmidt, telephone interview, May 21, 1987.

52. Telephone interview with Bob Greene, compliance manager at Wackenhut Corrections Corporation, June 30, 1989. Information in the rest of this paragraph is from Bob Greene.

53. Actually, this facility, a former college, was opened without any fences or armed guards, so its security at that point consisted mainly of supervision.

54. Another multi-security county jail was taken over by private management on October 1, 1985: the Butler County (Pennsylvania) Prison run by Buckingham Security Limited.

55. Bruce Cory, "From Rhetoric to Reality: Privatization Put to the Test," *Corrections Compendium*, May 1986, p. 11.

56. [Louisville] *Courier-Journal*, May 19, 1986.

57. Ibid.

58. Charles Ring, *Contracting for the Operation of Private Prisons: Pros and Cons* (College Park, MD: American Correctional Association, 1987), p. 33.

59. *Courier-Journal*, May 19, 1986.

60. Commonwealth of Virginia, "Correctional Privatization," pp. 57–58.

61. Commonwealth of Virginia, "Correctional Privatization," pp. 65, 80; *Courier-Journal*, May 19, 1986.

62. Ring, *Contracting*, p. 33.

63. Commonwealth of Virginia, "Correctional Privatization," p. 59.

64. Of these beds, 158 are kept available for prisoners of the U.S. Marshall.

65. As described earlier, Hidden Valley was previously under contract to the federal Bureau of Prisons as a training camp for Youth Corrections Act offenders. The state contract began the same year the federal contract ended. *Criminal Justice Newsletter*, June 16, 1986.

66. Ibid.

67. Site visit by author and interviews with county officials.

68. Cory, "Rhetoric to Reality," p. 13.

69. October 22, 1987, communication from David Myers, CCA Vice President, Facility Operations.

70. *New York Times*, May 21, 1985.

71. Samuel Jan Brakel, "Amended Proposal on 'Privatizing' Corrections," (American Bar Foundation, September 1986) p. 20.

72. Ibid., pp. 19–20.

73. National Criminal Justice Association, "Private Sector Involvement in Financing and Managing Correctional Facilities" (Washington, DC: National Criminal Justice Association, April 1987), p. 18.

74. The changes at Silverdale are in the following areas: security, medical services, recreation, classification, programs, case management, food services, maintenance, training and personnel, and chaplaincy. Brakel, "Amended Proposal," p. 16.

75. National Criminal Justice Association, "Private Sector Involvement," p. 18.

76. Ibid., p. 18.

77. Communication from David Myers, CCA, October 22, 1987.

78. National Criminal Justice Association, "Private Sector Involvement," p. 18.

79. *The New Mexican*, June 21, 1986.

80. Commonwealth of Virginia, "Correctional Privatization," p. 72. Also, David Myers, communication, October 22, 1987.

81. Corrections Corporation of America, press release, June 26, 1987.

82. Corrections Corporation of America, *1986 Annual Report*, p. 24.

83. *New Mexican*, June 21, 1986.

84. New Mexico Stat. Ann. 33–3–1 through 33–3–29 (1984). A 1985 statue also authorizes contracting at the state level: New Mexico Stat. Ann. 33–3–17 (1985).

85. All information on the New Mexico statute presented in this paragraph was taken from Ring, *Contracting for the Operation of Private Prisons*, Chapter 3.

86. *St. Paul Pioneer Press*, March 3, 1985.

87. Ibid.

88. Ibid.

89. *New York Times*, February 17, 1985.

90. National Criminal Justice Association, Exhibit 2.

91. Buckingham Security Limited, *Private Prison Management: First Year Report 1985–1986, Butler County, Pennsylvania* (Lewisburg, PA: Buckingham Security Ltd., 1986), p. 4.

92. *Hartford Courant*, April 1, 1984.

93. Commonwealth of Virginia, "Correctional Privatization," p. 73.

94. Buckingham Security Limited, *Private Prison Mangement*, p. 5.

95. National Criminal Justice Association, "Private Sector Involvement," p. 20.

96. Buckingham Security Limited, *Private Prison Management*, p. 6.

97. Ibid., pp. 6–7.

98. Ibid., p. 6.

99. Ibid., p. 3.

100. Ibid., p. 1.

101. Ibid., p. 2.

102. Phone conversations on: April 11, 1988, with Joseph Fenton, then at Buckingham Security; May 12, 1989, with Robert Thompson, Chairman of Butler County Commission; May 12, 1989, with Rick Jalotty, then Warden of Butler County Prison; May 12, 1989 with Charles Fenton, formerly warden of the prison under Buckingham. All of these sources

described the nonrenewal issue as "very political." Several sources reported that the union shop steward, a leader of the opposition to Buckingham, was a constant source of difficulty while working as a counselor under Buckingham's administration. When Buckingham eventually fired him, the incoming county commissioners created a new payroll position for him as "liaison" between the jail and the commission. After the contract expired, they made him Deputy Warden.

CHAPTER 3

1. This section is adapted with permission from Charles H. Logan, "Proprietary Prisons," in Lynne Goodstein and Doris L. MacKenzie, eds., *The American Prison: Issues in Research and Policy* (New York: Plenum, 1989).

2. Sources used include the following: Judith C. Hackett, Harry P. Hatry, Robert B. Levinson, Joan Allen, Keon Chi, and Edward D. Feigenbaum, "Contracting for the Operation of Prisons and Jails," *National Institute of Justice Research in Brief* (Washington, DC: Department of Justice, June 1987); Robert B. Levinson, "Okeechobee: An Evaluation of Privatization in Corrections," *Prison Journal* 65 (1985): 75–94; Charles H. Logan and Sharla P. Rausch, "Punish and Profit: The Emergence of Private Enterprise Prisons," *Justice Quarterly* 2 (1985): 303–318; Charles H. Logan, "The Propriety of Proprietary Prisons," *Federal Probation* 51 (1987): 35–40; Joan Mullen, "Corrections and The Private Sector," *National Institute of Justice Research in Brief* (Washington, DC: Department of Justice, March 1985); Charles Ring, *Contracting for the Operation of Private Prisons: Pros and Cons* (College Park, MD: American Correctional Association, 1987); and E. S. Savas, *Privatizing the Public Sector: How to Shrink Government* (Chatham, NJ: Chatham House Publishers, 1987).

CHAPTER 4

1. Jan Elvin, "A Civil Liberties View of Private Prisons," *Prison Journal* 65 (1985): 51 (emphasis added).

2. American Civil Liberties Union, *Policy Guide*, Policy #243, Board Minutes, April 12–13, 1986.

3. Cited in *Newsweek*, May 7, 1984.

4. Cited in Kevin Krajick, "Punishment for Profit," *Across the Board* 21 (March 1984): 27.

5. John J. DiIulio, Jr., "What's Wrong with Private Prisons," *Public*

Interest No. 92 (Summer 1988): 66–83; John J. DiIulio, Jr., "Prisons, Profits and the Public Good: The Privatization of Corrections," *Research Bulletin No. 1* (Huntsville, TX: Sam Houston State University Criminal Justice Center, 1986). DiIulio and I differ in our beliefs about the propriety of proprietary prisons. However, on virtually every other aspect of prison management, I am in total agreement with his views, which are having a profound effect on today's and tomorrow's thinking about corrections. Even on the matter at hand, I feel compelled to express appreciation and respect, before I attack. Many other critics of private prisons simply proclaim them to be "wrong" for ideological, moral, or "philosophical" reasons, without accepting the philosopher's obligation to examine and defend that judgment, as DiIulio does.

6. DiIulio, "Prisons, Profits and the Public Good," pp. 4–5.

7. DiIulio, "What's Wrong with Private Prisons," p. 82.

8. Ibid., p. 81.

9. DiIulio, "Prisons, Profits and the Public Good."

10. DiIulio, "What's Wrong with Private Prisons," pp. 78–89.

11. Ibid., p. 83.

12. This and portions of three other sections of this chapter were originally published in Charles H. Logan, "The Propriety of Proprietary Prisons," *Federal Probation* 51 (September 1987): 35–40, and reprinted in Charles H. Logan, "Proprietary Prisons," in Lynne Goodstein and Doris L. MacKenzie, eds., *The American Prison: Issues in Research and Policy* (New York: Plenum, 1989). Adapted with permission.

13. Peter M. Blau, *Exchange and Power in Social Life* (New York: John Wiley & Sons, 1967).

14. Ira P. Robbins, "Privatization of Corrections: Defining the Issues," *Judicature* 69 (April–May 1986): 331.

15. DiIulio, "What's Wrong with Private Prisons," p. 79.

16. Michael Walzer, "At McPrison and Burglar King It's . . . Hold the Justice," *New Republic*, April 8, 1985, p. 11.

17. I am indebted to Douglas McDonald for suggesting this term.

18. David M. Lawrence, "Private Exercise of Governmental Power," *Indiana Law Journal* 61 (1986): 647–695, at pp. 666–667.

19. Laurin A. Wollan, "Privatization of Criminal Justice," in *Proceedings of the 29th Annual Southern Conference on Corrections* (Tallahassee FL: School of Criminology, Florida State University, 1984), pp. 111–124.

20. E. S. Savas, *Privatizing the Public Sector: How to Shrink Government* (Chatham, NJ: Chatham House Publishers, 1987), p. 60.

21. William C. Collins, "Privatization: Some Legal Considerations from a Neutral Perspective," in *Collins: Correctional Law, 1986* (Olympia, WA: William C. Collins, 1986), pp. 81–93, at p. 85.

22. Ibid., p. 87.

23. Lawrence, *"Private Exercise of Governmental Power,"* pp. 648–649.

24. Ibid., p. 662.

25. Ronald A. Cass, "Privatization: Politics, Law and Theory" *Marquette Law Review* 71 (1988): 449–523, at 501. Citations to *Ward v. Village of Monroeville*, 409 U.S. 57 (1972); *Tumey v. Ohio*, 273 U.S. 510 (1927).

26. David N. Wecht [Note], "Breaking the Code of Deference: Judicial Review of Private Prisons," *Yale Law Journal* 96 (1987): 815 837.

27. Ibid., p. 834, note 102 and accompanying text.

28. Peter Greenwood, "Private Prisons: Are They Worth a Try?" *California Lawyer*, July/August 1982, pp. 41–42. Greenwood asserts that these functions account for less than 5 percent of current prison administration budgets, so it would not burden the state to retain full responsibility for their administration.

29. Ira P. Robbins, *The Legal Dimensions of Private Incarceration* (Washington, DC: American Bar Association, 1988), p. 54.

30. Courts may not welcome being drawn directly into the initial decision process themselves, however. According to a news report, Corrections Corporation of America "drew the ire of Hamilton County's Sessions Court judges when the company took inmates downtown to be charged for what Judge Richard Holcomb said were instances the company should have handled internally." The court objected to being asked by CCA to settle internal disputes that state prisons handled by withdrawal of privileges and denial of good time and other credits after internal administrative hearings. See *Chattanooga Times*, August 12, 1986.

31. Timothy L. Fitzharris, *The Desirability of a Correctional Ombudsman* (Berkeley, CA: Institute of Governmental Studies, 1973).

32. Richard A. Waples, "The Privatization of Prisons: The Wrong Solution for a Real Problem," presented at "A Critical Look at Privatization in Corrections," a conference sponsored by the Indiana Department of Corrections, Indianapolis, IN, January 29, 1988.

33. John W. Palmer, *Constitutional Rights of Prisoners*, 2nd ed. (Cincinnati: Anderson Publishing Co., 1977), p. 24.

34. Robbins, *Legal Dimensions of Private Incarceration*, p. 65.

35. Ibid., p. 449.

36. Ibid., pp. 317–318.

37. Ibid., pp 64–65.

38. Todd R. Clear and George F. Cole, *American Corrections* (Monterey, CA: Brooks/Cole, 1986), p. 319.

39. Including the ACLU. See William A. Donohue, *The Politics of the American Civil Liberties Union* (New Brunswick, NJ: Transaction Books, 1985).

40. Francis A. Allen, *The Borderland of Criminal Justice* (Chicago:

University of Chicago Press, 1964); David J. Rothman, *The Discovery of the Asylum* (Boston: Little, Brown, 1971); American Friends Service Committee, *Struggle for Justice* (New York: Hill & Wang, 1971).

41. Willard Gaylin, Ira Glasser, Steven Marcus, and David J. Rothman, *Doing Good: The Limits of Benevolence* (New York: Pantheon Books, 1981).

42. Bruce L. Benson, "Guns for Protection, and Other Private Sector Responses to the Government's Failure to Control Crime," *Journal of Libertarian Studies* 8 (1986): 75–109, at pp. 85–86.

43. A recent note in the *Yale Law Journal* discusses at length the advantages of using financial incentives, like bonuses and fines, to monitor and control private prisons. The author argues that by properly structuring their incentives, profit-seeking prisons can be powerfully motivated to maximize not just their profit, but also their effectiveness, as measured by recidivism. See James Theodore Gentry [Note], "The Panopticon Revisited: The Problem of Monitoring Private Prisons," *Yale Law Journal* 96 (1986): 353–375.

44. David J. Rothman, *Conscience and Convenience: The Asylum and Its Alternatives in Progressive America* (Boston: Little, Brown, 1980).

CHAPTER 5

1. Joan Mullen, Kent John Chabotar, and Deborah M. Carrow, *The Privatization of Corrections* (Washington, DC: National Institute of Justice, February 1985), p. 37.

2. Ibid., pp. 40–41.

3. National Institute of Justice, "Corrections and the Private Sector: A National Forum." Proceedings of a meeting sponsored by the National Institute of Justice, February 20–22, 1985, Washington, DC, p. 6.

4. Susan M. Duffy, "Breaking into Jail: The Private Sector Starts to Build and Run Prisons," *Barron's*, May 14, 1984, pp. 20–22.

5. James B. Jabobs, *New Perspectives on Prisons and Imprisonment* (Ithaca, NY: Cornell University Press, 1983), pp. 115–132.

6. Ibid., p. 126.

7. Timothy J. Flanagan and Susan L. Caulfield, "Public Opinion and Prison Policy: A Review," *Prison Journal* 64 (Fall/Winter, 1984): 31–46, at p. 37.

8. Richard Crane, Vice President, Legal Affairs, Corrections Corporation of America, testimony, November 13, 1985, U.S. Congress. House Committee on the Judiciary. *Privatization of Corrections. Hearings before the Subcommittee on Courts, Civil Liberties, and the Administration*

of Justice, 99th Cong., 1st and 2nd sessions, November 13, 1985, and March 18, 1986, Serial No. 40 (Washington, DC: U.S. Government Printing Office, 1986), p. 29.

9. Kevin Krajick, "Punishment for Profit" *Across the Board* 21 (March 1984): 20–27.

10. Ibid.

11. Ibid.

12. *Newsweek*, May 7, 1984.

13. *Hartford Courant*, April 1, 1984.

14. T. Don Hutto and G. E. Vick, "Designing the Private Correctional Facility," *Corrections Today* (April 1984), p. 85.

15. Crane, *Privatization of Corrections*, p. 33.

16. Construction itself took 90 days. Telephone interview with Bob Greene, Wackenhut Corrections Corporation, June 30, 1989.

17. The facility is the Central Texas Parole Violator Facility in San Antonio, which opened in January 1989. Information from Wackenhut Corporation, June 14, 1989.

18. George Camp and Camille Camp, "The Real Cost of Corrections: A Research Report" (South Salem, NY: Criminal Justice Institute, April 1985), p. 3

19. At Hidden Valley Ranch, when run by Electric Communications, Inc., the cook earned $4 less per hour than he did in the same job at a nearby San Francisco County boys' ranch. The warden earned one-third less than he did as warden at the federal prison in Terre Haute, Indiana. *San Jose Mercury News*, March 15, 1985.

20. Charles Ring, *Contracting for the Operation of Private Prisons: Pros and Cons* (College Park, Md: American Correctional Association, 1987), pp. 28–29.

21. Erik Larson, "Captive Company," *Inc.*, June 1988, p. 90.

22. Corrections Corporation of America, Company Report, April 3, 1987.

23. Gail Funke, "The Economics of Prison Crowding," *Annals*, 478 (1985): 88.

24. E. S. Savas, *Privatizing the Public Sector: How to Shrink Government* (Chatham, NJ: Chatham House Publishers, 1982), p. 24.

25. All quotes in this paragraph are from American Correctional Association, *Private Sector Operation of a Correctional Institution* (Washington, DC: U.S. Department of Justice, National Institute of Corrections, April 1985), p. 48.

26. Buckingham Security Limited, *Private Prison Management: First Year Report 1985–1986, Butler County, Pennsylvania* (Lewisburg, PA: Buckingham Security Ltd., 1986), p. 3.

27. Ibid., p. 5, with update via personal communication from Charles Fenton, Warden.

28. Ibid., pp. 4–5.

29. John Hanrahan, "Why Public Services Should Stay Public," *Des Moines Register*, March 31, 1983.

30. Kevin Krajick, "Prisons for Profit: The Private Alternative," *State Legislatures* 10 (1984): 9–14; *Philadelphia Inquirer*, April 16, 1984.

31. John D. Donahue, *Prisons for Profit: Public Justice, Private Interests* (Washington, DC: Economic Policy Institute, 1988), p. 4.

32. John J. DiIulio, Jr., "Prisons, Profits and the Public Good: The Privatization of Corrections," *Research Bulletin No.1* (Huntsville, TX: Sam Houston State University Criminal Justice Center, 1986), p. 3.

33. Ibid. See also John J.DiIulio, Jr., *Governing Prisons: A Comparative Study of Correctional Management* (New York: Free Press, 1987).

34. Peter F. Drucker, *Management: Tasks, Responsibilities, Practices* (New York: Harper & Row,1973), pp. 141ff.

35. Robert W. Poole, Jr., "Objections to Privatization," *Policy Review* 24 (1983): 106.

36. This also means that they can fully satisfy no one. For a discussion of this as it pertains to prisons, see Charles R.Tittle, "Prisons and Rehabilitation: The Inevitability of Disfavor," *Social Problems* 21 (1974): 385–395.

37. Poole, "Objections to Privatization," p. 107.

38. William L. Megathlin, Dennis D. Murphy, and Robert E. Magnus, *Feasibility of the Establishment of Regional Prisons* (Washington, DC: U.S. Department of Justice, National Institute of Corrections, May 1984) pp. 45–50.

39. Erwin O. Smigel, "Public Attitudes Toward Stealing as Related to the Size of the Victim Organization," *American Sociological Review* (1956): 320–327.

40. Peter Samuel, "Battling the Budget—Gracefully," *Reason* 16 (1984): 36.

41. Ibid., p. 38.

42. See Chapter 1.

43. Harry W. Miley, Jr., "Cost Analysis of State vs. Private Correctional Facilities," (Columbia, SC: University of South Carolina), p. 3.

44. American Correctional Association, *Private Sector Operation of a Correctional Institution* p. 47.

45. Information supplied by Bill McGriff, Hamilton County Auditor, October 27,1987.

46. Samuel, "Battling the Budget," p. 38.

47. Camille G. Camp and George M. Camp, *Private Sector Involvement*

in Prison Services and Operations (Washington, DC: U.S. Department of Justice, National Institute of Corrections, February 1984.)

48. Ibid., p. 5
49. Ibid., p. 7.
50. Ibid., p. 10.
51. Ibid., p. 12.
52. Moreover, the Camps noted that even those agencies not reporting cost savings "concluded that the operational benefits more than outweighed the cost factor." Ibid., p. 10.
53. Camille Camp and George Camp, "Correctional Privatization in Perspective," *Prison Journal* 65 (1985): 24.
54. Samuel, "Battling the Budget," p. 39.
55. U.S. Office of Management and Budget, *Enhancing Governmental Production Through Competition: Targeting for Annual Savings of One Billion Dollars by 1988* (Washington, DC: Office of Federal Procurement Policy, March 1984).
56. Savas, *Privatizing the Public Sector*, pp. 89–117.
57. American Correctional Association, *Private Sector Operation of a Correctional Institution*, p. 69.
58. Ibid., p. 67.
59. Ibid., p. 52.
60. Ibid., p. 49.
61. Dozier added 17.5 staff positions in 1982–83 and 32 positions the year after that. During the transition year, Eckerd reduced the staff at Okeechobee and concentrated on upgrading the physical facilities. The next year, the Foundation contributed $236,000 of its own money and returned the staff to above its previous level. Ibid., pp. 15, 48.
62. Judith C. Hackett, Harry P. Hatry, Robert B. Levinson, Joan Allen, Keon Chi, and Edward D. Feigenbaum, *Issues in Contracting for the Private Operation of Prisons and Jails* (Washington, DC: Department of Justice, October 1987), p. 53.
63. Mullen et al., *Privatization of Corrections*, p. 65.
64. *Philadelphia Inquirer*, August 12, 1984.
65. Bruce Cory, "From Rhetoric to Reality: Privatization Put to the Test," *Corrections Compendium*, May 1986, p. 12.
66. [Louisville] *Courier-Journal*, February 16, 1986.
67. Hackett et al., *Issues in Contracting*, pp. 52–53.
68. Mullen et al., *Privatization of Corrections*, p. 68.
69. *Philadelphia Inquirer* April 16, 1984.
70. Crane, *Privatization of Corrections*, p. 29.
71. Samuel Greengard, "Making Crime Pay," *Barrister Magazine* 13 (1986): 15.

72. *Money*, May 1986, p. 32.

73. John W.Moore, "Paying for Punishment" *National Journal* No. 11 (March 14, 1987): 616.

74. *Santa Fe New Mexican*, June 21, 1986.

75. *New Mexican*, August 16, 1987.

76. *Florida Times-Union*, November 24, 1985.

77. Ibid. The news account does not explain the discrepancy between the 12 percent differential for the per diem figures and the 22 percent differential for total next year's costs. It may be that the per diem figures referred only to the current jail facility, while the total next year's costs included a Jail Annex, planned for construction.

78. Interview with John Hutt, Bay County Commissioner, February 25, 1987.

79. Larson, "Captive Company," p. 90.

80. The fee is $28 for work release inmates.

81. Hackett et al., *Issues in Contracting*, p. 53.

82. All figures are from the *Cleveland Plain Dealer*, October 1, 1984.

83. *Philadelphia Inquirer*, April 16, 1984.

84. Lee Kravitz, "Tough Times for Private Prisons," *Venture* (May 1986): 56; Buckingham Security Limited, *Private Prison Management*, p. 4

85. Pennsylvania Legislative Budget and Finance Committee, *Report on a Study of Issues Related to the Potential Operation of Private Prisons in Pennsylvania* (Harrisburg, PA: Pennsylvania Legislative Budget and Finance Committee, 1985), p. 63.

86. Massachusetts Legislative Research Council, *Report Relative to Prisons for Profit*, July 31, 1986, pp. 80–81. See also Samuel Jan Brakel, "Privatization and Corrections," *Federal Privatization Project Issue Paper No. 7* (Santa Monica, CA: Reason Foundation, January 1989), pp. 10–11.

87. Norman A.Carlson, Director, Bureau of Prisons, testimony, March 18, 1986, U.S. Congress. House Committee on the Judiciary. *Privatization of Corrections. Hearings before the Subcommittee on Courts, Civil Liberties, and the Administration of Justice*, 99th Cong., 1st and 2nd sessions, November 13, 1985, and March 18, 1986, Serial No. 40 (Washington, DC: U.S. Government Printing Office, 1986), p. 133.

88. *Los Angeles Times*, March 29, 1985.

89. *Fresno Bee*, May 8, 1987.

90. For example, would the new facilities require financing, construction, and purchase or rental of land, which existing state prisons do not?

91. Hackett et al., *Issues in Contracting*, p. 6.

92. Before-and-after comparisons might seem, at first glance, to avoid some of the problems of cross-facility comparisons. Region and location remain the same, as does (usually) the inmate population. However, many

other things relevant to cost may change—indeed, it is frequently one of the goals of privatization to bring about these changes. The private company may renovate or build to increase capacity. It may introduce new programs. It is likely to be required to seek accreditation and thus to meet standards not previously met. Monitoring, which may be included in the cost of the contract, adds a dimension that makes the operation different than before. In short, even a before-and-after analysis does not compare the "same" facility under two forms of management, although it comes closer to it than a cross-facility comparison does.

93. E. S. Savas, "Municipal Monopolies Versus Competition in Delivering Urban Services," pp. 473–500, in W. D.Hawley and D. Rogers, eds., *Improving the Quality of Urban Management* (Beverly Hills, CA: Sage, 1974).

94. E. S. Savas, "How Much Do Government Services Really Cost?" *Urban Affairs Quarterly* 15 (1979): 23–42.

95. Ibid., p. 31, citing P. Kemper and J. M. Quigley, *The Economics of Refuse Collection* (Cambridge: Ballinger, 1976).

96. Ibid., p. 34.

97. Hidden costs are not the same as overexpenditures or unauthorized expenditures. Such expenditures also will not appear in a budget, which is a prospective authorization, but they will show up in account books at year's end (perhaps in a disguised form, if they are unauthorized). Hidden costs, however, appear in neither the budget nor the report of expenditures of the particular agency or institution in question.

98. This would parallel the 30 percent underestimate found in studies of governmental budget figures for refuse collection.

99. George Camp and Camille Camp, "The Real Cost of Corrections: A Research Report" (South Salem, NY: Criminal Justice Institute, 1985).

100. Ibid., p. 3.

101. The Correction Department gave $26,000 per inmate as the direct operating expense for its 11 jails in Fiscal Year 1984. When the Correctional Association included such costs as fringe benefits, debt financing, and interagency costs, they estimated the cost to be $40,000. See William G. Blair, "Inmate Cost is Put at $40,000 a Year," *New York Times*, December 27, 1984.

102. Camp and Camp, "Real Cost of Corrections," p. 3.

103. Cited in Morgan O. Reynolds, *Power and Privilege: Labor Unions in America* (New York: Universe Books, 1984), p. 194.

104. President Jimmy Carter's Commission on Pension Policy concluded that "If the government pension system were subject to the same funding requirements as private plans, the cost in 1980 would be 79.8% of payroll." Cited in Reynolds, *Power and Privilege*, p. 194.

105. American Correctional Association, *Private Sector Operation of a Correctional Institution*, p. 91.

106. Christine Bowditch and Ronald S. Everett, "Private Prisons: Problems within the Solution," *Justice Quarterly* 4 (1987): 441–453, at p. 449.

107. While "bankruptcy" may not be the right term, units of government do face the threat of financial collapse and preventing that from happening does carry a cost.

108. American Federation of State, County, and Municipal Employees, "Contracting Out in Local Government." Unpublished paper, March 1984.

109. Hackett, et al., *Issues in Contracting*, p. 52.

110. Government may create these hidden costs also, by paying less than subsistence wages or by underfunding pension plans.

111. All data in the following analysis were supplied by Bill McGriff, Hamilton County Auditor, in written and telephonic communications. The analysis is available as a separate report. See Charles H. Logan and Bill W. McGriff, "Comparing Costs of Public and Private Prisons: A Case Study, "*A National Institute of Justice Research in Action* (Washington, DC: Department of Justice, 1989). It also appears in Charles H. Logan, "Proprietary Prisons," in Lynne Goodstein and Doris L. MacKenzie, eds., *The American Prison: Issues in Research and Policy* (New York: Plenum, 1989). Adapted here by permission.

112. William D. Berry and David Lowery, "The Growing Cost of Government: A Test of Two Explanations," *Social Science Quarterly* 65 (1984): 735–749.

113. This is particularly common at the state level, but it happens at county and federal levels as well. Fringe benefits were included by Hamilton County in its prison budget, but are listed here on the right as a reminder that they are commonly taken from other budgets.

114. This experience is consistent with the research by Savas, cited earlier, showing that public administrators generally underestimate the cost of noncontracted refuse collection.

115. CCA is heavily insured and indemnifies the county against potential costs of litigation and legal damages.

116. After CCA took over, it subcontracted to a group of local doctors to visit the facility twice a week, In 1987, after the time of the auditor's report, the county health department hired a full-time physician, who now sees patients at the jail and prison as well as at the health department. CCA pays for that physician's services to the Penal Farm inmates (their contract with the private doctors having expired).

117. Hamilton County has four divisions and four administrators: finance, public works, health services, and human services.

118. General fund obligations were split off by the auditor from the total county obligations. General funds paid for the county's general government administration. Constitutional officers like the sheriff, registrar of deeds, tax collector, and clerk of court are separate legal entities, although they are part of the county's overall budget. While in many counties the sheriff handles both the jail and the prison out of his budget, in Hamilton County the Penal Farm was always under human services, and thus part of general administration.

119. *Corrections Compendium*, November 1986. This source did not indicate whether this includes capital costs.

120. U.S. Department of Justice, *1984 Census of State Adult Correctional Facilities* (Washington, DC: Bureau of Justice Statistics, August 1987), Tables 18 and 31 (combining data).

121. Another aspect of the methodology understates the savings in *percentage* terms, though not in *dollar* amounts. Certain costs (items 12–15 in Table 5.2) are identified in Table 5.3 as "continuing, noncontracted county costs." These costs are paid by the county directly and would be the same whether the prison were contracted or not. These costs were included in Table 5.2 (and therefore in Tables 5.3 and 5.4) in order to show as complete an accounting of the county's total correctional costs as possible. In Table 5.4, these costs were included on both sides of the comparison, but they might just as well have been *subtracted* from both sides. Had that been done, the percentage differences between contracting and direct county operation, shown in Table 5.4, would have been 4.3, 3.3, and 9.1 percent instead of 3.8, 3.0, and 8.1 percent. When this effect and the salary adjustment effect are combined, the new figures on percentage savings for the three years are 4.3, 7.9, and 13.1.

122. Besides monitoring, the superintendent now has time for additional duties that he did not have before the contract. For example, he supervises a new county program of electronic monitoring as an alternative to imprisonment for misdemeanants. Some of the time he would previously have spent as warden is now available for this sort of expansion of the county's total correctional program.

123. For a detailed discussion and evaluation of operational changes at the prison, see Samuel Jan Brakel, "Prison Management, Private Enterprise Style: The Inmates' Evaluation," *New England Journal on Criminal and Civil Confinement 14* (Summer 1988): 175–244.

124. Mullen et al., *Privatization of Corrections*, p. 81.

CHAPTER 6

1. Fern Shen, "Investors Hope to Spring Profit from Private Prison," *Hartford Courant*, April 1, 1984.

2. John D. Donahue, *Prisons for Profit: Public Justice, Private Interests* (Washington, DC: Economic Policy Institute, 1988), p. 14.

3. Quoted in *Philadelphia Inquirer*, February 1, 1986.

4. Dave Kelly, President, Council of Prison Locals, American Federation of Government Employees, statement entered into the record, U.S. Congress. House Committee on the Judiciary. *Privatization of Corrections. Hearings before the Subcommittee on Courts, Civil Liberties, and the Administration of Justice*, 99th Cong., 1st and 2nd sessions, November 13, 1985, and March 18, 1986, Serial No. 40 (Washington, DC: U.S. Government Printing Office, 1986) p. 18.

5. Charles W. Thomas, Lonn Lanza-Kaduce, Linda S. Calvert Hanson, and Kathleen A. Duffy, *The Privatization of American Corrections* (Gainesville, FL: Center for Studies in Criminology and Law, University of Florida, June 15, 1988), p. 209–210.

6. Todd R. Clear and George F. Cole, *American Corrections* (Monterey, CA: Brooks/Cole, 1986), p. 532.

7. Joan Mullen, Kent John Chabotar, and Deborah M. Carrow, *The Privatization of Corrections* (Washington, DC: National Institute of Justice, February 1985), p. 68.

8. Judith C. Hackett, Harry P. Hatry, Robert B. Levinson, Joan Allen, Keon Chi, and Edward D. Feigenbaum, *Issues in Contracting for the Private Operation of Prisons and Jails* (Washington, DC: Department of Justice, October 1987), p. 25.

9. *Los Angeles Time*, March 29, 1985.

10. *Cleveland Plain Dealer*, October 1, 1984.

11. James O. Finckenauer, *Juvenile Delinquency and Corrections: The Gap Between Theory and Practice* (Orlando, FL: Academic Press, 1984), p. 181.

12. Ernest van den Haag, "Prisons Cost Too Much Because They Are Too Secure," *Corrections Magazine*, April 1980, pp. 39–43.

13. Hackett et al., *Issues in Contracting*, p. 22.

14. John J. DiIulio, Jr., "Prisons, Profits and the Public Good: The Privatization of Corrections," *Research Bulletin No. 1* (Huntsville, TX: Sam Houston State University Criminal Justice Center, 1986), p. 4.

15. Ibid., p. 2.

16. Hackett et al., *Issues in Contracting*, p. 25.

17. *Los Angeles Times*, March 29, 1985.

18. This phrase, or one like it, is typical of the charge. See: Jan Elvin, "Private Prison Plans Dropped by Buckingham," *Journal: The National Prison Project*, Winter 1985, p. 11; Jody Levine, "Private Prison Planned on Toxic Waste Site," *Journal: The National Prison Project*, Fall 1985, pp. 10–11; Ira Robbins, "Privatization of Corrections: Defining the Is-

sues," *Judicature* 69 (1986): 327; John D. Donahue, *Prisons for Profit: Public Justice, Private Interests* (Washington, DC: Economic Policy Institute, 1988), p. 7.

19. Some of these details are included in one of the ACLU reports, but not in a way that detracts from its overall "horror story" tone. See Levine, "Private Prison Planned," pp. 10–11.

20. In the public sector, they could look at the state of Massachusetts, which located its Deer Island House of Correction on the same site as a sewage treatment plant. When plans were made to relocate the prison, those plans were made conditional on the ability to locate a garbage incinerator (a waste-to energy facility) at the same site as the prison. See *Boston Globe*, December 17, 1986, pp. 1,13.

21. 491 *F. Supp.* 1026 (1980).

22. See Donahue, *Prisons for Profit* p. 7; Levine, "Private Prison Planned," p. 10; Craig Becker and Amy Dru Stanley, "Incarceration Inc.: The Downside of Private Prisons," *Nation*, June 15, 1985, p. 729; J. Michael Keating, Jr., *Seeking Profit in Punishment: The Private Management of Correctional Institutions* (American Federation of State, County, and Municipal Employees, 1985), p. 15.

23. Hackett et al., *Issues in Contracting*, pp. 40–41.

24. Ibid., p. 41.

25. Corrections Corporation of America, *Company Report*, April 3, 1987, p. 10.

26. Federal Bureau of Prisons, *1986 Annual Report* (Washington, DC: Federal Bureau of Prisons), p. 11.

27. Telephone interview with Peggy Wilson, CCA, July 3, 1989.

28. Kevin Archer, "Off with Their Overhead," *Policy Review*, Fall 1989, p. 75.

29. Telephone interview with Bob Greene, Wackenhut Corrections Corporation, June 30, 1989.

30. Lee Kravitz, "Tough Times for Private Prisons," *Venture*, May 1986, p. 60.

31. Ibid.

32. DiIulio, "Prisons, Profits and the Public Good," p. 3.

33. Stephen Gettinger, "Accreditation on Trial," *Corrections Magazine*, February 1982, pp. 6–21, 51–55.

34. Accreditation has to be pursued, however, and a high rate of accreditation in a particular jurisdiction may be as much a reflection of political support for the pursuit as it is a reflection of quality. When Florida successfully won accreditation for all of its penal institutions, some experts objected to the impression created that Florida's prisons were somehow exemplary (see Gettinger, Ibid.). Florida was not so much special in the

quality of its prisons as in its system-wide commitment to *apply* for accreditation, an expensive and time consuming process.

35. Corrections Corporation of American, *Company Report*, p. 11.

36. Federal Bureau of Prisons, *1986 Annual Report*, p. 8.

37. *New York Times*, February 19, 1985.

38. A somewhat dated reference on this would be: Department of Justice, National Institute of Law Enforcement and Criminal Justice, *The National Manpower Survey of the Criminal Justice System: Executive Summary* (Washington, DC,: U.S, Government Printing Office, circa 1976), pp. 11-13. In that survey, the U.S. Department of Justice reported that nearly half of all juvenile correctional agencies provided no formal entry training to line staff; where they did provide training, it averaged about 30 hours in length, with less than one-fourth in excess of 40 hours. For staff in adult corrections, over half of the training programs were less than 100 hours. Subsequent training on the job was also rare: the Manpower Survey found that less than 10 percent of state correctional officers had attended in-service courses. Moreover, supervisors were not much better trained than line staff: only one-tenth of surveyed correctional agencies required that supervisors receive training in supervision either before or after appointment. Training levels of state corrections officers have generally increased considerably since the time of that survey.

39. Richard Crane, Vice President, Legal Affairs, Corrections Corporation of America, testimony, November 13, 1985, U.S. Congress. House Committee on the Judiciary. *Privatization of Corrections. Hearings before the Subcommittee on Courts, Civil Liberties, and the Administration of Justice*, 99th Cong., 1st and 2nd sessions, November 13, 1985, and March 18, 1986, Serial No. 40 (Washington, DC: U.S. Government Printing Office, 1986), p. 30.

40. American Correctional Association, *Private Sector Operation of a Correctional Institution* (Washington, D.C.: U.S. Department of Justice, National Institute of Corrections, April 1985), p. 12.

41. National Criminal Justice Association, "Private Sector Involvement in Financing and Managing Correctional Facilities" Washington, DC: National Criminal Justice Association, April 1987), p. 17.

42. Ibid.

43. John J. DiIulio, Jr., "Prison Discipline and Prison Reform," *Public Interest* No. 89 (Fall 1987): 73.

44. *Medina v. O'Neill*, 589 *F. supp.* 1028, 1031 (1984).

45. Who will train whom? In a survey of correctional agencies, Camille and George Camp found that 43 percent contracted with private agencies for staff training, placing that among the ten most frequently contracted services. See Camille G. Camp and George M. Camp, *Private Sector*

Involvement in Prison Services and Operations (Washington, D.C.: U.S. Department of Justice, National Institute of Justice, February 1984), p. 6.

46. George M. Camp and Camille Graham Camp, *Corrections Yearbook 1987* (South Salem, NY: Criminal Justice Institute, 1987), p. 42.

47. DiIulio, "Prison Discipline and Prison Reform," p. 89.

48. Clear and Cole, *American Corrections*, p. 302.

49. U.S. Department of Justice, Law Enforcement Assistance Administration, *Corrections: National Manpower Survey of the Criminal Justice System*, vol. 3 (Washington, DC: U.S. Government Printing Office, 1978), p. 45.

50. American Correctional Association, *1987 Directory of Juvenile and Adult Correctional Departments, Institutions, Agencies, and Paroling Authorities* (College Park, MD: American Correctional Association, 1987), pp. xxx–xxxi.

51. Crane, testimony, p. 29.

52. Samuel Jan Brakel, "Prison Management, Private Enterprise Style: The Inmates' Evaluation," *New England Journal on Criminal and Civil Confinement* 14 (Summer 1988): 175–244, at 195.

53. Crane, testimony, p. 38.

54. Samuel Greengard, "Making Crime Pay," *Barrister Magazine* 13 (1986): 14.

55. Ibid.

56. Becker and Stanley, "Incarceration Inc," p. 729.

57. *Chattanooga Times*, August 12, 1986.

58. Telephone interview with Bill McGriff, Hamilton County Auditor, August 14, 1987.

59. League of Women Voters, "CCA—First Year Report Card" (Bay County, FL: videotape, October 1986).

60. Kevin Krajick, "Punishment for Profit" *Across the Board* 21 (March 1984), pp. 25–27.

61. Ibid., p. 25.

62. Ibid.

63. *Philadelphia Inquirer*, August 12, 1984.

64. Ibid.

65. Krajick, "Punishment for Profit," p. 26.

66. American Correctional Association, *Private Sector Operation of a Correctional Institution*.

67. These figures are derived from Tables 8.1 and 8.2 of the ACA Report (Ibid). I extrapolated a weighted average turnover for all staff at Okeechobee from the ACA figures given separately for "counselors" and "other staff" in Table 8.2. The approximate ratio of these two categories was estimated from the data in Table 8.1.

68. Ibid., p. 92.

69. Ibid., p. 58.

70. Ibid., pp. 99–101.

71. All figures in this section are from Brakel, "Prison Management, Private Enterprise Style."

72. Camp and Camp, *Private Sector Involvement in Prison Services and Operation.*

73. Ibid., p. 5.

74. Ibid., pp. 9–10. The range of benefits mentioned included: improved administrative operations (more efficient operation, reduced training requirements, better accountability, better use of space); cost savings (fewer staff, lower costs): and improved services and conditions (better quality, unique service provided, decreased liability through better conditions).

75. The rest were miscellaneous. Ibid.

76. The rest distributed as follows: 39 percent process (supervision, bidding, red tape); 22 percent contracting relationships (quality control, payment, union or other labor problems); 5 percent cost-effectiveness. Ibid., pp. 11–13.

77. Hackett et al., *Issues in Contracting*, p. 51.

78. Charles Ring, *Contracting for the Operation of Private Prisons: Pros and Cons* (College Park, MD: American Correctional Association, 1987), p. 17.

79. The criticism that Robbins' report to the ABA creates a double standard has been leveled by others besides myself. See "Privatization Backers Criticize ABA for Issuing Negative Report," *Criminal Justice Newsletter* 19, No. 24 (December 15, 1988): 3–5.

80. Ira P. Robbins, The Legal Dimensions of Private Incarceration (Washington, DC: American Bar Association, 1988), pp. 271–279, especially note 727.

81. Nor does Robbins' report leave much room for later balance or compromise, at least with respect to the statutory provisions. Note in this connection that Robbins insists that his Model Statutes "must not be compromised" and "should not be negotiable." Robbins, *Legal Dimensions of Private Incarceration*, pp. 414–415.

82. See the statements by Linda Cooper and Charles Logan in "Privatization Backers Criticize ABA," p. 4.

83. This implication was not lost on at least one member of the American Bar Association committee that was proposing a formal resolution and report based on Robbins' report to the ABA. In a letter to the committee, this member, an opponent of private prisons, wrote: "The resolution itself is correct in urging caution. More importantly, if followed, the report makes privatization very difficult." The letter made clear the writer's

complete opposition to private prisons, In the absence of a condemnation of the concept (which he preferred), he would settle for a report that made privatization as difficult as possible.

CHAPTER 7

1. Michael A. Kroll, "Prisons for Profit," *Progressive*, September 1984, pp. 18–22.

2. Jess Maghan and Edward Sagarin, "The Privatization of Corrections: Seeking to Anticipate the Unanticipated Consequences." Paper presented to American Society of Criminology, San Diego, CA, November 1985, pp. 44–46: Russ Immarigeon, "Private Prisons, Private Programs, and their Implications for Reducing Reliance on Imprisonment in the United States." *Prison Journal* 65 (1985): 60–74; Christine Bowditch and Ronald S Everett, "Private Prisons: Problems within the Solution," *Justice Quarterly* 4 (1987): 451.

3. Jan Elvin, "Private Prison Plans Dropped by Buckingham," *Journal: The National Prison Project* Winter 1985, p. 50.

4. Ibid.

5. [New York] *Newsday*, July 30, 1984.

6. Institutions Etc., "If You Think This Sounds Good, Wait'll You Hear About Discount Gas Chambers," *Investigative Newsletter on Institutions/Alternatives* 6 (November 1983): 6–8.

7. *Florida Times-Union*, September 23, 1984.

8. J. Michael Keating, Jr., *Seeking Profit in Punishment: The Private Management of Correctional Institutions* (American Federation of State, County, and Municipal Employees, 1985), p. 29.

9. Abt Associates, Inc., *American Prisons and Jails* (Washington, DC: U.S. Government Printing Office, 1980).

10. Alfred Blumstein, Jacqueline Cohen, and William Gooding, "The Influence of Capacity on Prison Population: A Critical Review of Some Recent Evidence," *Crime and Delinquency* 29 (January 1983): 1–51.

11. Ibid., p. 50.

12. Paul Starr, *The Limits of Privatization* (Washington, DC: Economic Policy Institute, 1987).

13. Maghan and Sagarin, "Privatization of Corrections," pp. 60–61.

14. Edward Sagarain and Jess Maghan, "Should States Opt for Private Prisons?" A debate with Charles Logan in the *Hartford Courant*, January 12, 1986.

15. Harmon L. Wray, Jr., "Cells for Sale," *Southern Changes* 8 September 1986): 6.

16. Herbert J. Hoelter, "Private Presentence Reports: Boon or Boondoggle?" *Federal Probation* 48 (1984): 53.

17. David M. Lawrence, "Private Exercise of Governmental Power," *Indiana Law Journal* 61 (1986): 653.

18. John P. Conrad, "Corrections and its Constituencies," *Prison Journal* 64 (Fall/Winter 1984): 47–48.

19. Bruce L. Benson, "Guns for Protection and Other Private Sector Responses to the Government's Failure to Control Crime," *Journal of Libertarian Studies* 8 (1986): 77.

20. U.S. Department of Justice, *Sourcebook of Criminal Justice Statistics—1986* (Washington, DC: Bureau of Justice Statistics, 1987), Table 2.11, pp. 86–87.

21. Joseph E. Jacoby and Christopher S. Dunn, "National Survey on Punishment for Criminal Offenses" (Bowling Green, OH: Bowling Green State University, 1987).

22. Benson, "Guns for Protection," p. 79, note 22.

23. Ibid., p. 79.

24. Ibid., pp. 81–83.

25. Richard Berk, Harold Brackman, and Selma Lesser, *A Measure of Justice: An Empirical Study of Changes in the California Penal Code, 1955–1971* New York: Academic Press, 1977).

26. Benson, "Guns for Protection," p. 82.

27. Dave Kelly, President, Council of Prison Locals, American Federation of Government Employees, statement entered into the record, U.S. Congress. House Committee on the Judiciary. *Privatization of Corrections. Hearings before the Subcommittee on Courts, Civil Liberties, and the Administration of Justice*, 99th Cong., 1st and 2nd sessions, November 13, 1985 and March 18, 1986, Serial No. 40 (Washington, DC: U.S. Government Printing Office, 1986) p. 17. Emphasis shifted from first occurrence of "self-interest."

28. Warren I. Citkins, "Privatization of the American Prison System: An Idea Whose Time Has Come?" *Notre Dame Journal of Law, Ethics and Public Policy* 2 (1986): 455.

29. Morgan O. Reynolds, *Power and Privilege: Labor Unions in America* (New York: Universe Books, 1984), p. 183.

30. John M. Wynne, Jr., *Prison Employee Unionism: The Impact on Correctional Administration and Programs* (Washington, DC: U.S. Department of Justice, NILECJ, January 1978), pp. 184–185.

31. Ibid., pp. 227–228.

32. Ibid., p. 217. I am grateful to Bruce Benson for drawing my attention to this reference.

33. James B. Jacobs, *New Perspectives on Prisons and Imprisonment* (Ithaca, NY: Cornell University Press, 1983), p. 118.

34. Ibid., pp. 130–131.

35. Wray, p. 4.

36. *Tennessean*, September 11, 1985.

37. Joan Mullen, Kent John Chabotar, and Deborah M. Carrow, *fThe Privatization of Corrections* (Washington, DC: National Institute of Justice, Feburary 1985), p. 73.

38. It is the government, not the Hilton Inn, that for decaded has chosen to cram more "guests" into each "room," rather than to expand its facilities.

39. Corrections Corporation of America, press release, June 26, 1987.

40. Corrections Corporation of America, press release, July 7, 1987.

CHAPTER 8

1. Joan Mullen, "Corrections and the Private Sector," *Prison Journal* 65 (1985): 1.

2. Edward Sagarin and Jess Maghan, "Should States Opt for Private Prisons?" A debate with Charles Logan in the *Hartford Courant*, January 12, 1986.

3. John J. DiIulio, Jr., "What's Wrong with Private Prisons," *Public Interest* No. 92 (Summer 1988): 73.

4. John M. Wynne, Jr., *Prison Employee Unionism: The Impact on Correctional Administration and Programs* (Washington, DC: U.S. Department of Justice, NILECJ, January 1978, pp. 170–171.

5. American Federation of State, County, and Municipal Employees, "Contracting Out in Local Government," unpublished paper, March 1984.

6. Robert Behn, "The False Dawn of the Sunset Laws," *Public Interest* 49 (Fall 1977): 103–118.

7. Robert J. Schmidt, panel presentation on "Assessments of Private Corrections," at the National Conference on Alternatives to Jail and Prison Overcrowding, sponsored by the University of Florida, Orlando, March 10, 1988.

8. American Correctional Association, *Private Sector Operation of a Correctional Institution* (Washington, DC: U.S. Department of Justice, National Institute of Corrections, April 1985), p. 16.

9. Gene Kassebaum, Billy Wayson, Joseph Seldin, Gail Monkman, Peter Nelligan, Peter Meyer, and David Takeuchi, *Contracting for Cor-*

rectional Services in the Community (Washington, DC: U.S. Department of Justice, May 1978), Vol. 1, summary.

10. Jess Maghan and Edward Sagarin, "The Privatization of Corrections: Seeking to Anticipate the Unanticipated Consequences." Paper presented to American Society of Criminology, San Diego, CA, November 1985, p. 53.

11. John D. Donahue, *Prisons for Profit: Public Justice. Private Interests* (Washington DC: Economic Policy Institute, 1988), p. 18.

12. U.S. Congress. House Committee on the Judiciary. *Privatization of Corrections. Hearings before the Subcommittee on Courts, Civil Liberties, and the Administration of Justice*, 99th Cong., 1st and 2nd sessions, November 13, 1985, and March 18, 1986, Serial No. 40 (Washington, DC: U.S. Government Printing Office, 1986), p. 140 (statement of Norman A. Carlson, Director, Federal Bureau of Prisons, submitted with testimony on March 18, 1986).

13. Robert Mathias and Diane Steelman, "Controlling Prison Populations: An Assessment of Current Mechanisms." Unpublished paper, National Council on Crime and Delinquency, 1982.

CHAPTER 9

1. Cited in Warren I. Cikins, "Privatization of the American Prison System: An Idea Whose Time Has Come?" *Notre Dame Journal of Law, Ethics and Public Policy* 2 (1986): 462.

2. Judith C. Hackett, Harry P. Hatry, Robert B. Levinson, Joan Allen, Keon Chi, and Edward D. Feigenbaum, *Issues in Contracting for the Private Operation of Prisons and Jails* (Washington, DC: Department of Justice, October 1987), p. 25. Note, however, that the restriction to minimum security facilities, while mentioned in the body of the report, does not appear in the summary of recommendations.

3. Ibid., p. 25. Of course, there is also community resistance to the location of prisons when government runs them. While government may be exempt from some zoning laws and can use force (i.e., eminent domain) to overcome community opposition, private agencies must rely on persuasion. Some communities find the prospect of new jobs and added property taxes hard to resist.

4. David M. Lawrence, "Private Exercise of Governmental Power," *Indiana Law Journal* 61 (1986): 666, note 77.

5. Connie Mayer, "Legal Issues Surrounding Private Operation of Prisons," *Criminal Law Bulletin* 22 (1986): 318.

6. Hackett et al., *Issues in Contracting*, p. 13.

7. Massachusetts Legislative Research Council, *Report Relative to Prisons for Profit. House Report No. 6225* (Boston: Massachusetts House of Representatives, July 31, 1986), p. 100.

8. Telephone interview with Bob Greene, Wackenhut, June 30, 1989.

9. Most deadly force in prisons is exercised by inmates, not officers. A common complaint among corrections officers is that they are surrounded by inmates who are often better armed than their keepers.

10. Buckingham Security Limited, *Private Prison Management: First Year Report 1985–1986, Butler County, Pennsylvania* (Lewisburg, PA: Buckingham Security Ltd., 1986), p. 6.

11. Samuel Jan Brakel, "Prison Management, Private Enterprise Style: The Inmates' Evaluation," *New England Journal on Criminal and Civil Confinement* 14 (Summer 1988): 175–244, at 188.

12. *Washington Post*, August 9, 1987.

13. *Washington Post*, February 5, 1988.

14. Commonwealth of Virginia, "Study of Correctional Privatization" (Richmond, VA: Secretary of Transportation and Public Safety, 1986), pp. 57–58.

15. At Dozier School for Boys, a "comparison" (but not truly comparable) state run facility, the escape rates for those three years were 10.6, 8.0, and 6.3 per 100. American Correctional Association, *Private Sector Operation of a Correctional Institution* (Washington, DC: U.S. Department of Justice, National Institute of Corrections, April 1985), p. 58.

16. All information for this paragraph is from Brakel, "Prison Management, Private Enterprise Style," pp. 187–189. Brakel indicates some slight uncertainty in the escape data. A conflicting set of figures shows 10 escapes from within the prison in 1985, the same number in 1986, and a drop to 7 in 1987.

17. Mary R. Woolley, "Prisons for Profit: Policy Considerations for Government Officials," *Dickinson Law Review* 90 (Winter 1985): 324–327.

18. Ibid.

19. Morgan O. Reynolds, *Power and Privilege: Labor Unions in America* (New York: Universe Books, 1984), p. 195.

20. Research cited in Ralph de Toledano, *Let Our Cities Burn* (New Rochelle, NY: Arlington Hosue, 1975), pp. 84–86.

21. John M. Wynne, Jr., *Prison Employee Unionism: The Impact on Correctional Administration and Programs* (Washington, DC: U.S. Department of Justice, NILECJ, January 1978), pp. 223–224.

22. de Toledano, *Let Our Cities Burn*, p. 46.

23. James B. Jacobs, *New Perspectives on Prisons and Imprisonment* (Ithaca, NY: Cornell University Press, 1983) p. 142.

24. Wynne, *Prison Employee Unionism*, p. 202.

25. Ibid., p. 221.

26. Woolley, "Prisons for Profit," pp. 326–327.

27. Hackett et al., *Issues in Contracting*, p. 11.

28. "Hamilton County, Tennessee, Corrections Facilities Agreement," September 20, 1984, section 13 (4), p. 37.

29. Wynne, *Prison Employee Unionism*, p. 204.

30. Ibid., p. 203.

31. Ibid., p. 223.

32. U.S. Office of Management and Budget, *Enhancing Governmental Productivity Through Competition: Targeting for Annual Savings of One Billion Dollars by 1988* (Washington, DC: Office of Federal Procurement Policy, March 1984), p. 11.

CHAPTER 10

1. J. Michael Keating, Jr., *Seeking Profit in Punishment: The Private Management of Correctional Institutions* (American Federation of State, County, and Municipal Employees, 1985), p. 43.

2. Ira Robbins, "Should Private Firms Run Prisons for Profit?" [New York] *Newsday*, March 31, 1985.

3. Charles W. Thomas, Lonn Lanza-Kaduce, Linda S. Calvert Hanson, and Kathleen A. Duffy, *The Privatization of American Corrections* (Gainesville, FL: Center for Studies in Criminology and Law, University of Florida, June 15, 1988), p. 142; Ira Robbins, *The Legal Dimensions of Private Incarceration* (Washington, DC: American Bar Association, 1988), p. 118.

4. Actually, Section 1983 applies only to states and not to the federal government. However, it is discussed here as though applying to both levels because it is very similar in logic to so-called *Bivens* actions against the federal government. See Thomas, p. 114, note 71.

5. *Medina v. O'Neill*, 589 F. Supp. 1028 (1984).

6. *Medina V. O'Neill*, 838 F.2d 800 (5th Cir. 1988) at 800.

7. 589 F. Supp. at 1028.

8. Or in a *Bivens*-type action against the federal government.

9. Robbins, *Legal Dimensions of Private Incarceration*, pp. 72, 118.

10. Ibid., p. 11, note 375.

11. Quoted in "Privatization Backers Criticize ABA for Issuing Negative Report," *Criminal Justice Newsletter*, December 15, 1988, p. 4.

12. In reply to this criticism, Robbins has quoted a statement by Tom Beasley, chairman of Corrections Corporation of America, promising that CCA "will protect every political figure associated with the prison system by means of a multi-million dollar insurance policy which will be sufficient . . . to finance all litigation, pay all claims and judgments, and in general insulate those officials from personal liability." (See "Robbins Responds to Critics of His Report on Privatization," *Criminal Justice Newsletter*, February 1, 1989, p. 6.)

This citation, however, does more to refute than to support Robbins' claim that contractors have promised to reduce or eliminate governmental *liability*. The statement by Beasley is a forceful reminder to government officials that they, personally, remain liable along with their agencies. CCA does not promise to "immunize" these officials against liability, but to "insulate" them from the cost of that liability, through indemnification, insurance, and payment of legal fees. Since CCA will charge government for the cost of this insulation, it might seem that nothing has been gained, but that is not the case. While liability for risks remains, it is still possible to reduce the risks themselves and to reduce the cost of protecting against the risks. This will be explained shortly.

13. Ira Robbins, Testimony to President's Commission on Privatization, Washington, DC, December 22, 1987, unpublished transcript, pp. 294–295.

14. Third-party rights can be created in intergovernmental contracts as well as public-private contracts. See Robbins, *Legal Dimensions of Private Incarceration*, pp. 142–143, note 436.

15. Ibid., pp. 141–149, 418–423.

16. Ibid., p. 149 (emphasis added).

17. Thomas et al., *Privatization of American Corrections*, p. 93.

18. Ibid., p. 95, note 32.

19. Ibid., pp. 89–90.

20. Ibid., p. 91.

21. However, if private prisons are required to carry insurance at levels too much higher than the liability of the state, this may create unnecessary problems. This will be discussed below, in the section on "Insurance and Indemnification."

22. October 28, 1987, interview with Richard Crane, then Vice President for Legal Affairs at Corrections Corporation of America.

23. Ibid.

24. Bruce Cory, "From Rhetoric to Reality: Privatization Put to the Test," *Corrections Compendium*, May 1986, p. 10.

25. National Criminal Justice Association, "Private Sector Involvement in Financing and Managing Correctional Facilities" (Washington, DC: National Criminal Justice Association, April 1987), p. 20.

26. Buckingham Security Limited, *Private Prison Management: First Year Report 1985–1986, Butler County, Pennsylvania* (Lewisburg, PA: Buckingham Security Ltd., 1986), p. 9.

27. See "CCA Settles Lawsuit," press release, October 3, 1988.

28. Roger Hanson reports that prisoner grievances account for 7 percent of all U.S. district court cases and 12 percent of the dockets of U.S. courts of appeals. Hanson estimates the costs of processing these cases at well over $100 million a year. By comparison, the total budget of the entire federal judiciary is $950 million. See Roger A. Hanson, "What Should Be Done When Prisoners Want to Take the State to Court?" *Judicature* 70 (December 1986/1987): 223–227, at 223 and 225.

29. Contact Center, Inc., *Inmate Lawsuits: A Report on Inmate Lawsuits Against State and Federal Correctional Systems Resulting in Monetary Damages and Settlement* (Lincoln, NE: Contact Center, Inc., 1985). I am grateful to Charles Thomas for drawing my attention to this report.

30. Ibid, p. 14.

31. Ibid. Calculated from figures presented on p. 14.

32. Ibid, p. 1. This survey identified 87 lawsuits lost and 161 settled for money over a two-year period in 1984 and 1985. In the year ending June 30, 1985, over 22,000 civil rights actions were filed in district and appeals courts. That does not include the smaller number of tort claims filed in state courts.

33. Corrections Corporation of America, *1986 Annual Report*, p. 31.

34. *Chattanooga Times*, August 12, 1986.

35. *Los Angeles Times*, March 29, 1985.

36. Pricor, *Prospectus*, July 23, 1987.

37. Information supplied by the Wackenhut Corporation.

38. "Bay County Detention Facilities Contract between Corrections Corporation of America and Bay County, Florida, September 3, 1985," pp. 32–33.

39. Thomas W. Beasley, Chairman, CCA. Transcript of testimony to President's Commission on Privatization, Washington, DC, December 22, 1987, p. 287.

40. Contact Center, Inc., *Inmate Lawsuits*.

41. Camille G. Camp and George M. Camp, *Private Sector Involvement in Prison Services and Operations* (Washington, DC: U.S. Department of Justice, National Institute of Justice, February 1984), p. 6.

42. Robbins, *Legal Dimensions of Private Incarceration*, pp. 238–239.

43. Brian B. Evans, "Private Prisons," *Emory Law Journal* 36 (Winter 1987): 253–283, at p. 273, note 106.

CHAPTER 11

1. Joseph P. Kalt, "Public Goods and the Theory of Government," *Cato Journal* 1 (Fall 1981): 565–584.
2. The high reelection rate of sheriffs, in spite of the deplorable condition of many of their jails, casts doubt on their political accountability in practice, at least on this score.
3. E. S. Savas, "How Much Do Government Services Really Cost?" *Urban Affairs Quarterly* 15 (1979): 23–41, at p. 30.
4. In Washington, these officials are regarded as the "summer help" by the lower echelons of civil service bureaucrats, who form a kind of permanent government.
5. Morgan O. Reynolds, *Power and Privilege: Labor Unions in America* (New York: Universe Books, 1984), p. 181.
6. John M. Wynne, Jr., *Prison Employee Unionism: The Impact on Correctional Administration and Programs* (Washington, DC: U.S. Department of Justice, NILECJ, January 1978), p. 203.
7. *Wall Street Journal*, July 22, 1987, p. 20.
8. Site visit by author and interviews with county officials.
9. *News-Herald*, Panama City, August 6, 1987.
10. *News-Herald*, Panama City, June 26, 1987.
11. Judy S. Grant and Diane Carol Bast, *Corrections and the Private Sector: A Guide for Public Officials* (Chicago: Heartland Institute, 1986), p. 13.
12. [Louisville] *Courier-Journal*, June 9, 1986.
13. Commonwealth of Virginia, "Study of Correctional Privatization" (Richmond, VA: Secretary of Transportation and Public Safety, 1986), p. 58.
14. Cited in Joan Mullen, Kent John Chabotar, and Deborah M. Carrow, *The Privatization of Corrections* (Washington, DC: National Institute of Justice, February 1985), pp. 73–74.
15. American Correctional Association, *Private Sector Operation of a Correctional Institution* (Washington, DC: U.S. Department of Justice, National Institute of Corrections, April 1985), p. 11.
16. Herbert J. Hoelter, "The Private Presentence Report: Issues for Consideration," *Prison Journal* 65 (1985): 57. Emphasis in original.

17. John P. Conrad, "Corrections and its Constituencies," *Prison Journal* 64 (Fall/Winter 1984): 47–48.

18. Judith C. Hackett, Harry P. Hatry, Robert B. Levinson, Joan Allen, Keon Chi, and Edward D. Feigenbaum, *Issues in Contracting for the Private Operation of Prisons and Jails* (Washington, DC: National Institute of Justice, October 1987), p. 43.

19. Ibid., pp. 50–51.

20. American Correctional Association, *Private Sector Operation of a Correctional Institution* (Washington, DC: U.S. Department of Justice, National Institute of Corrections, April 1985), p. 79, note 4 and accompanying text.

21. Ibid., p. 99.

22. Ibid., p. 78.

23. National Criminal Justice Association, "Private Sector Involvement in Financing and Managing Correctional Facilities" (Washington, DC: National Criminal Justice Association, April 1987), p. 17.

24. Interview with Floyd Fuller, Superintendent of Corrections, Hamilton County, Tennessee, October 27, 1987.

25. National Criminal Justice Association, p. 20.

26. National Criminal Justice Association, "Private Sector Involvement," p. 10; J. Michael Keating, Jr., *Seeking Profit in Punishment: The Private Management of Correctional Institutions* (American Federation of State, County, and Municipal Employees, 1985), p. 46.

27. Interview with Robert Schmidt, Supervisor of Detention Services, Immigration and Naturalization Service, May, 21, 1987.

28. At the Volunteers of America Regional Correction Center, a contracted jail for women serving Ramsey County, Minnesota, inmates are asked to complete an evaluation questionnaire at the time of their release. The questionnaire asks about safety, food, physical facilities, and program results. The results are available to county officials and are used by the contractor to make changes. One other function of the questionnaire is to allow departing inmates to vent their feelings. (Telephone interview with Bill Nelson, VOA, Roseville, MN, October 15, 1987.)

29. Inmate evaluations of one county prison (Silverdale) were described in chapter 6, "Issues of Quality." See Samuel Jan Brakel, "Prison Management, Private Enterprise Style: The Inmates' Evaluation," *New England Journal on Criminal and Civil Confinement* 14 (Summer 1988): 175–244.

30. See Samuel Jan Brakel, " 'Privatization' in Corrections: Radical Prison Chic or Mainstream Americana?" *New England Journal on Criminal and Civil Confinement* 14 (Winter 1988): 1–39, at 27.

31. The Massachusetts Department of Mental Health was recently quoted as deploring the worsening conditions of state institutions, with the comment, "If private psychiatric hospitals we license did this, we'd close them down" (*National Review*, September 16, 1988, p. 11).

32. Interview with T. Don Hutto, Nashville, October 28, 1987.

33. See *Corrections Compendium*, November 1986, p. 14.

34. Estimate by Howard Messing, *NIJ Reports*, July/August 1987. Some unpublished figures provided by Messing, however, indicate that, of jails under court order, 24 percent had a Master appointed, which would imply far more than 60 such jails.

35. U.S. Department of Justice, *Crime and Justice Facts, 1985* (Washington, DC: Bureau of Justice Statistics), p. 26.

36. John J. DiIulio, Jr., *Governing Prisons: A Comparative Study of Correctional Management* (NY: Free Press, 1987), p. 246.

37. William C. Collins, "Privatization: Some Legal Considerations from a Neutral Perspective," in *Collins: Correctional Law, 1986* (Olympia, WA: William C. Collins), p. 93.

38. Samuel Jan Brakel, " 'Mastering' the Legal Access Rights of Prison Inmates," *New England Journal on Criminal and Civil Confinement* 12 (Winter 1986): 1–69, at pp. 8–9. Also see Samuel Jan Brakel, "Prison Reform Litigation: Has the Revolution Gone Too Far?" *Judicature* 70 (June/July 1986): 5–6, 64–65, at p. 64.

The state of New Mexico, with a relatively small prisoner population but operating under a consent decree, recently reported payments of $1.8 million to support the activities of a court-appointed monitor, his support staff, and his consulting experts and investigators. When the cost of state attorneys and inmate legal expenses are included, the direct costs of the consent decree come to over $4 million. These figures are given in an annual report, but they are probably cumulative over the four years since the special master's appointment, rather than annual costs. See *The Annual Report of the New Mexico Corrections Department for the Seventy-Fifth Fiscal Year, July 1, 1986, through June 30, 1987* (Santa Fe: New Mexico Corrections Department), p. 16.

39. Lawyers have been known to pursue appointment as a special master in order to retire from all other practice with a source on long-term income.

40. Like contractors, masters are not elected but chosen. The manner of their choosing, however, differs significantly. Contractors are chosen by or subject to final approval by officials who are either elected or politically appointed and are thus vulnerable to political removal, while special masters are chosen by federal judges with lifetime tenure. Whereas contractors are chosen in a process that is public, competitive, and usually guided by preannounced criteria that are at least subject to legislative

determination, special masters are chosen by judges in an informal and subjective fashion from a limited field of insiders.

41. Hackett et al., *Issues in Contracting*, pp. 49–50.

42. For an elaborate discussion of monitoring and structured incentives for private prisons, see James Theodore Gentry, "The Panopticon Revisited: The Problem of Monitoring Private Prisons," *Yale Law Journal* 96 (1986): 353–375.

CHAPTER 12

1. John Hanrahan, "Why Public Services Should Stay Public." *Des Moines Register*, March 31, 1983.

2. If it were, it would be a stronger argument against unions than against contracting. A Rand study of racketeering in New York garbage collection found that "unions have been essential to racketeer control. That is to say, only where a corrupt union has been available, or created, have racketeers been able to establish an industrywide influence." See Peter Reuter, *The Value of a Bad Reputation: Cartels, Criminals, and Barriers to Entry* [Report No. P-6835] (Santa Monica, CA: The Rand Corporation, December 1982).

3. Bernard J. McCarthy, "Keeping an Eye on the Keeper: Prison Corruption and its Control," *Prison Journal* 64 (Fall/Winter 1984): 113–125.

4. Ira Robbins, "Privatization of Corrections: Defining the Issues," *Judicature* 69 (1986): 331.

5. Professor Robbins' faith in the superiority of governmental over private management of prisons is all the more remarkable coming from a man who, a few years earlier, likened America's prison system to that described in Aleksandr Solzhenitsyn's *Gulag Archipelago*. While Robbins saw many similarities between the two penal systems, he acknowledged no fundamental differences, admitting only to differences of degree. From a perspective so negative toward America's governmentally run prisons, to anticipate that privately run prisons would be worse is to imagine great horrors indeed. See Ira P. Robbins, "Beyond Freedom and Dignity: Aleksandr Solzhenitsyn and the American Gulag," *Michigan Law Review* 78 (1980): 763–789.

6. J. Michael Keating, "Thoughts about Prisons for Profit," in American Federation of State, County, and Municipal Employees, *Does Crime Pay?* (Washington, DC: American Federation of State, County, and Municipal Employees, 1985), p. 17.

7. Harmon L. Wray, Jr., "Cells for Sale," *Southern Changes* 8 (September 1986): 5.

8. Edward Sagarin and Jess Maghan, "Should States Opt for Private Prisons?" A debate with Charles Logan in the *Hartford Courant*, January 12, 1986.

9. John DiIulio, Jr., "Prisons, Profits and Public Good: The Privatization of Corrections," *Research Bulletin No. 1* (Huntsville, TX: Sam Houston State University Criminal Justice Center, 1986), p. 3.

10. John J. DiIulio, Jr., "What's Wrong with Private Prisons," *Public Interest* No. 92 (Summer 1988): 66–83, at pp. 71–72.

11. Gustave de Beaumont and Alexis de Tocqueville, *On the Penitentiary System in the United States and its Application in France* (Carbondale, IL: Southern Illinois University Press, 1964), p. 68.

12. D. Smith, *Police Systems in the United States*, 2nd ed. (New York: Harper & Row, 1960), p. 143. Cited in Gilbert Geis, "The Privatization of Prisons: Panacea or Placebo?" in Barry J. Carroll, Ralph W. Conant, and Thomas A. Easton, eds., *Private Means—Public Ends: Private Business in Social Service Delivery* (New York: Praeger, 1987), pp. 76–97, at pp. 81–82.

13. Malcolm Braly, *False Starts: A Memoir of San Quentin and Other Prisons* (Boston: Little, Brown, 1976).

14. Roger Morris, *The Devil's Butcher Shop: The New Mexico Prison Uprising* (New York: Franklin Watts, 1983) pp. 143–144.

15. *Milwaukee Journal*, February 1, 1989.

16. One possible exception to this generalization is that private contractors in the nineteenth century frequently went bankrupt. This could be seen as an abuse in itself (avoidance of responsibility), or it could be seen as the termination of other abuses. Unlike contractors, states that historically could not or would not raise the revenues necessary to run humane, or even viable, institutions did not go bankrupt. They merely reduced expenditures and worsened conditions further, or turned the problem over to private contractors. The issue of bankruptcy among contemporary contractors is discussed in the next chapter.

17. E. R. Cass, "Jails for Profit," *Corrections Today* 50 (October 1988): 84, 86.

18. Ibid., p. 86.

19. Ideally, there would also be a random or broadly representative selection of time periods, jurisdictions, and prisons.

20. William C. Collins, "Privatization: Some Legal Considerations from a Neutral Perspective," in *Collins: Correctional Law, 1986* (Olympia, WA: William C. Collins), p. 81.

21. Judith C. Hackett, Harry P. Hatry, Robert B. Levinson, Joan Allen,

Keon Chi, and Edward D. Feigenbaum, *Issues in Contracting for the Private Operation of Prisons and Jails* (Washington, DC: Department of Justice, October 1987, p. 49.

22. Joan Mullen, Kent John Chabotar, and Deborah M. Carrow, *The Privatization of Corrections* (Washington, DC: National Institute of Justice, February 1985), p. 73.

23. Robert W. Poole, Jr., "Objections to Privatization," *Policy Review* 24 (1983): 114.

CHAPTER 13

1. William D. Berry and David Lowery, "The Growing Cost of Government: A Test of Two Explanations," *Social Science Quarterly* (September 1984): 735–749.

2. E. S. Savas, *Privatizing the Public Sector: How to Shrink Government* (Chatham, NJ: Chatham House Publishers, 1982), p. 93.

3. Joan Mullen, Kent John Chabotar, and Debroah M. Carrow, *The Privatization of Corrections* (Washington, DC: National Institute of Justice, February 1985), p. 68.

4. Thomas E. Burke, "Research: Corrections Corporation of America Company Report," Boston, April 3, 1987, p. 2. See also Corrections Corporation of America quarterly and annual reports.

5. Martin Tolchin, "Privately Operated Prison in Tennessee Reports $200,000 in Cost Overruns," *New York Times*, May 21, 1985, p. A14. See also Russ Immarigeon, "Private Prisons, Private Programs, and their Implications for Reducing Reliance on Imprisonment in the United States," *Prison Journal* 65 (1985): 67; Charles Ring, *Contracting for the Operation of Private Prisons: Pros and Cons* (College Park, MD: American Correctional Association, 1987), pp. 33–34; John D. Donahue, *Prisons for Profit: Public Justice, Private Interests* (Washington, DC: Economic Policy Institute, 1988).

6. Charles Ring, *Contracting for the Operation of Private Prisons*, p. 34.

7. National Criminal Justice Association, "Private Sector Involvement in Financing and Managing Correctional Facilities" (Washington, DC: National Criminal Justice Association, April 1987), p. 18; Judith C. Hackett, Harry P. Hatry, Robert B. Levinson, Joan Allen, Keon Chi, and Edward D. Feigenbaum, *Issues in Contracting for the Private Operation of Prisons and Jails* (Washington, DC: Department of Justice, October 1987), p. 53.

8. Telephone interview with Bill McGriff, Hamilton County Auditor, November 11, 1987.

9. Erik Larson, "Captive Company," *Inc.*, June 1988, p. 90.

10. Philip B. Taft, Jr., "Private Vendors, Part II: Survival of the Fittest," *Corrections Magazine* 9 (February 1983). p. 43.

11. Ibid., p. 42

12. Jess Maghan and Edward Saragin, "The Privatization of Corrections: Seeking to Anticipate the Unanticipated Consequences." Paper presented to American Society of Criminology, San Diego, CA, November 1985, pp. 43–44.

13. *Insight*, December 7, 1987, pp. 34–36.

14. James Theodore Gentry, "The Panopticon Revisited: The Problem of Monitoring Private Prisons," *Yale Law Journal* 96 (1986): 370.

15. Ibid., p. 369.

16. Thomas Coughlin, "The New York Experience," in American Federation of State, County, and Municipal Employees, *Does Crime Pay?* (Washington, DC: American Federation of State, County, and Municipal Employees,1985), p. 32.

17. *U.S. News and World Report*, December 23, 1985, p. 39.

18. Hackett, et al., *Issues in Contracting*, p. 40

19. [Louisville] *Couier-Journal*, March 19, 1985.

20. Corrections Corporation of America, *1986 Annual Report*, p. 24.

21. Paul Starr, *The Limits of Privatization* (Washington, DC: Economic Policy Institute, 1987), p. 5.

22. Ibid., p. 6.

23. Hans F. Sennholz, "Privatizing Federal Programs," *Freeman*, June 1987, pp. 223–228.

24. Ibid., p. 405.

25. Ibid., pp. 404–405.

26. Ibid., p. 409.

CHAPTER 14

1. Barry Bozeman, *All Organizations Are Public: Bridging Public and Private Organizational Theories* (San Francisco: Jossey-Bass, 1987), chap. 6.

2. James M. Buchanan and Robert D. Tollison, eds., *The Theory of Public Choice—II* (Ann Arbor, MI: University of Michigan Press, 1984).

3. American Federation of State, County, and Municipal Employees,

Passing The Bucks (Washington, DC: American Federation of State, County, and Municipal Employees, 1983).

4. For discussion of this concept see: George Smith, "Justice Entrepreneurship in a Free Market," *Journal of Libertarian Studies* 3 (Winter 1979): 405–426; Randy Barnett, "Pursuing Justice in a Free Society: Part One—Power vs. Liberty," *Criminal Justice Ethics* 4 (Summer/Fall 1985; 50–72; Randy Barnett, "Pursuing Justice in a Free Society: Part Two—Crime Prevention and the Legal Order," *Criminal Justice Ethics* 5 (Winter/ Summer 1986): 30–53; Bruce L. Benson, *The Enterprise of Law: Avoiding Anarchy and Leviathan* (San Francisco: Pacific Research Institute on Public Policy, 1990); Murray N. Rothbard, *For a New Liberty* (New York: Collier Macmillian, 1973): 215–241.

5. For example, John Locke, Adam Smith, John Stuart Mill, and Thomas Jefferson.

6. For example, Frederic Bastiat, Herbert Spencer, Ludwig von Mises, Friedrich Hayek, John Hospers, and Robert Nozick.

7. For example, Lysander Spooner, Benjamin Tucker, and Murry Rothbard.

8. Robert Nozick, *Anarchy, State and Utopia* (New York: Basic Books, 1974), p. 109. Most social scientists, following Max Weber, regard the de jure claim of monopoly over the legitimate use of force as a defining characteristic of states as they exist in the real world. Nozick, however, accepts the hypothetical case of a purely de facto monopoly as constituting a minimal state. (See Nozick, pp. 117–118. Actually, the monopoly of force is used by Nozick to define an "ultraminimal" state. The "minimal" state requires another feature [taxes, basically] that is not relevant here.) Nozick argues, further, that there is an advantage to having only one such agency, in that this will preempt the fewest individuals in the exercise of their right to punish those who violate the rights of others.

In Chapter 4, I argued that even if individuals have some kind of contract with the state, in a Lockean sense, whereby they transfer to the state their individual right to punish criminals, it may still be legitimate for a government agency to then "subcontract" with private firms to exercise this authority on behalf of the state. In this chapter, I ask what would happen if individuals bypassed the government middleman and contracted directly with private companies to enforce their rights and to punish those who transgressed against them.

9. Rothbard, *For a New Liberty*, pp. 215–241.

10. David D. Friedman, *The Machinery of Freedom: Guide to Radical Capitalism* (New Rochelle, NY: Arlington House, 1978).

11. See note 4, *supra*.

12. Randy Barnett, "Restitution: A New Paradigm of Criminal Justice," in Randy Barnett and John Hagel III, eds., *Assessing the Criminal: Restitution, Retribution, and the Legal Process* (Cambridge. MA: Ballinger, 1977), pp. 349–383, at p. 354.

13. Rothbard, *For a New Liberty*, pp. 231–234.

14. "Relatively autonomous" here means "not subject to a high degree of direct government regulation." Prisons in a libertarian society would certainly, however, be strongly constrained by the rule of law.

15. Rothbard, *For a New Liberty*, p. 259.

16. Barnett, however, proposes that a victim's right to compensation would become unowned property, available to be claimed, or "homesteaded," by any entrepreneur. (See Barnett, "Restitution," p. 368.) Barnett argues only for restitution and against punishment, but the homesteading argument could apply as well to a punishment right.

17. Murray N. Rothbard, "Punishment and Proportionality," in Barnett and Hagel, eds., *Assessing the Criminal*, pp. 259–270, at p. 260.

18. Ibid., p. 259.

19. A market in punishment could develop, in which brokers would seek to profit by buying the right to punish as cheaply as possible from victims selling it as dearly as possible to offenders or others.

20. Randy Barnett and John Hagel III, "Assessing the Criminal: Restitution, Retribution and the Legal Process," in Barnett and Hagel (eds.), *Assessing the Criminal*, pp. 1–31.

21. Ibid.

22. Andrew von Hirsch, *Doing Justice: The Choice of Punishments* (New York: Hill and Wang, 1976).

23. Von Hirsch's rationale for the justice model, however, is not purely retributivist. Unlike Kant, von Hirsch see deservedness only as necessary, but not sufficient, to justify punishment. There is supposedly a "countervailing moral consideration"—specifically, "the principle of not deliberately causing human suffering where it can possibly be avoided" (von Hirsch, *Doing Justice*, p. 553). Accepting this principle, von Hirsch argues that for punishment to be justified, it must also be shown to have a deterrent effect. A utilitarian element has been added.

Von Hirsch's compromise is internally inconsistent, and thus is weaker than a purely retributivist justification. The principal that punishment for wrongdoing is deserved, and the principal against all avoidable suffering, are logically incompatible. To say that *some* suffering (i.e., punishment) may sometimes be deserved is to say that we do *not* believe that *all* avoidable infliction of pain *should* be avoided. The justice model is stronger when the utilitarian requirement of deterrence is dropped.

24. Rehabilitation might be proposed as an individual good in itself, rather than as a method of crime control. This, however, would be coercive state paternalism, which is also incompatible with libertarian principles. For a few exceptions that do not include criminals, see John Hospers. "Libertarianism and Legal Paternalism," in Tibor R. Machan, eds., *The Libertarian Reader* (Totowa, NJ: Rowman and Littlefield, 1982), pp. 135–144.

25. To say that rights and their corollary duties must be "socially constructed" does not conflict with libertarian postulates of natural law, at least not for secular libertarians. Nonreligious libertarians recognize that to speak of a "natural right" is to use a verbal shorthand. They do not believe that a natural right is literally given by God or by nature in some teleological sense. They understand that a right, like all mental constructs, is humanly defined. When they speak of something as a "natural" right, they are saying that it must be *treated* as absolute and inalienable, *as if* it were given by nature or by God.

26. This view—that sanctions express and uphold values—does much to explain the role of mercy as a counterpart of desert. Justice and mercy are not necessarily in conflict. They may be reconciled by noting their relationship to the value we seek to uphold. In certain cases (e.g., a starving person steals a small amount of food), punishment, though deserved, might seem so unfair that its imposition would not serve to uphold the value at stake (here, property rights). Rather, such punishment would discredit and thereby weaken that value. To "temper justice with mercy" in such a case (e.g., by suspending a sentence) is not so much a comprise between conflicting values as it is a formulation designed to uphold as effectively as possible the relevant legal value.

27. J. Roger Lee, "The Arrest and Punishment of Criminals: Justification and Limitations," in Machan, *Libertarian Reader*, pp. 86–97, at p. 95.

28. Barnett and Hagel, "Assessing the Criminal." p. 15.

29. Ibid., p. 13.

30. John Hospers, "Retribution: The Ethics of Punishment," in Barnett and Hagel, *Assessing the Criminal*, pp. 181–209, at pp. 204–206.

31. Richard A. Epstein. "Crime and Tort: Old Wine in Old Bottles," in Barnett and Hagel, *Assessing the Criminal*, pp. 231–257.

32. Lee, "The Arrest and Punishment of Criminals."

33. J. Roger Lee and Laurin A. Wollan, Jr., "The Libertarian Prison: Principles of Lassiez-Faire Incarceration." *Prison Journal* 65 (Autumn/Winter 1985): 108–121.

34. Ibid., p. 108.

35. Lee, "The Arrest and Punishment of Criminals," p. 91.

36. Ernest van den Haag, *Punishing Criminals* (New York: Basic Books, 1975), p. 15.

37. I leave this fate unspecified. Public welfare? Private charity? Starvation? The answer is irrelevant here: only let it be the same inside as outside.

38. John Price, "Political Enterprise in a Prison: The Free Market Economy of La Mesa Penitenciaria," *Crime and Delinquency* 19 (April 1973): 218–227.

39. Ibid., p. 218.

40. The description here draws heavily from Edgar May, "Maine: Was Inmate Capitalism Out of Control?" *Corrections Magazine* 7 (May 1981): 17–23; and Jeffrey Shedd, "Making Good(s) Behind Bars," *Reason* (March 1982): 23–32.

41. May, "Maine," p. 19.

42. Shedd, "Making Good(s)," p. 25.

43. Ibid., p. 26.

44. In federal prisons, about one-third of prisoners participate in prison industry programs, but in state prisons it is less than 10 percent.

45. May, "Maine," p. 18.

46. Shedd, "Making Good(s)," p. 26.

47. Ibid., p. 25.

48. May, "Maine," p. 20.

49. Shedd, "Making Good(s)," p. 27.

50. May, "Maine," p. 20.

51. Ibid., p. 18.

52. Shedd, "Making Good(s)," p. 29.

53. Ibid., p. 32 (emphasis in original).

54. David B. Kalinich, *The Inmate Economy* (Lexington, MA: D.C. Heath, 1980).

55. Roger Morris, *The Devil's Butcher Shop* (New York: Franklin Watts, 1983).

56. Kevin Krajick, "People in Prison Do Not Run Businesses," *Corrections Magazine*, February 1981, pp. 22–23.

57. See John J. DiIulio, Jr., *Governing Prisons: A Comparative Study of Correctional Management* (New York: Free Press, 1987).

58. *Detroit News*, April 23, 1989.

59. A jurisdiction might even contract with a private company to establish a new facility or to take over an existing one for a specified period of time, with the understanding that at the end of this period the facility would revert to direct government control. The contract could include training of government employees and managers by the contractors. A

jurisdiction considering this arrangement would have to expect it to be more costly, at least in the short run, than a contract that was either long-term or indefinitely renewable subject to rebidding.

60. Outside of the federal system and a few states that pursue accreditation vigorously.

Selected Bibliography

American Correctional Association. 1985. *Private Sector Operation of a Correctional Institution* (Washington, DC: U.S. Department of Justice, National Institute of Corrections).

Anderson, Patrick, Charles R. Davoli, and Laura J. Moriarty. 1985. "Private Corrections: Feast or Fiasco?" *Prison Journal* 65(2): 32–41.

Auerbach, Barbara J., George E. Sexton, Franklin C. Farrow, and Robert H. Lawson. 1988. *Work in American Prisons: The Private Sector Gets Involved* (Washington, DC: National Institute of Justice).

Bacas, Harvey. 1984. "When Prisons and Profits Go Together." *Nation's Business* (October): 62R–63R.

Barnett, Randy. 1986. "Pursuing Justice in a Free Society: Part Two—Crime Prevention and the Legal Order." *Criminal Justice Ethics* 5 (Winter/Spring): 30–53.

―――. 1985. "Pursuing Justice in a Free Society: Part One—Power vs. Liberty." *Criminal Justice Ethics* 4 (Summer/Fall): 50–72.

―――. 1979. "Justice Entrepreneurship in a Free Market: Comment." *Journal of Libertarian Studies* 3 (Winter): 439–451.

Bast, Diane Carol. 1986. "In Defense of Private Prisons" (Chicago: Heartland Institute).

Becker, Craig, and Amy Dru Stanley. 1985. "Incarceration Inc.: The Downside of Private Prisons." *Nation* (June 15): 728–730.

Benson, Bruce L. 1990. *The Enterprise of Law: Avoiding Anarchy and Leviathan* (San Francisco: Pacific Research Institute on Public Policy).

Borna, Shaneen. 1986. "Free Enterprise Goes to Prison." *British Journal of Criminology* 26(4): 321–334.

Bowditch, Christine, and Ronald S. Everett. 1987. "Private Prisons: Problems within the Solution." *Justice Quarterly* 4: 441–453.

Brakel, Samuel Jan. 1989. "Privatization and Corrections." *Federal Privatization Project Issue Paper No. 7* (Santa Monica, CA: Reason Foundation).

———. 1988. "Prison Management, Private Enterprise Style: The Inmates' Evaluation." *New England Journal on Criminal and Civil Confinement* 14(2): 175–244.

———. 1988. " 'Privatization' in Corrections: Radical Prison Chic or Mainstream Americana?" *New England Journal on Criminal and Civil Confinement* 14 (Winter): 1–39.

Camp, Camille, and George Camp. 1985. "Correctional Privatization in Perspective." *Prison Journal* 65(2): 14–31.

Cikins, Warren I. 1986. "Privatization of the American Prison System: An Idea Whose Time Has Come?" *Notre Dame Journal of Law, Ethics and Public Policy* 2(2): 445–464.

Collins, William C. 1986. "Privatization: Some Legal Considerations from a Neutral Perspective." In *Collins: Correctional Law, 1986* (Olympia, WA: William C. Collins), pp. 81–93.

———. 1985. "Contracting for Correctional Services: Some Legal Considerations" (Washington, DC: National Institute of Corrections).

Cory, Bruce. 1986. "From Rhetoric to Reality: Privatization Put to the Test." *Corrections Compendium* (May): 1, 10–14.

Council of State Governments and Urban Institute. 1987. *Issues in Contracting for the Private Operation of Prisons and Jails*. Executive Summary and Final Report (Washington, DC: Department of Justice, National Institute of Justice).

Cullen, Francis T., Jr. 1986. "The Privatization of Treatment: Prison Reform in the 1980's." *Federal Probation* 50(1): 8–16.

DiIulio, John J., Jr. 1988. "What's Wrong with Private Prisons," *Public Interest* No. 92 (Summer): 66–83.

Donahue, John D. 1988. *Prisons for Profit: Public Justice, Private Interests* (Washington, DC: Economic Policy Institute).

Duffy, Susan M. 1984. "Breaking into Jail: The Private Sector Starts to Build and Run Prisons." *Barron's* (May 14): 20–22.

Dunham, Douglas W. [Note]. 1986. "Inmates' Rights and the Privatization of Prisons." *Columbia Law Review* 86: 1475–1504.

Ellison, W. James. 1987. "Privatization of Corrections: A Critique and Analysis of Contemporary Views." *Cumberland Law Review* 17(3:): 683–730.

Elvin, Jan. 1985. "A Civil Liberties View of Private Prisons." *Prison Journal* 65(2): 48–52.

Evans, Brian B. 1987. "Private Prisons". [Note]. *Emory Law Journal* 36 (Winter): 253–283.

Fenton, Joseph. 1985. "A Private Alternative to Public Prisons." *Prison Journal* 65(2): 42–47.

Field, Joseph E. [Note]. 1987. "Making Prisons Private: An Improper Delegation of Governmental Power." *Hofstra Law Review* 15 (Spring): 649–675.

Fitzgerald, Randall. 1988. *When Government Goes Private* (New York: Universe Books), pp. 93–119, "Streamlining Our Justice System."

Gage, Theodore. 1982. "Cops, Inc." *Reason* (November): 23–28.

Geis, Gilbert. 1987. "The Privatization of Prisons: Panacea or Placebo?" In Barry J. Carroll, Ralph W. Conant, and Thomas A. Easton, eds., *Private Means—Public Ends: Private Business in Social Service Delivery* (New York: Praeger), pp. 76–97.

Gentry, James Theodore [Note]. 1986. "The Panopticon Revisited: The Problem of Monitoring Private Prisons." *Yale Law Journal* 96: 353–375.

Grant, Judy S. 1986. "Prisons for Profit." *Hamline Journal of Public Law and Policy*, 7(1): 123–141.

Grant, Judy S., and Diane Carol Bast. 1986. *Corrections and the Private Sector: A Guide for Public Officials* (Chicago: Heartland Institute).

Immarigeon, Russ. 1987. "Privatizing Adult Imprisonment in the U.S.: A Bibliography." *Criminal Justice Abstracts* (March): 123–139.

———. 1985. "Private Prisons, Private Programs, and their Implications for Reducing Reliance on Imprisonment in the United States." *Prison Journal* 65(2): 60–74.

Joel, Dana. 1988., "A Guide to Prison Privatization." *Backgrounder* No. 650 (Washington DC: Heritage Foundation).

Kay, Susan L. 1987. "The Implications of Prison Privatization on the Conduct of Prisoner Litigation under 42 U.S.C. Section 1983." *Vanderbilt Law Review* 40(4): 867–888.

Keating, J. Michael, Jr. 1986. *Public Ends and Private Means: Accountability among Private Providers of Public Social Services.* NIDR Report No. 2 (Washington, DC: National Institute for Dispute Resolution).

Krajick, Kevin. 1984. *Private Financing and Management of Prisons and Jails* (New York: Edna McConnell Clark Foundation, n.p.)

———. 1984. "Punishment for Profit," *Across the Board* 21(3): 20–27.

———. 1984. "Prisons for Profit: The Private Alternative." *State Legislatures* 10(4): 9–14.

Kravitz, Lee. 1986. "Tough Times for Private Prisons." *Venture* (May): 56–60.

Larson, Erik. 1988. "Captive Company." *Inc.* June: 86–92.

Lauter, David. 1985. "The Plunge into Private Justice." *National Law Journal* (March 11).

Lawrence, David M. 1986. "Private Exercise of Governmental Power." *Indiana Law Journal* 61: 647–695.

Lee, J. Roger, and Laurin A. Wollan, Jr. 1985. "The Libertarian Prison: Principles of Laissez-Faire Incarceration." *Prison Journal* 65(2): 108–121.

Liebmann, George. 1975. "Delegation to Private Parties in American Constitutional Law." *Indiana Law Journal* 50: 650–719.

Logan, Charles H. 1989. "Proprietary Prisons." In Lynne Goodstein and Doris L. Mackenzie, eds., *The American Prison: Issues in Research and Policy* (New York: Plenum).

————.1987. "The Propriety of Proprietary Prisons." *Federal Probation* 51(3): 35–40.

Logan, Charles H., and Bill W. McGriff. 1989. "Comparing Costs of Public and Private Prisons: A Case Study." *National Institute of Justice Research in Action* (Washington, DC: Department of Justice).

Logan, Charles H. and Sharla P. Rausch. 1985. "Punish and Profit: The Emergence of Private Enterprise Prisons." *Justice Quarterly* 2(3): 303–318.

McConville, Sean. 1988. "The Privatization of Penal Services." (Strasbourg: Draft Report for the Council of Europe, Eighteenth Criminological Research Conference).

————. 1987. "Aid from Industry? Private Corrections and Prison Crowding." In Stephen Gottfredson and Sean McConville, eds., *America's Correctional Crisis: Prison Populations and Public Policy* (Westport, CT: Greenwood Press), pp. 221–242.

McDonald, Douglas, ed. 1990. *Private Prisons and Public Interest.* (New Brunswick, NJ: Rutgers University Press).

May, Edgar. 1981. "Maine: Was Inmate Capitalism Out of Control"? *Corrections Magazine* 7 (May): 17–23.

Mayer, Connie. 1986. "Legal Issues Surrounding Private Operation of Prisons." *Criminal Law Bulletin* 22(4): 309–325.

Miller, Jerome. 1986. "The Private Prison Industry: Dilemmas and Proposals." *Journal of Law, Ethics and Public Policy* 2: 465–477.

Mullen, Joan. 1985. "Corrections and the Private Sector." *Prison Journal* 65(2): 1–13.

————. 1985. "Corrections and the Private Sector," *National Institute of Justice Research in Brief* (Washington, DC: Department of Justice).

Mullen, Joan, Kent John Chabotar, and Deborah M. Carrow. 1985. *The*

Privatization of Corrections (Washington, DC: National Institute of Justice).

National Criminal Justice Association. 1987. "Private Sector Involvement in Financing and Managing Correctional Facilities" (Washington, DC: National Criminal Justice Association).

Palumbo, Dennis J. 1986. "Privatization and Corrections Policy." *Policy Studies Review* 5(3): 598–605.

Pennsylvania Legislative Budget and Finance Committee. 1985. *Report on a Study of Issues Related to the Potential Operation of Private Prisons in Pennsylvania* (Harrisburg, PA: Pennsylvania Legislative Budget and Finance Committee).

Ring, Charles. 1987. *Contracting for the Operation of Private Prisons: Pros and Cons* (College Park, MD: American Correctional Association).

Robbins, Ira P. 1988. "The Impact of the Nondelegation Doctrine on Prison Privatization." *UCLA Law Review* 35: 911–952.

———. 1988. *The Legal Dimensions of Private Incarceration* (Washington, DC: American Bar Association).

———. 1986. "Privatization of Corrections: Defining the Issues." *Judicature* 69(6): 324–331.

Roper, Brian A. 1986. "Market Forces, Privatization and Prisons: A Polar Case for Government Policy." *International Journal of Social Economics* 13(1): 77–92.

Savas, E. S. 1987. "Privatization and Prisons." *Vanderbilt Law Review* 40 (May): 889–899.

Shedd, Jeffrey. 1982. "Making Good(s) Behind Bars." *Reason* (March): 23–32.

Smith, George. 1979. "Justice Entrepreneurship in a Free Market." *Journal of Libertarian Studies* 3 (Winter): 405–426.

Starr, Paul. 1987. *The Limits of Privatization* (Washington, DC: Economic Policy Institute).

Steinberg, Sheldon S., J. Michael Keating, and James J. Dahl. 1981. *Potential for Contracted Management in Local Correctional Facilities*. Report to National Institute of Corrections (Washington, D.C.).

Stewart, James K. 1986. "Costly Prisons: Should the Public Monopoly be Ended"? In Patrick B. McGuigan and Jon S. Pascale eds., *Crime and Punishment in Modern America* (Washington, DC: Institute for Government and Politics of the Free Congress Research and Education Foundation), pp. 365–387.

Taft, Philip B., Jr. 1983. "Private Vendors, Part II: Survival of the Fittest." *Corrections Magazine* 9 (February): 36–43.

_____. 1982. "Private Vendors, Part I: The Fiscal Crisis in Private Corrections." *Corrections Magazine* 8 (December): 27–32.

Thomas, Charles W., and Linda S. Calvert Hanson. 1989. "The Implications of 42 U.S.C. Section 1983 for the Privatization of Prisons." *Florida State University Law Review* 16(4): 933–962.

Thomas, Charles W., Lonn Lanza-Kaduce, Linda S. Calvert Hanson, and Kathleen A. Duffy. 1988. *The Privatization of American Corrections* (Gainesville: FL: Center for Studies in Criminology and Law, University of Florida).

Travis, Lawrence F., III, Edward J. Latessa, Jr., and Gennaro F. Vito. 1985. "Private Enterprise in Institutional Corrections: A Call for Caution." *Federal Probation* 49(4): 11–16.

The Urban Institute. 1989. *Comparison of Privately and Publicly Operated Corrections Facilities in Kentucky and Massachusetts* (Washington, D.C.: Urban Institute).

Virginia, Commonwealth of. 1986. "Study of Correctional Privatization." (Secretary of Transportation and Public Safety).

Voison, Elizabeth. 1985. "Privatization and Prisons." *City and State* (April): 1, 30.

Walzer, Michael. 1985. "At McPrison and Burglar King It's . . . Hold the Justice." *New Republic* (April 8): 10–12.

Wecht, David N. [Note]. 1987. "Breaking the Code of Deference: Judicial Review of Private Prisons." *Yale Law Journal* 96: 815–837.

Wooley, Mary R. 1985. "Prisons for Profit: Policy Considerations for Government Officials." *Dickinson Law Review* 90 (Winter) 307–331.

Young, Peter. 1987. *The Prison Cell* (London: Adam Smith Institute).

Index